The Economics of
Federal Credit Programs

The Economics of Federal Credit Programs

BARRY P. BOSWORTH
ANDREW S. CARRON
ELISABETH H. RHYNE

THE BROOKINGS INSTITUTION
Washington, D.C.

Copyright © 1987 by
THE BROOKINGS INSTITUTION
1775 Massachusetts Avenue, N.W., Washington, D.C. 20036

Library of Congress Cataloging-in-Publication data:

Bosworth, Barry, 1942–
  The economics of federal credit programs.

  Includes bibliographical references and index.
    1. Government lending—United States.   2. Loans—
United States—Government guaranty.   3. Credit
control—United States.   I. Carron, Andrew S.
II. Rhyne, Elisabeth.   III. Title.
HJ8119.B67   1987   336.3′44′0973   85-48205
ISBN 0-8157-1038-0
ISBN 0-8157-1037-2 (pbk.)

9 8 7 6 5 4 3 2 1

THE BROOKINGS INSTITUTION is an independent organization devoted to nonpartisan research, education, and publication in economics, government, foreign policy, and the social sciences generally. Its principal purposes are to aid in the development of sound public policies and to promote public understanding of issues of national importance.

The Institution was founded on December 8, 1927, to merge the activities of the Institute for Government Research, founded in 1916, the Institute of Economics, founded in 1922, and the Robert Brookings Graduate School of Economics and Government, founded in 1924.

The Board of Trustees is responsible for the general administration of the Institution, while the immediate direction of the policies, program, and staff is vested in the President, assisted by an advisory committee of the officers and staff. The by-laws of the Institution state: "It is the function of the Trustees to make possible the conduct of scientific research, and publication, under the most favorable conditions, and to safeguard the independence of the research staff in the pursuit of their studies and in the publication of the results of such studies. It is not a part of their function to determine, control, or influence the conduct of particular investigations or the conclusions reached."

The President bears final responsibility for the decision to publish a manuscript as a Brookings book. In reaching his judgment on the competence, accuracy, and objectivity of each study, the President is advised by the director of the appropriate research program and weighs the views of a panel of expert outside readers who report to him in confidence on the quality of the work. Publication of a work signifies that it is deemed a competent treatment worthy of public consideration but does not imply endorsement of conclusions or recommendations.

The Institution maintains its position of neutrality on issues of public policy in order to safeguard the intellectual freedom of the staff. Hence interpretations or conclusions in Brookings publications should be understood to be solely those of the authors and should not be attributed to the Institution, to its trustees, officers, or other staff members, or to the organizations that support its research.

9.95

Foreword

FOR HALF A CENTURY after the Great Depression, government credit programs quietly expanded in response to the demands of homeowners, farmers, small-business owners, and students, among others. Recently, though, events have pushed these programs into the public spotlight. Some programs face enormous cost increases at a time of budgetary austerity. The economic depression that hit the farm economy in the 1980s has raised the spectre of widespread defaults on federally guaranteed farm loans and threatened the viability of the farm credit system. The subsidy costs of other programs continue to grow rapidly, adding to the U.S. budget deficit. In addition, the Reagan administration has focused attention on the loan programs with its proposal to reduce the deficit, temporarily, by selling a portion of the government portfolio. Finally, because many of the lending agencies compete directly with private institutions, they have played a prominent role in the debate over public versus private provision of services.

Loans issued or guaranteed by the federal government totaled more than $700 billion at the end of 1986. If loans made by government-sponsored enterprises are included, the total surpasses the one trillion dollar mark. These loan programs developed under financial market conditions far different from those that exist today. Yet no coherent reporting system exists for evaluating the need for these programs or the risks and costs they impose on taxpayers.

In this study, Barry P. Bosworth, Andrew S. Carron, and Elisabeth H. Rhyne evaluate the economic justifications for government credit programs. They clarify such basic issues as how to measure the subsidy cost of a loan program, how government lending affects economic activity, and when a loan program may be justified. The study assesses recent policy initiatives to impose user fees on government-sponsored loans, to sell off existing loan assets, and to include all federal loan programs within the U.S. budget.

The authors examine loan programs in four areas—housing, small business, agriculture, and education—that illustrate the diversity of the policy issues. They propose a new method of including loan programs in the budget, one that highlights the full cost to taxpayers and reduces opportunities to camouflage those costs. They also review new directions in government credit, covering the growing role of state and local programs and recent suggestions to use government loans as part of an industrial policy to renovate the U.S. economy.

Barry P. Bosworth is a senior fellow in the Brookings Economic Studies program; Andrew S. Carron is a vice president of First Boston Corporation; and Elisabeth H. Rhyne is project development advisor for the U.S. Agency for International Development in Kenya. They are grateful to Shannon P. Butler, Michael K. Kuehlwein, and Sheila E. Murray for research assistance. They appreciate the helpful comments on earlier drafts by Arthur Hauptman, Alice M. Rivlin, Charles L. Schultze, and an anonymous reviewer. Jeanette Morrison, Brenda B. Szittya, and Caroline Lalire edited the manuscript; Almaz S. Zelleke verified its factual content; and Florence Robinson prepared the index. Kathleen Elliott Yinug provided administrative assistance. Financial support was provided by a grant from the Andrew W. Mellon Foundation.

The views expressed in this book are those of the authors and should not be ascribed to the persons or the organization whose assistance is acknowledged or to the trustees, officers, or other staff members of the Brookings Institution.

BRUCE K. MACLAURY
President

January 1987
Washington, D.C.

Contents

Text Tables

Appendix Tables

Text Figures

Appendix Figure

The Economics of
Federal Credit Programs

CHAPTER ONE

Introduction and Assessment

FEDERAL CREDIT PROGRAMS are among the least understood areas of government involvement in the economy. In these programs, the government acts much like a bank, raising funds or directing their flow to provide credit on terms it specifies to borrowers it selects. In the sheer volume of the loans there is at least the potential for a substantial impact on the allocation of income and resources within the economy. In several areas—especially housing, education, and agriculture—the loans constitute the principal tool of federal policy. Yet the goals of the programs are often ill-defined and contradictory, and despite the substantial cost to taxpayers, little or no effort has been made to evaluate either the current need for such programs or their effectiveness.

A substantial portion of the funds that now move through U.S. capital markets originates in government credit programs. The outstanding volume of loans supported by government or government-sponsored agencies exceeded a trillion dollars at the end of fiscal 1985.[1] In the 1980–85 period, federally assisted lending, net of repayments, averaged $88 billion annually, or 17 percent of all funds raised in U.S. capital markets.[2] In addition, state and local governments have recently entered the loan business in a big way, financing loans to private firms and individuals through tax-exempt bonds. Their annual private-purpose lending rose from $11 billion in 1976 to $88 billion in 1985.[3] Government has become the nation's largest financial intermediary.

Federal credit programs have grown over the last half century in response to a variety of perceived needs. First conceived to shore up

---

1. *Special Analyses, Budget of the United States Government, Fiscal Year 1987*, pp. F-66, F-72.
2. Ibid., p. F-80.
3. Ibid., p. F-52; and *Special Analyses, Fiscal Year 1986*, p. F-50.

1

weak financial markets during the Great Depression, they were subsequently expanded to strengthen those markets in hopes of avoiding a repetition of the 1930s experience. Later programs represented efforts to promote certain national goals, such as the spread of homeownership or access by students to higher education, or to provide help to specific groups of individuals, such as veterans or disaster victims. Credit programs also reflect political interest in aiding specific industries, such as agriculture or synthetic fuels, or bailing out faltering enterprises, such as Lockheed, Chrysler, and New York City.

During the depression and the immediate postwar period, the credit programs were extremely successful in meeting these needs. As a result, credit markets are far stronger and more integrated than they once were. Homeownership is far more widespread than it would have been without federal credit programs. Many students have been able to go to college because of government loans. Remote rural communities have access to electricity because of subsidized federal loans. There have even been some recent successes: Lockheed, Chrysler, and New York survived their financial crises.

But the hallmark of the government credit programs at present is controversy. Opponents of some programs argue that they no longer serve a real need. Budget-minded critics point out that although most government credit programs were not intended to provide a subsidy, many now do. The rapid growth of government-assisted credit has also increased fears that these programs are crowding out other, nonassisted borrowers, distorting the allocation of capital in the economy. Meanwhile, the system under which the programs are administered prevents Congress from obtaining information needed for reasonable judgments about their effectiveness or cost.

A substantial controversy also surrounds the issue of the actual effect of the credit programs on the economy. The public debate is dominated by two groups who share the view that these programs have a strong impact on resource use, comparable to direct expenditures. They differ only in their views as to the desirability of such activities. One group believes that the credit programs constitute a beneficial intervention to correct market failures that disadvantage specific borrowers. The other group believes that they are an unwarranted intrusion of government into well-functioning capital markets.

A third view, held primarily by academic economists, is that many of these programs actually have little or no impact on resource use. In this view, the federal credit agencies are, to a large extent, simply another financial intermediary, competing with commercial banks and other lending institutions, raising funds in one market to relend in another. Although they alter the pattern of financing, the economic effect of such loans is far less than that of a direct government expenditure.

In this study we argue that the issue can be resolved by focusing on the subsidy cost of a loan program. Unsubsidized loans may represent a competitive challenge to private financial institutions, but they do not distort the pattern of resource use in the economy. Subsidized loans, however, impose a direct cost on taxpayers and an indirect cost on other borrowers who are forced out of the credit markets or compelled to pay a higher rate of interest. Those costs must be accounted for in evaluating the net benefits of the programs.

The remainder of this chapter outlines the chief forms of credit assistance, their basic rationales, and our proposals for reform. The conceptual issues involved in an evaluation of the economic effects of government credit assistance are the subject of chapter 2. The individual programs are examined in more detail in chapters 3 through 6. Chapter 7 outlines a system of accounting for the credit programs that yields a more direct measure of their costs to taxpayers and their impact on the economy. The final chapter looks at the recent development of state and local government credit programs and the potential use of loan programs in industrial policy.

Forms of Credit Assistance

In federal budget documents, four different types of government credit assistance are distinguished: loan guarantees, direct loans, government-sponsored enterprises, and tax-exempt state and local bonds to finance private sector activities.[4]

Loan guarantees, which accounted for $410 billion of the government credit outstanding in 1985, are privately held loans for which the government guarantees to pay all or part of the principal and interest in the event of a default.[5] The category of loan guarantees includes both

4. The volume of lending and the outstanding stock are reported each year in *Special Analyses* of the federal budget documents.

5. *Special Analyses, Fiscal Year 1987*, p. F-72. The terms *loan guarantee* and *guaranteed loan* are used interchangeably.

loan insurance—on those loans for which the government charges the private parties a fee to cover the cost of the program—and true guarantees, for which the government absorbs the cost of potential defaults. Loan guarantees are most common for housing finance and small business loans. Some loans, such as those for students, that are classified as loan guarantees also include an explicit interest rate subsidy besides the guarantee.

Direct loans are originated and serviced by government agencies. Private lenders play no role in the process. Normally such loans, which are implicitly government guaranteed, involve a greater degree of subsidy than simple loan guarantees because, besides the cost of a guarantee, most credit agencies do not charge the borrower enough interest to cover their administrative and borrowing costs. These loans, the outstanding volume of which totaled $257 billion in 1985, are at the center of the controversy over the budgetary treatment of government credit programs.[6] The largest direct loan programs are operated by the Department of Agriculture and the Export-Import Bank.

Government-sponsored enterprises are private financial institutions established and chartered by the federal government. There are five such programs: the Farm Credit System, the Federal Home Loan Bank System, the Federal National Mortgage Association, the Federal Home Loan Mortgage Corporation, and the Student Loan Marketing Association. Except for the Farm Credit System, these institutions do not normally initiate new loans, concentrating instead on maintaining secondary markets for the resale of mortgages and student loans, offering secondary loan guarantees (on securities backed by pools of existing mortgages), and providing credit to private lending institutions. The Farm Credit System issues marketable bonds to support the agricultural loans of its member cooperative associations. The government-sponsored agencies held $418 billion in loan assets in 1985, of which $48 billion represented loans included in other programs.[7]

The most rapidly growing source of government-assisted credit has been state and local governments. Because their bonds are exempt from federal income tax, these governments can raise funds in financial markets at interest rates 20 to 40 percent below similar federal government securities. State and local governments have used this low-cost financing to establish their own financial institutions, which make below-market-rate loans to favored borrowers. These private-purpose bond

6. Ibid., p. F-66.
7. Ibid., pp. F-73–F-74.

Table 1-1. *Federal Government Participation in Domestic Capital Markets, Fiscal Years 1975, 1980, 1985*
Billions of dollars unless otherwise specified

Loan category	1975	1980	1985
Total funds loaned in U.S. credit markets	178.0	354.5	768.6
Federally assisted lending	27.0	79.9	110.3
Direct loans	12.8	24.2	28.0
Guaranteed loans	8.6	31.6	21.6
Government-sponsored enterprise			
loans	5.6	24.1	60.7
Participation rate (percent)	15.2	22.5	14.4
Total funds borrowed in U.S. capital			
markets	178.0	354.5	768.6
Total government borrowing	64.8	123.5	276.8
Federal borrowing[a]	50.9	70.5	197.3
Guaranteed loans	8.6	31.6	21.6
Government-sponsored enterprise			
borrowing	5.3	21.4	57.9
Participation rate (percent)	36.4	34.8	36.0
Tax-exempt state and local bond issues[b]	30.5	54.5	178.2
Private purpose	8.9	32.5	88.4
Public purpose	21.6	22.0	89.8

Source: *Special Analyses, Budget of the United States Government, Fiscal Year 1985*, pp. F-5, F-38, and *Special Analyses, Fiscal Year 1987*, pp. F-52, F-80.
a. Includes financing of unified budget deficit.
b. New issues on a calendar year basis.

issues have been concentrated in three areas: business, housing, and education loans. In general, the state or local agency assumes no responsibility for repayment, even in the event of default. The interest subsidy costs are paid by the federal government through the loss of tax revenue, which was estimated to have exceeded $8 billion annually by 1985.[8]

Table 1-1 shows annual net lending within these major categories of credit assistance for fiscal 1975, 1980, and 1985. Federally assisted lending rose sharply as a share of total credit market activity throughout the last half of the 1970s—from 15 percent of net funds loaned in U.S. credit markets in 1975 to a peak of 22 percent in 1980. Recently, there has been some decline in the federal share, but the drop has been due more to a rapid rise in the total size of the market than to a slowdown in government activity. If federal borrowing to finance the budget deficit is included, the federal government absorbed or influenced between one-

8. *Special Analyses, Fiscal Year 1987*, table G-2. The $8 billion represents the sum of individual line items.

third and one-half of all funds moving through the capital markets in 1980–85.

Although the categories shown in table 1-1 are suited to the available accounting data, from an analytical perspective it is more useful to distinguish among the credit assistance programs on the basis of the mechanism that is used to influence credit terms. The most direct form of assistance is an interest rate subsidy. It is also the easiest to evaluate because borrowers can be expected to respond to the subsidy in a fashion similar to a simple change in the market interest rate.

The government may also influence credit terms by altering the risk characteristics of private loans, providing either a loan guarantee or insurance. In the case of a guarantee, the government provides a subsidy equivalent to the fee that would be required to purchase private insurance against default. A government-operated loan insurance program, on the other hand, need not involve a subsidy if the fee charged the borrower is sufficient to cover all costs of the program.

Finally, the government may attempt to change the relative structure of interest rates faced by different classes of borrowers by altering the composition of assets in financial markets, buying up assets in one market (mortgages, for example) financed by the sale of securities in another (government agency securities). The object of such a maneuver is for the increased supply of funds to lower the interest rate in the target market at the cost of a higher rate on government securities. The exchange of one asset for another appears not to involve a subsidy. The government is merely acting much like private financial intermediaries, raising funds in one market to invest in another.

Loan insurance and asset-exchange programs that do not involve a subsidy, or cost to the government, are a lesser cause for public concern. In such cases, the government is doing nothing that private investors should not be able to do for themselves in well-functioning markets. Thus in evaluating the economic effect of credit programs we focus on the amount of subsidy associated with guarantees and the partial payment of interest costs.

The Rationales for Government Credit Programs

A clear identification of the goals of the various credit programs is critical to an evaluation of their performance. There is, as well, a significant link between the goals of a credit program and the specific form of credit assistance that is likely to be most effective. In this study we shall emphasize three important objectives of the credit programs: to improve the efficiency of markets by correcting market imperfections and encouraging innovations, to reallocate resources toward activities that are judged to have a public value greater than that reflected in private decisions, and to redistribute income by providing a transfer to selected firms and individuals.

Credit Market Imperfections

We often speak of the capital market as though it were a single market with one rate of interest. In fact, of course, there are a large number of markets specializing in a wide range of financial instruments that vary substantially in their credit terms—interest rate, maturity, and collateral requirements. In competitive capital markets, however, funds can move freely among these markets so as to equate the net return on all types of loans. Interest rates will differ among borrowers only because of differences in defaults and the administrative costs of originating and servicing the loans. To insure against defaults, lenders can form pools of dissimilar assets. For the portfolio as a whole, default becomes a highly predictable cost based on average experience plus a systemic risk component common to all assets.

Credit markets are not, however, perfect. It is often alleged that some borrowers lack equal access to credit and that they are charged an interest rate that is excessive even after adjusting for differences in default and administrative costs. Credit market imperfections may take a variety of forms. First, borrowers may lack access to national credit markets. Federal regulations, for example, restrict interstate banking, so that borrowers dependent on their local bank may find that funds available for loans are contracting at the time they are most in need. Agricultural credit programs are commonly justified on this ground.

Second, some types of loans do not have effective insurance markets because the information needed to assess risk is lacking. Such information is readily available for large national firms, but difficult to obtain for individuals and small businesses—particularly when there is no standard form for loan contracts. Ineffective insurance markets present severe problems for borrowers, such as students, who cannot provide a marketable form of collateral.[9] The lack of both insurance against default and standardization of loan contracts may limit the development of a resale market for some financial instruments. Thus, from the perspective of the lenders, such loans are illiquid and their riskiness uncertain, requiring a compensatory increase in the interest rate or a shortening of the loan maturity.

At their inception, some of the federal credit programs provided financial services that were unavailable from private institutions. Examples include the resale markets for residential mortgages and student loans, mortgage-backed securities, Federal Housing Administration mortgage insurance, and some of the insurance programs of the Export-Import Bank. Most of these programs facilitate the trading of financial instruments among investors. To the extent that they reduce transaction costs, they do result in some reallocation of credit toward sectors such as housing, but a shift of credit flows that results from lower transaction costs improves the productivity of capital rather than misallocates it.

In establishing these programs the government played an important role in demonstrating that they could be operated profitably. Private firms, in turn, began to offer the same services, benefiting both from the information that the levels of risk were manageable and from the establishment of already functioning markets in which they could participate. It does not often happen, however, that the government can play such a demonstration role. It can do so only when it can take advantage of economies of scale not available to the private sector or when the private sector misestimates the risks involved in a particular market.

Programs aimed at improving the efficiency of capital markets do not normally require a subsidy. By furnishing services the private market lacks, the government should be able to provide borrowers with a lower interest rate than available elsewhere, while imposing no net costs on taxpayers. Insurance programs can charge a fee to offset costs, and arbitrage between markets is a potentially profit-making activity. As we shall argue in later chapters, programs that identify specific market failures and design measures to overcome them have been the most successful of the government's initiatives in the credit area.

---

9. The provision of insurance in financial markets is also severely constrained by problems of moral hazard and adverse selection. Moral hazard occurs when the existence of insurance itself reduces the degree of effort that the lender or borrower will make to ensure that the loan is repaid. Problems of adverse selection arise when the lender knows more than the insurer about the risks of individual loans and purchases insurance only for loans of greater-than-average risk.

The chief danger encountered by these market-correcting programs is that at the time when they should be fostering the development of private alternatives, they may instead stifle them by using special privileges afforded to government. They may offer the services at a price so low that private firms will be unable to compete. This issue arises most often with respect to loan insurance and the secondary market activities of government-sponsored agencies.

Resource Reallocation

Credit programs can be used to induce firms or industries to engage in or to expand certain economic activities that have public benefits in excess of those that accrue to the private parties. Examples include the synthetic fuels program, education credits, low-cost rental housing loans, and loans for environmental waste treatment equipment. Unlike market-correcting programs, resource reallocation programs are subsidized, either by a loan guarantee or by a below-market rate of interest.

For a variety of reasons, these programs are often ineffective in achieving their goals. First, the assistance may go to borrowers who would, in the absence of the program, have received credit from the private market anyway. It is difficult, and often undesirable, to design a program so that only marginal new borrowers are eligible. Second, borrowers may use the loans to expand some activity other than the one intended. Student education loans, for example, may simply reduce the financial contribution of parents. Finally, the benefits of the subsidy may accrue to the lenders as a larger profit, rather than to the borrowers.

The programs also involve substantial costs beyond the obvious cost to taxpayers of providing the subsidy. A loan subsidy program does not increase the total supply of funds to capital markets. All it does is provide an advantage to one group of borrowers relative to others. Some marginal borrowers are crowded out of the market, as market interest rates rise to a higher level than would exist in the program's absence.[10] Because of the multitude of federal programs aimed at marginal borrowers, the government is often working against itself, as subsidies extended to one group neutralize the subsidies to another. To the extent that a particular program succeeds, it transfers resources to uses that the private market would have valued less highly. Unless the assisted borrowers generate

10. Even when the government provides a direct loan it does so by entering the market to borrow more on its own account and then turning around and lending the funds to a private borrower.

substantial social and economic benefits, the shift in allocation implies a reduction in the overall efficiency of resource use. Because of the potential costs to others imposed by these programs it is important that the public benefits be strongly justified and that the effectiveness of the programs be closely monitored.

Income Redistribution

Some credit programs have as their main objective the simple transfer of income to a specific class of borrower rather than a change in economic behavior. The focus of a true income redistribution program is not on what a recipient would have done in the absence of credit, but only on whether the recipient fits the eligibility characteristics. Programs that involve a strong emphasis on income redistribution include the Veterans' Administration mortgage guarantee program, some programs of the Farmers Home Administration, and the various types of disaster loans.[11]

It is difficult to evaluate these programs on an economic basis because the decision to assist certain groups is usually based on political or humanitarian considerations, not economic ones. The question confronting designers of this type of program is not whether to intervene, but whether credit is the most appropriate form of assistance, as opposed to a grant, tax credit, or other form of aid.

On the other hand, such decisions should reflect a full understanding of their costs. In most respects costs are the same as those for resource reallocation programs: subsidy costs to taxpayers and higher interest costs to other borrowers. Thus an accurate system of accounting for costs is still important.

Although the objectives of government credit programs can be differentiated clearly in principle, individual programs often reflect an intermingling of motives. Such a mixing of motives can be particularly insidious when an income transfer or resource reallocation program masquerades for purposes of public discourse as a market-perfecting program—directing attention away from its costs.

The Evolution of Government Credit Programs

The initial involvement of government in credit markets was triggered by the financial collapse that accompanied the Great Depression of the

11. Recipients of VA mortgage insurance do have to buy a home to qualify, but because the Federal Housing Administration offers essentially the same insurance in an unsubsidized form, the VA program is primarily a simple income transfer to veterans.

1930s. When it emerged from the depression, the American financial system had not merely recovered from a disaster, it had been fundamentally restructured. Before the depression, the system had been characterized by regional divisions and was oriented primarily toward commerce and industry and the wealthy. Afterwards it was on its way to becoming a modern, nationwide system offering services that most Americans both desired and could afford. Government credit programs helped ease that transition, and several such programs became ongoing parts of the new system.

The early programs aimed at stemming further decline and providing relief to institutions and individuals that had already suffered losses. The Reconstruction Finance Corporation loaned money to banks and helped them stay open. The Home Owners' Loan Corporation purchased and rescheduled delinquent mortgages from banks, and the Federal Farm Mortgage Corporation provided a similar function for farmers. These agencies helped private financial institutions to stay afloat and kept families from losing their homes and farms.

By the end of the 1930s, the relief functions of federal credit had dwindled, and most of the agencies that provided them were soon liquidated. The emphasis shifted toward correcting perceived failures of private capital markets and developing mechanisms to ensure that the financial system would be safe from another collapse. Among such programs were the Federal Deposit Insurance Corporation, the Securities and Exchange Commission, and such large credit programs as the Federal Home Loan Bank System, a government-sponsored enterprise empowered to lend to savings and loan institutions; Federal Housing Administration mortgage insurance to create lender confidence in long-term amortizing mortgages; and the Commodity Credit Corporation to provide crop financing to farmers. The Export-Import Bank opened its doors in 1934 to promote U.S. exports, and in 1938 the Federal National Mortgage Association (Fannie Mae) was created to develop a resale market for residential mortgages. A battery of federal programs to meet the special needs of agriculture included, besides the Commodity Credit Corporation, the Rural Electrification Administration; an expanded Farm Credit System, which furnished a range of services to creditworthy farmers; and the Farmers Home Administration, which served smaller, more marginal farmers. Most programs were intended to be self-financing; no substantial government subsidy was involved.

Today, the main volume of loan activity continues to be concentrated in those sectors that were singled out for attention in the 1930s: agricul-

Table 1-2. *Federal Government Loans by Major Program Area,*
Fiscal Year 1985
Billions of dollars

Category	Outstanding loans	New issues	Net change in outstanding loans
Direct loans			
Foreign military sales	19.1	4.0	1.9
Agriculture	127.1	22.5	12.0
Education	16.1	1.3	0.5
Housing and Urban Development	29.4	15.6	13.3
Small Business Administration	9.4	1.4	−0.1
Export-Import Bank	16.9	1.6	−0.6
Deposit insurance corporations	5.4	0.8	0.3
Other programs	34.0	17.2	0.7
Total	257.4	64.4	28.0
Loan guarantees			
Agriculture	11.2	4.0	0.3
Education	35.8	8.5	3.9
Housing and Urban Development[a]	202.8	22.8	12.9
Veterans' Administration	130.6	11.5	5.2
Small Business Administration	9.1	2.5	0.2
Export-Import Bank	5.1	4.4	−0.5
Other programs	15.8	1.8	−0.4
Total[a]	410.4	55.5	21.6
Government-sponsored enterprises			
Student Loan Marketing Association	11.6	3.1	2.1
Federal National Mortgage Association	145.5	39.6	27.8
Farm Credit System	69.1	44.1	−7.8
Federal Home Loan Bank System[b]	192.1	165.2	43.7
Total	418.3	252.0	65.8
Loans included in other categories	48.4	0.0	5.1
Net lending	369.9	252.0	60.7

Source: *Special Analyses, Fiscal Year 1987*, tables F-19, F-20, F-21.
a. Excludes secondary guaranteed loans and guaranteed loans held as direct loans.
b. Includes Federal Home Loan Mortgage Corporation loans.

ture, housing, small business, and export sales. As shown in table 1-2, agriculture accounts for half of outstanding direct loans, with business-related loans representing another 20 percent. More than three-fourths of outstanding loan guarantees are in the mortgage market, as are 80 percent of the activities of government-sponsored agencies. In fact, in 1985 more than 60 percent of the outstanding government-assisted credit (excluding tax-exempt bonds) belonged to agencies existing at the end of the 1930s. The inclusion of the Veterans' Administration mortgage guarantee program, created in 1946, would raise that ratio to 75 percent.

The stability of the basic administrative structure notwithstanding, new programs have proliferated, each oriented toward a specific subsector of borrowers or activities. There are about 350 separate government credit programs.[12] The Farmers Home Administration alone now administers more than twenty programs, all aimed at the broad target population of relatively low-income rural dwellers, but each offering a different service. Many of the programs that first appeared during the 1960s, when the usefulness of credit programs in combating poverty was being tried, are more heavily subsidized than their predecessors. In addition, some of the established direct loan programs came, during the 1960s, to embody large subsidies, as the government failed to raise loan rates in step with increases in its own borrowing costs.

Significant recent developments have been the student loan programs and highly targeted loans to businesses, such as Lockheed, Chrysler, and the synthetic fuels industry. The student loan program was originally established in the 1960s, but during the last half of the 1970s it was expanded to include middle- and upper-income students, and the magnitude of the government subsidy was sharply increased. In the Lockheed and Chrysler bailouts, the government loan guarantees provided emergency, confidence-restoring actions, similar to those of the Reconstruction Finance Corporation and other agencies during the 1930s. Unlike the earlier examples, however, financial confidence was not the fundamental problem for Lockheed and Chrysler; rather it was economic viability. A return to profitability was assured by later, quieter government policies, including the awarding of defense contracts and the imposition of automobile import quotas. The Synthetic Fuels Corporation, also the beneficiary of federal loan guarantees, is gradually being dismantled without ever having become fully operational.

Current Need for Government Credit

Private capital markets have evolved in ways that make them far more capable of servicing the diverse needs of private borrowers than they

12. Clifford M. Hardin and Arthur T. Denzau, *Closing the Backdoor on Federal Spending: Better Management of Federal Credit,* no. 64 (St. Louis: Washington University, Center for the Study of American Business, 1984), p. 2.

were fifty years ago. The existence of a national capital market makes it possible to absorb financial risk through portfolio diversification in ways that were not possible in the 1930s. Capital now flows freely between different regions of the country, and active resale markets increase the liquidity of most types of assets.

Government credit programs have played a positive role in stimulating these innovations. Such efforts have been particularly useful when the government has aimed at promoting an integration of capital markets and assuring access of local borrowers to a national market. The standardization of loan contracts and the development of secondary resale markets have also increased the liquidity of specific financial claims, such as mortgages and student loans. The programs' very success, however, has eliminated some of the rationale for their continued existence.

Among the various programs the government-sponsored enterprises, such as the Federal National Mortgage Association, have proved a particularly effective means of enhancing market performance. Often owned and financed by private individuals and institutions, their links to the government take the form of assurances of support in severe crises in return for some responsibility for operating in accord with national goals. The mixture of private ownership, which provides a motive to minimize costs, with a public policy orientation has generally worked well. The criticisms that have been leveled against these programs— overdependency on government and excessive competition with private lenders—are less serious than that of failing to serve the intended goals.

In the past, these enterprises received some direct subsidies, such as an exemption from income taxation, but since the 1960s there has been a steady trend toward eliminating subsidies and allowing the institutions to stand on their own. The question of whether their liabilities have an implicit guarantee because of the link to government is controversial, but in our judgment it does not constitute a large subsidy and differs only modestly from the implied guarantee against failure of any large private financial or nonfinancial institution.

Another form of federal assistance that is clearly appropriate to improve the functioning of specific markets is loan insurance in cases in which private insurance against default has failed to develop. Again, such programs need not involve a subsidy, and the government should charge a fee to cover default losses.

Unsubsidized programs, even large ones, that improve the operation of private financial markets should not be feared as sources of crowding out or misallocation of resources. They involve transformations of certain financial assets from one form to another that leave the price and quantity of credit virtually unchanged. As long as the government's costs are fully reflected in loan terms, borrowers' and investors' own decisions will provide the primary judgment on the need for each program.

The question remains, however, whether government should be in the business of direct lending—operating its own lending agencies. From an economic perspective there is little difference between a loan program, such as that for student loans, that relies on private lenders to originate and service the loan, and direct lending, such as agricultural loans of the Farmers Home Administration. The government and private lenders are both acting as financial intermediaries, raising funds from savers to lend to borrowers. The source of the funds, public or private, has no effect on the long-term cost to the government, or to other participants in the market. But although there may be no economic reason for selecting one over the other, there are several administrative and accountability features that make reliance on private lenders preferable in most cases. First, many credit programs are intended to support rather than supplant the borrower-lender relationship. Keeping private lenders involved is in accord with this objective. Second, private lenders are more expert than the government at handling a loan throughout its life. The government has an especially poor record in loan collections. And finally, the costs to the government of externally serviced loans are easier to see because the payment of a fee for servicing the loan does not become mingled with loan disbursements and repayments.

An exception to the administrative advantages of using private lenders arises for programs involving large loans to a few borrowers. Such loans often take the form of bond issues rather than bank loans. If they are financed as direct loans through Treasury borrowings, the number of nonstandard, government-backed securities circulating in the credit markets is minimized. Loan recipients and the government do not have to pay the premium required for the lack of standardization. This was the original rationale behind the Federal Financing Bank, which now finances most such programs, such as those of the Rural Electrification Administration, the Export-Import Bank, and foreign military sales.

A final exception, discussed in the chapter on student loans, would be a repayment program tied to the borrower's income and for which there is no physical collateral. In those unusual circumstances the government might be able to provide a superior vehicle for collection of loan repayments—the Internal Revenue Service.

Loan Subsidies

The concerns of Congress and the Administration should be focused on those loan programs that, for a variety of reasons and in a variety of ways, provide a subsidy. Most such programs have taken on the subsidy role inadvertently. When the programs were established, loan rates were typically equal to, or slightly in excess of, government borrowing costs. As time went by, however, the government failed to raise its loan rates in step with market interest rates.[13] Except for the Federal Housing Administration (FHA) mortgage insurance program, it also failed to charge borrowers a fee to cover expected future default costs on loan guarantees. In addition, it ignored administrative costs in setting loan rates. The result is a haphazard variation of interest rates that bears no logical relationship to the professed goals of different programs.

Subsidies may be justified in two situations: to promote the purchase of public goods that generate public benefits in excess of those that accrue to the private purchasers, and to redistribute income. The "public good" argument is used to justify loan programs for small business, new energy technologies, agriculture, and education. The government hopes to induce private parties to undertake a specific activity at the cost of a small reduction in its price. What it fears is that it will end up paying the private parties for something they would have done in any case or, even worse, that the borrowers will take the subsidy and do something completely different. Credit subsidies are particularly susceptible to a simple substitution of public for private credit or a redirection of the funds to other uses.

The rationale for using credit policies to redistribute income is similar to the argument favoring in-kind transfer payments, such as food stamps, medical care, and housing allowances, over cash grants: the government wishes to dictate the use to which the income payment will be put. These programs are politically popular because a credit subsidy is less evident

13. To an increasing extent the government is tying the loan rate within individual programs to Treasury financing costs. This reform has simply institutionalized a subsidy, however, because it ignores administrative and default costs. Examples of programs whose original loan terms were comparable to market rates are the Rural Electrification Administration loans and the student loan program.

in the federal budget than a direct payment is. Veterans' Administration mortgage guarantees, disaster loans, and the rural housing programs of the Farmers Home Administration are examples of such programs.

Over the years, little effort has been made to undertake a systematic review of the costs and benefits of the subsidized loan programs or to adjust their operations in light of that analysis. The loan guarantee program of the Small Business Administration, for example, began as a market-perfecting program in an area where private lenders were believed to have overestimated the risk of default. Experience, however, has shown that the actual rate of SBA loan defaults is high. By failing to charge a fee to cover those losses, the government converted the program to a subsidy and allowed the guarantee to evolve into a simple income transfer for small businesses.

In other cases the subsidy is a historical accident. The Rural Electrification Administration, for example, originally charged a rate close to the government's own borrowing cost. As market rates rose, however, the loan rate was not adjusted in step. A similar situation has emerged for the student loan program, in which the loan rate remains constant and the size of the subsidy varies randomly in response to changing market interest rates.

In general, we believe that loan subsidies are an inefficient means of promoting a reallocation of resources or a redistribution of income. As discussed in subsequent chapters, we find it is difficult to show that the subsidized programs achieve their aims and generate benefits sufficient to justify the costs.

There may be sound reasons for subsidizing specific activities or groups, but a requirement that the receipt of the subsidy be dependent on taking out a loan seems inappropriate. By using more direct means of making the payment, government can avoid the diversion of funds into other uses that so dilutes the impact of the programs. For example, a targeted grant program combined with an unsubsidized loan program is likely to be more successful in expanding access to higher education than the current loan program, which is heavily subsidized but not available to all students. Combining two objectives in a single program leads to inevitable tensions that limit success in both directions. In the case of the student loan program, the tension between one objective—correcting a capital market imperfection to provide all students with access to credit—and the other—subsidizing the target group of low-income students—means either that subsidy costs are too high or that some students have no access to credit.

In a few cases, a loan subsidy may be appropriate. For example, left to their own devices, private markets will discriminate on the basis of such characteristics as race or sex whenever it is profitable to do so. Regulation of the private banking industry is often a clumsy means of preventing discrimination, and a subsidized federal program targeted on affected groups may be a more effective way to assure access to credit to all borrowers. Still, loan subsidies are appropriate only when the specific problem they address is directly related to the operation of credit markets. There are few cases in which that is true.

Crowding Out

In general, credit programs should not be defended on the grounds that they increase the level of total demand or employment in the economy. Supporting federal credit because it increases demand is as inappropriate as supporting defense spending because it increases employment. A desire to increase total demand or employment does not constitute an argument for favoring a specific type of expenditure or class of borrowers. Nor should an evaluation of government credit programs be based on whether they increase the total supply of resources in capital markets. That supply is determined by national rates of saving.[14] The proper context for an evaluation of the credit programs is the allocation of the nation's resources among competing uses. If government assists one class of borrowers to obtain credit that they would not otherwise receive, the cost of credit to other borrowers must rise to "crowd out" an equivalent amount of unassisted lending.

In practice, however, the amount of crowding out of alternative resource uses may be much different than that implied by the mere volume of assisted loans. First, much of the credit assistance is absorbed in a simple substitution by borrowers of public for privately supplied credit with no net change in their expenditures. FHA or VA mortgages, for example, are highly substitutable with conventional mortgages, and changes in the volume of such loans cannot be interpreted as implying a net change in mortgage demand or home purchases.

In addition, many of the efforts of government to expand credit in

14. In today's financial markets international flows of capital are also of growing importance.

individual markets may be undone by the arbitrage activities of private investors. For example, a government agency may attempt to expand the total supply of mortgage credit by purchasing mortgages financed by an equivalent sale of government securities. Such an asset exchange will tend to reduce mortgage interest rates relative to those on government securities, but in response private investors will withdraw from the mortgage market and purchase higher-yielding government securities, reversing much of the initial change in interest rates. In later chapters we shall argue that this private arbitrage among markets is so extensive as to negate most of the allocative effect of unsubsidized credit programs.

Reliable estimates of the crowding-out effects of government credit programs can be obtained only by measuring the magnitude of the subsidy embedded in the credit programs and estimating the sensitivity of expenditures, as opposed to loan demand, to a change in the cost of credit. Both of these parameters vary enormously across the various loan programs, making any generalization meaningless. In later chapters we demonstrate how such estimates can be obtained for individual loan programs.

Budget Accounting

Tabulating the amounts of government credit extended is no easy matter. There is no common accounting system for tracking and reporting loan defaults and delinquencies, and loans are often rescheduled so as to delay the appearance of default costs. The costs that are reported each year are associated with servicing the stock of existing loans and are difficult to use in estimating the costs of new loans. Such practices stand in sharp contrast to those required by government regulation of private financial institutions.

When government undertakes a subsidy program, it is important to ensure that the benefits equal or exceed the costs. Most benefit-cost analyses of government programs involve some ambiguity because the *benefits* are often elusive and difficult to quantify. For loan subsidies, however, the situation is even worse because the *costs* are also elusive. Measuring costs is difficult because the budget system, with its emphasis of cash-flow accounting, records the volume of a loan as an outlay, equivalent to a direct expenditure, and records repayments in future years as a negative outlay, failing to note that the value of the repayments is often less than the original value of the loan. Thus it is impossible to identify the subsidy element within the regular budget.

The inclusion of the loan accounts within the unified budget also raises substantial opportunities to use financial gimmicks to camouflage the underlying fiscal condition of the government. For example, it is possible, for a time, to hide an excess of spending over income by selling financial assets in the private market—reported as a negative outlay. Yet from an economic perspective, it makes no difference that the government has financed a deficit by selling a financial asset rather than by issuing debt.

The issue of how best to identify the subsidy and report it in the budget is discussed in chapters 2 and 7. The value of the subsidy can be measured either as the benefit to the borrower or the cost to the government. The benefit approach requires a comparison with the alternative private market interest rate available to the borrower. Under the cost approach the subsidy is defined as the difference between receipts obtained from the borrower and the costs to the government. Those costs include the cost of raising funds, of administration, and of defaults.

In perfectly competitive capital markets the two estimates of the subsidy would be identical because government could not offer an unsubsidized loan at any lower rate than private lenders. If there are some private market imperfections, however, the benefit approach will generally yield a higher estimate of the subsidy. We prefer to use a cost-based estimate because it excludes the effects of market imperfections: a program that benefits borrowers without imposing a cost on government is not classified as a subsidy. Also, the cost approach provides a more direct link to the government budget, and in some cases, such as student loans, no comparable private market rate is available.

An additional question arises as to whether the subsidy should be valued and reported on an annual basis or capitalized over the life of the loan, providing a present discounted value of the future subsidy costs. Subsidy costs will usually be incurred in each year of a loan's existence. For evaluating the impact of the subsidy on resource use and on the budget, it is more useful to capitalize those annual costs to obtain the present value of the subsidy at the time the loan is made. The present value of the subsidy multiplied by the loan-to-value ratio provides an estimate of the decline in the price of the target good or activity. That is the measure required to evaluate the impact on demand and thus resource use. The use of the present discounted value of the subsidy also forces the government to recognize, in the budget, the full cost of a loan at the time it is made.

All of this leads us to emphasize that it is the magnitude of the subsidy, not loan volume, that should be the primary focus of budgetary attention. From an economic perspective, unsubsidized loans do not distort the allocation of resources. Furthermore, a loan, which will be repaid, is not the same as an expenditure, and the inclusion of loans in the unified budget, offset by repayments on old loans, simply confuses the effort to identify their fiscal impact and their ultimate cost to taxpayers.

The current system of accounting for credit programs is so lax that it hides the crossover from market improvement to subsidy. The resulting lack of attention to the subsidy costs and their relationship to potential benefits is an even more serious problem than the budgetary distortion alone.

We suggest that, contrary to current practice, all loan agencies should be moved off-budget and reorganized to parallel, in their accounting, the practices of private and government-sponsored financial institutions—income-expense, rather than cash-flow, accounting. The government would be required to make a payment to these agencies, equal to the present discounted value of any required subsidy, at the time a loan is made. That payment would go into a reserve, the earnings from which would reimburse the loan agency for future subsidy costs (both interest and default). In effect, the government would be contracting with essentially private lending institutions. Such a procedure would provide Congress with a direct measure of the budget costs of loans, enabling it to evaluate the costs relative to the benefits before making a commitment. Congress might then choose to eliminate some programs entirely or, in other cases, reduce the magnitude of the subsidy provided.

At present, the lack of reliable information on the operations of the credit agencies frustrates efforts to evaluate their performance. Rational judgments could be made if each lending agency were required to develop data on the administrative and default costs that, in conjunction with the government borrowing rate, define the cost of operating each loan program.

Summary

Subsequent chapters analyze individual loan programs, highlighting several features of government-assisted credit that are important in evaluating its impact on the economy. Five major conclusions emerge from that review. First, from the perspective of their influence on resource use, the effect of the loan programs is best measured by the magnitude of the subsidy embedded in the loans, not the volume of loan activity.

Second, while the magnitude of the subsidy varies widely across programs, the chief subsidy costs (and hence reallocation effects) are concentrated in a relatively small number of programs. Because of that diversity the aggregate volume of government-assisted credit is a particularly useless index of its economic impact and a misleading guide to the magnitude of the problems it raises.

Third, the most successful programs are those that have maintained a focus on improving the efficiency of capital markets and have avoided large subsidy elements. Loan subsidies are an inefficient means, compared with more direct methods available to government, of altering resource use or transferring income to specific groups in society. Federal chartering of financial institutions has been one successful method of minimizing the subsidy element because such institutions are required to be self-sufficient. They do have some comparative advantages over fully private institutions, but those advantages fall in the same category as deposit insurance, the lender-of-last-resort functions of the Federal Reserve, and preferential tax treatment of some private institutions. As discussed in subsequent chapters, the quantitative magnitude of the implicit subsidy is small and not out of line with the competitive advantages granted for private institutions. The government has also acted in recent years to remove some of the forms of preferential treatment by subjecting most of the agencies to taxation.

Fourth, it has been difficult for the subsidized programs to maintain a focus on the original objectives because the costs to the government are indirect and poorly represented in the budget. The lack of accountability has allowed some of the programs, such as those of the Department of Agriculture and the Small Business Administration, to expand beyond their original charter to extend subsidized credit to politically powerful groups.

Finally, the credit programs have far less impact on the allocation of resources in the economy than either their proponents or opponents believe. In many cases the result is simply a reshuffling of credit as the government credit agencies compete with private financial intermediaries for loan business. The issues for resource allocation are specific to a few programs—particularly those for agriculture, small business, and student loans—where the magnitude of the subsidy is unusually large.

CHAPTER TWO

The Economic Effects of Government Credit

THE EFFECTS OF government credit programs are a subject that generates substantial controversy, and they lie at the center of the debate over how the credit programs should be treated in the federal budget. Some critics of the programs argue that, in their economic impact, loans are virtually identical with direct expenditures by the government: both create demands on resources, absorb credit market funds, and drive up interest rates. As such, the credit programs represent an undesirable intrusion of government into well-functioning capital markets. These critics see including loan outlays in the federal budget, on a par with other expenditures, as a necessary recognition of their equivalent impact. They believe, moreover, that the greater visibility conferred on loans by their inclusion in the budget will exercise a constraining influence.

By contrast, the defenders of the programs view existing credit markets as highly imperfect, unfairly denying credit to otherwise well-qualified applicants. They argue that government credit programs represent a desirable intervention to correct private market failures that disadvantage specific borrowers. While agreeing with critics that the credit programs have a powerful effect on the economy, defenders tend to minimize their costs, pointing out that the vast majority of the loans are repaid. They argue that a loan is quite different from an expenditure and has no place in budget totals.

A third viewpoint, held mainly by academic economists, is that many government credit programs have little or no impact on the total demand for resources in the economy. The credit agencies are essentially equivalent to, and competitive with, privately owned financial intermediaries such as banks, raising funds in one market to relend in another. The issue for them is the influence of the programs on the allocation of credit and thereby the allocation of resources. From that perspective the primary interest is in the magnitude of the government *subsidy*

23

conferred by a loan program and how the subsidy affects ultimate spending decisions. These economists have concluded that in their influence on resource use, the loan programs are most similar to tax subsidies, such as the investment tax credit. If the government made loans at competitive market rates, private lenders might resent the competition, but the programs would impose no costs on taxpayers, and the economic impact would be limited to changes in the pattern of credit market intermediation. Neither the overall level of interest rates nor demand for credit would be changed. From this third viewpoint it is the cost of the loan subsidy, not the volume of loans, that should be included in the budget.

Determining the impact of credit programs on real resource use, as opposed to their effects on competition among lenders, revolves around two issues. First, are capital markets sufficiently imperfect that the government can alter the allocation of credit among borrowers without paying a subsidy? And second, how do borrowers respond in their expenditure decisions to lower interest rates that result from either subsidized or unsubsidized programs?

The first issue arises, for example, when a government agency simply buys existing private credit claims such as mortgages or other loans and finances the purchase by selling an equal amount of public securities. Such asset exchanges involve no subsidy, for the credit agencies act much like a private financial intermediary, raising funds in one market to relend in another. Although the total amount of debt outstanding (public plus private) is not affected, the change in its composition may lower the interest rate in the private market relative to that on public debt. Yet in changing the composition of assets in the market, the government agency appears to be doing nothing that private investors cannot do for themselves. The loan purchases of the Student Loan Marketing Association (Sallie Mae) are one such program.

A closely related activity of the agencies leaves private assets in place in the market but attempts to alter the interest rate structure by sponsoring the development of secondary markets to improve the assets' marketability. The effort to develop a secondary resale market for mortgages comparable to that for government and corporate debt, for example, was designed to make mortgages more attractive to private investors. Similarly, the agencies have created new financial instruments that blend the characteristics of private and public securities.[1]

1. An example here is the mortgage pools operated by the Federal National Mortgage

Loan subsidy programs, however, are not dependent for their economic effects on credit market imperfections. The government may provide a direct interest rate subsidy to borrowers, or it may seek to alter the interest rate structure indirectly by providing a guarantee against default as a means of increasing the attractiveness of the loans to investors. Student and small business loans are examples of such programs. Subsidized loan programs raise issues that are very similar to those encountered in evaluating tax subsidies. How sensitive are the expenditure decisions of borrowers to changes in loan costs? And to what extent do the subsidies accrue to activities that would have been undertaken in any case? Loan guarantees do, however, raise some additional problems because they are most valuable for the most risky or least viable projects, and because they reduce the lenders' incentives to evaluate the economic viability of an investment proposal thoroughly. Although loan guarantees appear to have a low cost to taxpayers, they may more greatly distort private behavior than outright interest subsidies do.

In the following sections, we examine in greater detail the effects on resource allocation of three main types of credit programs: asset exchanges, interest rate subsidies, and loan guarantees. Asset exchanges are examined first because they are at the heart of the debate over the efficiency of private capital markets. Can government, simply by varying the composition of assets in financial markets, alter the interest rates charged different borrowers? The chapter then examines subsidized loan programs and discusses the methodological issues involved in measuring the subsidies. An effective measure of the subsidy makes it possible to compare interest rate subsidies and loan guarantees with one another and with other types of government programs. Finally, we address the special aspects of loan insurance and guarantees.

Asset Exchange Programs

Two conflicting views of how capital markets operate—as a homogeneous whole, or as a collection of segmented individual markets—have played a critical role in the continuing debate over government

---

Association (Fannie Mae) and other mortgage market institutions. Securities are issued that represent a pass-through of the principal and interest earned on a pool of residential mortgages. Instead of holding a specific mortgage, the investor has purchased a share in a pool of mortgages.

credit programs. The first might be labeled the undifferentiated-markets hypothesis. It sees financial markets as highly fluid and competitive, with active arbitrage among individual submarkets. Individual investors are assumed to move their funds among markets in search of the maximum expected yield (exclusive of risk and liquidity premiums). They will buy and sell securities until all expected future yields are equal.

According to this school of thought, the ability of investors to arbitrage across markets and to diversify their portfolios, thereby reducing the risks of individual loans, means that the differences in interest rates between individual markets are independent of the relative quantities of assets outstanding in those markets: assets are close substitutes for one another, and the supply of funds to an individual market is highly responsive to changes in relative interest rates. Rates of return on assets of comparable maturity will differ only because of differences in administrative costs of originating and servicing loans and perceived differences in their risk and liquidity.

In such circumstances a swap of financial assets among markets—the purchase of assets in one market financed by an equivalent sale in another—does not significantly affect interest rates. A credit agency is doing nothing that private investors could not do for themselves.

By contrast, the segmented-markets, or "preferred habitat," hypothesis asserts that interest rates are affected by changes in the relative quantities of assets in the various markets. One version of this theory holds that different classes of lenders and borrowers have strong preferences for specific types of assets or assets of specific maturities. For example, savings and loan associations specialize in mortgage lending because of regulatory restrictions and an economic advantage that is derived from economies of scale and their knowledge of local markets. Life insurance companies direct many of their funds into long-term assets with the object of balancing the maturity of their assets and liabilities. Some arbitrage may occur across markets, but since the participants have well-defined preferences, shifts in the composition of financial claims among markets will alter interest rates.

This issue is important because, if existing capital markets are highly fragmented, with extensive barriers to the flow of credit between individual markets, resources are being wasted. That is, scarce savings are not being allocated among alternative projects so as to equalize the benefits of an additional dollar of investment in each area. If, for example, lenders cannot achieve the full benefits of diversifying their loan portfolios across a wide range of projects, individual borrowers or areas of activity may be denied the use of credit, even though the expected benefits exceed those of competing uses that are financed.

In such a segmented capital market structure, the government could have a powerful influence on resource use—comparable to that of fiscal and monetary policy—simply by borrowing funds in one market to relend in another. In fact, such activities could be highly profitable since the government would earn a higher return in the markets where credit is scarce than it would pay in the markets where credit is plentiful.[2]

Much traditional analysis in monetary economics, with its emphasis on the supply of and demand for money, is consistent with the undifferentiated-markets view. In essence, all bonds are lumped together in a homogeneous whole and interest rate differentials are related only to the maturity and risk characteristics of the underlying securities. Yet participants in the financial markets clearly believe that financial structure does matter and that interest rates in individual markets are not independent of the volume of claims on those markets. This second view of the financial markets has been greatly extended by the development of portfolio theory by Tobin, Markowitz, and others, and by the work that has been done to highlight the importance of financial intermediaries.[3]

In an appendix to this book we summarize the empirical research that has been done by proponents of each of these two versions of how capital markets operate. That survey reveals that the different conclusions reached by the two sets of observers reflect a basic difference in the type of analysis used. Studies that focus on movements in interest rates generally conclude that financial markets are highly integrated, with substantial arbitrage between individual markets. All interest rates tend to move up and down together over the business cycle in ways that are uncorrelated with changes in the relative quantities of assets outstanding.

2. These contrasting views of the capital markets are relevant to a wide range of financial market issues other than the effect of federal credit programs. They have been prominent in the research on the term structure of interest rates, and they arise with respect to government intervention in foreign exchange markets.

3. J. Tobin, "Liquidity Preference as Behavior towards Risk," *Review of Economic Studies*, vol. 25 (February 1958), pp. 65–86; Harry M. Markowitz, *Portfolio Selection: Efficient Diversification of Investments* (John Wiley and Sons, 1959); James S. Duesenberry, "A Process Approach to Flow-of-Funds Analysis," in National Bureau of Economic Research, *The Flow-of-Funds Approach to Social Accounting: Appraisal, Analysis, and Applications* (Princeton University Press, 1962), pp. 173–89; and Raymond W. Goldsmith, *Financial Intermediaries in the American Economy since 1900* (Princeton University Press, 1958).

In addition, interest rate differentials, adjusted for differences in risk and maturity, seem to reflect little more than differences in the costs of servicing various types of loans.

By contrast, studies that attempt to explain changes in the mix of assets which investors hold in their portfolios—a quantity approach— generally conclude that, although interest rates do affect the structure of the portfolio, the effects are small, implying a substantial degree of market segmentation.[4] The conclusion that assets are not close substitutes for one another leads, in turn, to the policy implication that changes in the relative supplies of securities should be an effective means of altering relative costs of financing.

In our own research, also reported in the appendix, we argue that these conflicting results can be traced to problems in the statistical methods used to analyze the data. An alternative methodology produces a greater degree of consistency between the interest rate and quantity approaches. We find that there is a substantial degree of market segmentation in the short run because of lags in investors' adjustments to changes in interest rates. However, the adjustment lags appear to be of short duration—less than one year. Thus over the longer term financial markets appear to be highly integrated, allocating funds to the markets where the net returns are greatest. During the last several decades interest rate differences among assets of comparable maturity have remained quite stable. The change in the interest rate structure that has occurred appears, from our statistical results, to be explainable by reference to various measures of the riskiness of different types of loans. The variation that remains is only weakly associated with changes in the mix of outstanding assets, and it is too small to leave room for a major influence from changes in the asset mix.

The equalization of the net return to investors across different classes of loans, after adjusting for differences in expenses, is illustrated in table 2-1 for a sample of U.S. commercial banks over the period 1970–79. The gross interest income varied from a low of 7.8 percent for marketable securities to a high of 19.3 percent for credit card debt. Differences in operating and default costs accounted for most of the variation in loan

4. The statistical regressions use interest rates to explain changes in the composition of the portfolio. The small, although significant, interest rate coefficients imply large coefficients on quantities when the equations are reversed to put an interest rate on the left-hand side.

Table 2-1. *Commercial Banks' Net Return on Loans, by Loan Category, 1970–79*[a]
Percent

	Loan function category				
Item	Invest-ment	Real estate mortgage	Install-ment	Credit card[b]	Commer-cial and other
Gross yield	7.77	8.22	10.96	19.30	8.81
Less: Operating expense	0.16	0.75	3.46	11.19	1.12
Net income before loss	7.60	7.47	7.50	8.10	7.69
Less: Loss reserve[b]	0.00	0.08	0.48	1.84	0.36
Less: Cost of funds[c]	4.64	4.66	4.64	4.72	4.66
Net profit	2.96	2.74	2.38	1.54	2.67

Source: Federal Reserve Bank of New York, *Functional Cost Analysis* (New York: FRBNY, annually), 1970–79 issues.

a. The data are from major commercial banks (those with more than $200 million of deposits).
b. Entries are based on data from 1971 to 1979 only because data for 1970 are unavailable.
c. Varies among categories because of differences in weights attached to individual banks.

rates, however, so that, net of costs, yields were very similar over a wide range of different types of loans.[5]

We conclude that purchases of private assets financed by a sale of government securities will have only a transitory influence on the cost of borrowing in the private market. Because expanded lending under such credit programs does not alter borrowing costs, it follows that such lending affects the allocation of real resources in a relatively minor way.

One key implication of this conclusion is that, in broad terms, existing capital markets are highly efficient. Thus opportunities for profitable arbitrage among markets by the government are limited. Private investors are equally capable of exploiting such opportunities, and at least among the major markets, they appear to have done so.

Of course, existing government programs are an important feature of today's capital market structure. Particularly for those programs whereby government has sought to expand secondary resale markets and provide insurance against default, the government presence may be crucial to an efficient market operation. The implication is not that eliminating current

5. Loss reserves were calculated as a simple average of actual experience over the previous five years. There is some variation in the average cost of funds because the weight attached to each bank depended on the volume of its activity in the specific loan category. The low net return to credit cards is accounted for by losses in the early years, when start-up costs and competition were most intense in this newly developing market.

secondary market programs would have no effect, only that their expansion at the margin would not.

It should also be noted that this analysis is a highly aggregate one that examines arbitrage only among large markets, such as those for mortgages, corporate bonds, and government securities. Other, smaller markets, such as student loans or agricultural credit, may be more isolated, and additional market-perfecting activities may be possible.

In sum, if the government believes that unexploited opportunities exist to narrow interest rate differentials among markets, it should be able to do so without a cost to taxpayers. That is precisely the logic behind the government-sponsored enterprises. In evaluating credit programs whose justification rests on the ground of correcting failures of the private credit market, it should be sufficient to ensure that they are not subsidized. Unnecessary programs will fade away simply because there will be no demand for the services they provide.

Subsidized Credit

Evaluating the economic effects of loan subsidies involves four steps: measuring the magnitude of the subsidy, determining whether the borrower or the lender benefits from the subsidy, calculating the effect of the lower price of credit on loan volume, and calculating the effect on expenditures. Differences of view on each of these steps contribute to the dispute about the ability of government credit programs to achieve their goals. In addition, as discussed in chapter 1, some loan programs are simply intended to be an indirect means of transferring income to individual classes of borrowers; no effort is being made to promote any specific economic activity. Those income effects, however, depend on many of the same factors that influence resource utilization.

Measures of the Interest Rate Subsidy

There are two distinctly different concepts of the interest rate subsidy: the cost to the government and the benefit to the borrower. Under the first concept the subsidy (s_g) is represented as the sum of the government's cost of raising funds (i_g), its administrative expenses (a), the expected costs of default (d), and an allowance for profit (p) on invested capital, minus the interest rate charged the borrower (i_b):[6]

$$s_g = i_g + a + d + p - i_b.$$

The credit agency is viewed more or less as a private bank, and the subsidy is the payment needed to keep it in business.

Under the benefit concept the subsidy (s_b) is measured as the difference between the cost to the borrower of a comparable loan in the private market (i_p) and that charged under the government program:

$$s_b = i_p - i_b.$$

In an economy of perfect capital markets the benefit-to-the-borrower and cost-to-the-government measures of the subsidy would correspond closely. The government could not provide unsubsidized credit at any lower cost than a private entity. In actual practice, however, several points argue against the benefit-based measure. For one thing, the benefit-based measure depends on acceptance of the argument that existing markets are perfectly competitive. For another, under the benefit approach, activities that impose no costs on the government can nevertheless be labeled subsidies. Furthermore, in some situations—student loans, for example—the absence of private lending rules out the possibility of defining a comparable rate.

Finally, the cost-based measure of the subsidy, as shown in chapter 7, can be more directly tied into the government budget process. Thus in the following chapters we use the cost to the government as the basic measure of the subsidy.[7]

Applying the cost-based measure to specific programs raises several methodological issues. The basic cost of funds (i_g) should be the cost to the Treasury of borrowing for a period equal to the average maturity of the loans being financed. While the cost of funds is readily observable, administrative costs (a) are not. Often they are not allocated among individual programs by the loan agencies; in some cases, the costs of

---

6. The cost of a loan to the borrower includes elements other than the interest rate, such as the down payment or initial finance charges. For the purposes of this discussion, however, it is sufficient to view these other costs as equivalent to an add-on to the interest rate.

7. The Office of Management and Budget estimates a measure of the subsidy that is based on the benefits to the borrower, but it is not incorporated into the budget. See *Special Analyses, Budget of the United States Government, Fiscal Year 1986*, pp. F-31–F-38.

servicing loans are included with the administrative expenses of other agency activities. Yet as shown in table 2-1, loan servicing can be a substantial element of the cost of a loan.

Default costs (d) pose the greatest measurement problems. Expected default costs are, of necessity, speculative, but the previous experience of the agency should provide some guidance.[8] In many cases, though, the agencies engage in accounting practices that camouflage loan losses—refinancing loans that are delinquent and reporting them as new loans.

Finally, the calculation of the subsidy includes an allowance for profit (p). For a private institution, that would be the profit rate multiplied by the ratio of its own capital to total loan assets, the capitalization ratio. For government agencies, the capitalization ratio may appear very low because of their reliance on the Treasury as a financial backstop and because they are not subject to the same financial regulations as private institutions. Failure to include such an allowance, though, may ignore an important hidden element of subsidy in comparing government loan agencies with their private counterparts. In later chapters we consider this issue in some detail for government-sponsored agencies, but it is a refinement that is not fully reflected in some calculations of the subsidy element of direct loans because the relevant data are lacking.

A further question arises as to whether the subsidy costs should be reported on an annual basis or capitalized over the life of the loan—the present discounted value (PDV). Interest rate subsidies differ from most other government subsidy programs in that only a small portion of the subsidy will be paid in the year in which the loan is made and the funds are spent.[9] Thus there may be little association between the timing of budget payments and the actual impact on demand for real resources. The present discounted value of the subsidy is equivalent, at the time the loan is made, to a capital grant or transfer payment to the borrower.[10] As later chapters show, the present discounted value of a loan subsidy,

8. Estimating default costs is examined in greater detail below in the section on loan guarantees.

9. This issue does arise in the measurement of tax subsidies, and most studies do attempt to report them on a present-discounted-value basis. In other expenditure programs the government occasionally subsidizes operating costs (Amtrak, for example), but it usually prefers one-time capital grants.

10. Either of two interest rates could be used to discount the future subsidy payments. The interest rate charged the borrower should be used if the purpose is to measure the benefits to him. But the government cost of funds is most appropriate in arriving at a PDV of the future budget costs. For simplicity, we base our calculations in later chapters on the cost to the government.

expressed as a percent of the loan value, is a useful means of comparing the costs of widely diverse loan programs. For instance, the value of the subsidy is high—between 50 and 100 percent—for student loans and for some programs of the Farmers Home Administration; it is low for the government-sponsored agencies.

The Beneficiaries of Interest Rate Subsidies

The benefits of a loan subsidy may accrue either to lenders or borrowers.[11] How much borrowers will gain, in the form of a lower interest rate or a larger volume of loans, depends on the sensitivity to interest rate changes of both loan supply and loan demand. Interest rate subsidies increase the volume of loans most in markets where the loan supply is highly interest-elastic—the asset in question is a close substitute for other assets in lenders' portfolios. In such markets borrowers receive most of the subsidy benefit, both in the form of lower interest rates and in the form of increased volume of lending because lenders will greatly expand the loan supply in exchange for a small increase in their return. On the other hand, in markets where the loan supply is inelastic (low asset substitution), little new loan volume will be generated by interest rate subsidies, and lenders will receive most of the subsidy benefit in the form of a higher interest rate.

A similar analysis can be made for variations in the interest elasticity of loan demand. The interest elasticity of loan demand, however, depends on both the interest elasticity of the underlying expenditure decision and the alternative sources of finance available to the borrower—the potential for substituting public for private credit. Again, if the demand for loans is highly elastic, the increase in loan volume will be relatively large. But, in that case, a large portion of the interest subsidy will accrue to lenders. On the other hand, an inelastic demand implies a small increase in loan volume and means that borrowers rather than lenders will gain, primarily from lower interest payments. Thus while a high elasticity of loan supply both increases the quantity of lending and transfers most of the subsidy to borrowers, variations in the

11. The material in this section relies heavily on the analysis in Rudolph G. Penner and William L. Silber, "The Interaction between Federal Credit Programs and the Impact on the Allocation of Credit," *American Economic Review*, vol. 63 (December 1973), pp. 838–52.

elasticity of demand create a conflict between the objectives of increasing loan volume and reducing the interest costs to existing borrowers.

In the first section of this chapter we argued that the supply of funds to individual markets is likely to be highly elastic in all but the very short run. Thus, at least on the supply side, the basic market conditions support the argument that interest rate subsidies are likely to be important tools for reallocating resources and redistributing income to specific classes of borrowers.[12] The chief uncertainties result from a lack of knowledge about the effect on demand.

Effect on Loan Demand

The belief that a dollar of loans is equivalent to a dollar of expenditures is a common misconception among both proponents and opponents of federal credit programs. In many situations, however, borrowers may simply substitute government-supplied credit for that available from private lenders or use fewer of their own financial resources, with little or no change in their expenditures. In addition, the revenue from the loan is fungible in that it can be spent on items other than that for which it was intended. A student loan, for example, may allow parents to make fewer cutbacks in their own consumption plans. There is an expenditure effect in such cases, but it may be far removed from the targeted area.

This potential for substitution of government credit for private credit suggests that the volume of loan demand is a poor guide to measuring the impact of loan subsidies on resource allocation. While the volume of loans may be useful as a measure of the effect of a subsidy on income redistribution (all borrowers will receive the subsidy), the effect on resource use requires a direct measure of the change in expenditures.

Expenditure Demand

An interest rate subsidy is most easily seen as a reduction in the price of the targeted good, and its effect on real expenditures can be evaluated in two ways. For loans such as mortgages in which receipt of the subsidy

12. Although the introduction of an interest rate subsidy is unlikely to change the underlying elasticity of supply, the same cannot be said for loan guarantee programs. If no effective private insurance previously existed, the loan guarantee will increase the marketability of the asset in secondary markets. Thus the guarantee will raise the degree of substitutability with other assets.

is conditional upon continued ownership of the asset to which it is tied, the subsidy is most appropriately thought of as a reduction in the cost of using the asset for each period in the future—its rental price.[13] In the absence of taxes, the rental price (c) of an asset, such as a house, is equal to its acquisition price (P_k) multiplied by a fraction equal to the rate of interest (i), plus the rate of depreciation (d), minus any expected capital gain resulting from a change in its price ($\dot{P}_k$):

$$c = P_k (i + d - \dot{P}_k).$$

For example, if the value of an asset depreciates 10 percent a year, the interest rate is 10 percent, and inflation is 7 percent a year, the rental price is 13 percent of the acquisition price. If the government is willing to provide a 1 percent interest rate subsidy on a loan equal to 75 percent of the property value, the effective interest rate drops to 9.25 percent, and the cost of holding the asset for one period falls to 12.25 percent—a 6 percent decline in price. Even though taxes complicate the calculation, it is feasible to estimate the effective price reduction of an interest rate subsidy for a wide range of assets with different rates of taxation and depreciation.[14]

For loans that are not tied to continued ownership of an asset, such as student loans, the reduction in price is more easily computed as the present discounted value of the subsidy multiplied by the loan-to-value ratio. For example, if the present discounted value of the subsidy component of a ten-year student loan equals 50 percent, and the loan amount covers 50 percent of annual education costs, there is a net reduction of 25 percent in the price of education.

The final step in the calculation of the expenditure impact of a loan subsidy requires information on the sensitivity of the expenditure to a change in price. Are tuition costs, for example, an important factor in decisions to attend college? Such information is not easy to obtain. Statistical techniques can be applied to historical data to disentangle the effects of price changes from other factors such as changes in income, and an enormous number of studies have attempted to do so for spending

13. For example, most subsidized housing and agricultural loans are not assumable by the purchaser if the property is resold.

14. Such calculations also demonstrate the greater importance of interest costs for long-lived assets, such as housing, which have low depreciation rates. The annual rate of depreciation of the housing stock has been estimated at about 2 percent. In the above example, lowering the depreciation rate from 10 percent to 2 percent changes the implied price reduction from 6 percent to 15 percent.

in various sectors of the economy. The results are often ambiguous, yielding a range of probable effects rather than a firm value. Still, in later chapters we use these estimates to illustrate the effects of loan subsidies on agricultural investments and college enrollment.

This uncertainty about the effect of price changes is, of course, not unique to government credit programs. The same doubts complicate evaluating the impact of a wide range of other public policy measures, such as tax subsidies. The advantage of focusing on the price effects of credit subsidies is that it places them within an analytical framework that has proved useful for evaluating other programs and for which ongoing economic research does reduce the uncertainties.

Income Effects

Government loan subsidies might also be viewed as a simple transfer of income to borrowers. Individuals who would have made the expenditure even without subsidized credit receive a windfall income gain, in the form of a lower loan cost, that they are free to dispose of as they please. This income gain for inframarginal purchasers occurs in all price subsidy programs. The only differences here are that the income gain is a function of loan volume rather than expenditures, and that it is paid out in successive years over the life of the loan rather than being received at the time of purchase, as with an investment tax credit. Thus the subsidy is most usefully viewed as an addition to wealth equal to the present discounted value of the future stream of subsidy payments.

Because the recipients of the subsidy are likely to resemble other economic agents in their response to a windfall income gain, the existing studies of how increased wealth affects spending are useful guides. A subsidy to individuals will augment their wealth and lead to increased outlays on a broad range of consumer goods and services. There is little reason to expect the windfall to be spent on the subsidized activity to any greater extent than would be true for an increase in income derived from any other source.

Finally, it is important to remember that subsidized loan programs, while they increase the demand for loans in specific markets, do not provide for a matching increase in the total supply of credit. Subsidies enable some borrowers to obtain loans only by forcing others out of the markets. If fiscal and monetary policy are seen as specifying a fixed target for total demand, a loan subsidy program must raise interest rates in other markets to reduce demand by an amount equal to the increase in the targeted sector. Because many of the subsidized programs are aimed at marginal borrowers, they will be forcing out of the market borrowers who are indistinguishable in many respects from those they seek to help.

Loan Guarantees and Insurance

Loan guarantees raise more complex issues than either simple interest rate subsidies or asset exchanges. The economic effects are similar to those involved in an exchange of public for private debt. Although the private asset is not removed from the market, it becomes, from the lender's perspective, similar to public debt.[15] The guarantee lowers the interest cost to the borrower both by reducing the lender's concern with its risk and by increasing the marketability of the asset in secondary resale markets—its liquidity. Unlike most secondary market purchases of existing loans, however, loan guarantees are made at the time the loan is negotiated, and thus they raise additional concerns about their impact on the behavior of both the borrower and the lender. Three different types of government guarantee programs can be distinguished.[16]

A *loan insurance* program, such as Federal Housing Administration mortgage insurance, requires borrowers to pay a fee equal to expected future costs. If it is an actuarially sound program, the government is doing nothing that a well-functioning capital market should not be expected to do for itself; insuring default risk is conceptually no different from insuring casualty risk.

In *categorical guarantees,* the government insures broad categories of loans against default but does not collect a fee sufficient to cover costs. Such guarantees, found in Veterans' Administration mortgages, student loans, and small business credit, include a clear element of subsidy to the borrower.

15. Direct loans of federal credit agencies also, of course, incorporate a loan guarantee, but in most cases they are not sold in the market. The subsidy cost of the guarantee and its impact on borrower behavior, however, are the same as for guarantors of privately negotiated loans.

16. The distinctions among loan insurance, in which borrowers bear the cost, general category loan guarantees, in which government pays for the insurance, and special-project loan guarantees are suggested in Congressional Budget Office, *Loan Guarantees: Current Concerns and Alternatives for Control* (CBO, 1978).

Finally, *special-project guarantees* are sometimes provided for large ventures or to categories of borrowers where the small number of loans limits the ability to reduce risk exposure by holding a widely diversified portfolio. In most of these programs, no effort is made to charge a fee that is related to the probability of default, and the lack of comparable previous projects makes an estimate of the default risk speculative. Recent examples are the extension of loan guarantees for energy demonstration projects.

These special-project guarantees have tended to heighten existing concerns about how guarantees affect the behavior of borrowers and lenders. Because resources are scarce, society needs some means of screening investment projects—sorting out the good from the bad. In a private market economy, that function is performed by the lender. In the presence of loan guarantees, screening may not occur or may fall to the program administrators, who are poorly equipped to make such judgments. As a result, resources may be squandered on ill-conceived projects.

Loan Insurance

To a greater extent than is often realized, private markets are capable of absorbing a large volume of risky loans by pooling loans with diverse risk and through equity financing, where the lender (insurer) participates in the gains as well as the losses.[17] The basic principle of default insurance can be illustrated by assuming that an insurer is concerned both with the mean expected loss (best guess) and with the risk of more extreme outcomes. If the insurer is visualized as forming a subjective probability distribution of the possible losses, the mean or expected default loss $(\overline{D})$ is simply the loss under each possibility (D_i) times the probability of that outcome (P_i):

$$\overline{D} = \sum_{i=1}^{m} D_i \, P_i,$$

where m is the total number of possible outcomes. Assume further that risk is associated with the dispersion, or standard deviation (σ), of the possible outcomes,

17. The same principle is involved when investors diversify a stock portfolio to reduce the risk of large price changes for a single stock.

$$\sigma^2 = \sum_{i=1}^{m} (D_i - \overline{D})^2 P_i.$$

The dispersion of possible losses can be quite broad for a single loan, but holding a broadly diversified portfolio of individual loans will substantially reduce the overall risk. Although the expected default cost of the total portfolio is simply the sum of the expected costs of the underlying individual loans, the standard deviation of the total is not the sum of the individual standard deviations. Instead, it depends on the covariance of potential default costs among assets as well as their individual variances.[18]

If the probabilities of default for individual loans display zero or negative covariance, the variance of default costs for the overall portfolio can be reduced nearly to zero by holding a large enough portfolio. In such a case the cost of default becomes a predictable element in the cost of lending to a broad class of borrowers.[19] Lenders may provide their own insurance by holding a widely diversified portfolio or by purchasing insurance in the market.

However, if individual default rates are uniformly affected by outside events, such as general business conditions, they have a common or systematic risk that cannot be fully offset by diversification. In that case either the risk must be transferred to others who are less risk-averse, or

18. Specifically, the standard deviation of the overall portfolio is given by

$$\sigma = \sum_{j}^{n} \sum_{k}^{n} A_j A_k r_{jk} \sigma_j \sigma_k,$$

where n is the total number of assets in the portfolio, A_j and A_k are the proportions invested in assets j and k, σ_j and σ_k are the deviations about the expected default costs of the jth and kth assets, and r_{jk} is the correlation between the distribution of potential losses for assets j and k. A correlation coefficient of 1.0 implies that potential default costs of the two assets vary in exact proportion to one another; a coefficient of zero implies the absence of any correlation; and a negative coefficient implies an inverse correlation.

19. The risk-absorbing nature of portfolio diversification is illustrated by considering what one would be willing to pay for the opportunity to win $1,000 on the single flip of a coin versus the opportunity to win $10 each on 100 coin flips. Both have the same expected value, $500, but the second is a low-risk proposition. Important contributions in this area were made by Markowitz, *Portfolio Selection;* William F. Sharpe, "Capital Asset Prices: A Theory of Market Equilibrium under Conditions of Risk," *Journal of Finance*, vol. 19 (September 1964), pp. 425–42; and John Lintner, "Security Prices, Risk, and Maximal Gains from Diversification," *Journal of Finance*, vol. 20 (December 1965), pp. 587–615.

investors must be compensated by receiving a higher return. In such situations the fee charged in the private market will exceed actual default costs in order to provide a higher return to risk takers.

In the following sections of this study, it has sometimes proved useful to decompose the variance of the default cost into three components: one that can be offset by diversification within the industry (individual-specific); the second, across industries or markets (industry risk); and the third, economywide (systematic risk). Lenders can also control their risk exposure by collecting or purchasing information about potential borrowers that is useful in predicting future default rates.[20] Thus quite apart from the risk of uncertainty of default, insurance fees should reflect predictable differences in expected default rates among classes of borrowers. In addition, rather than charging different interest rates for various risk classes of borrowers, lenders may simply deny credit to borrowers beyond a certain risk threshold.[21] Finally, lenders can reduce their losses in the event of default by requiring borrowers to provide collateral.

Two special problems limit the ability of even well-functioning markets to provide insurance: moral hazard and adverse selection. Moral hazard occurs when the existence of insurance affects the degree of effort that the lender or borrower makes to ensure repayment: the lender invokes the guarantee rather than expending effort to collect from the borrower. Adverse selection occurs when the purchaser of insurance (the lender) knows more than the insurer does about the risks of individual loans and purchases insurance only for those loans of greater-than-average risk. Both problems exist because there is less-than-perfect information in markets; both tend to drive up the costs of insurance or inhibit its development.[22]

20. With respect to the costs of collecting such information, households and small business may compete at a significant disadvantage relative to large nationally known firms.

21. This is not an optimal profit-maximizing strategy, but it is alleged to exist in some local markets where community goodwill is an important competitive factor. The full adjustment of interest rates to reflect risk on some individual loans may attract unfavorable public comment.

22. These problems and their implications for the efficient operation of markets are discussed in a survey article by Joseph E. Stiglitz, "Information and Economic Analysis: A Perspective," *Economic Journal*, vol. 95 (1984 Supplement, *Conference Papers, 1985*), pp. 21–41. See also William C. Hunter, "Moral Hazard, Adverse Selection, and SBA Business Loan Guarantees," in Congressional Budget Office, *Conference on the Economics of Federal Credit Activity*, pt. 2: *Papers* (CBO, 1981), pp. 233–80.

The provision of insurance by the government cannot solve these problems. The government faces the same difficulties as private lenders in obtaining the information required to establish fees that vary with the degree of risk. Instead of dealing with them, it usually resorts to charging a uniform fee for all cases and relies upon minimum standards for admission to the program. Some problems of adverse selection can be controlled by making insurance mandatory, but such action implies a cross-subsidy from low-risk to high-risk borrowers. There is evidence that information such as the loan-to-value ratio, the income, regional location, and race of the borrower, and the previous record of the lender are useful predictors of default rates, yet the federal credit agencies have not used such information to set different insurance fees for various categories of borrowers.[23] Some characteristics, such as race and sex, cannot legally be used to differentiate among borrowers. As long as private insurance is available, however, the low-risk borrowers can opt out of the government program, automatically limiting the cross-subsidy.

Government-sponsored loan insurance is normally advocated for those situations where the qualifying criteria for private insurance are perceived as too strictly drawn relative to expected default costs. For example, the section 203(b) program of the Federal Housing Administration initially offered mortgage insurance at lower cost and at higher loan-to-value ratios than was available from private insurers. The primary program has thus far covered its cost without any budgetary support from the government.

In general, actuarially sound government insurance programs can provide a useful stimulus to innovation in the private insurance market without implying substantial budget costs. Although there may be a small element of subsidy in programs such as mortgage and deposit insurance because of the greater credibility of government insurance in the event of severe loss, these programs have improved the stability of the financial system. In a sense, such programs have self-limiting features. If private markets can supply the insurance, the government program will have little effect on resource use, and the lower-cost private insurers will attract the low-risk loans. As capital markets become more sophisticated, however, it becomes increasingly difficult

23. For example, see James R. Barth, Joseph J. Cordes, and Anthony M. J. Yezer, "Federal Government Attempts to Influence the Allocation of Mortgage Credit: FHA Mortgage Insurance and Government Regulations," in CBO, *Conference on the Economics of Federal Credit Activity,* pt. 2: *Papers,* pp. 159–232.

to find areas where such a government-sponsored program could operate successfully.

Categorical Loan Guarantees

Categorical loan guarantees differ from loan insurance only in that the government pays at least part of the cost of the insurance. By providing a subsidy, the government goes beyond the goal of correcting market imperfections and tilts the balance toward specific types of loans. There are, however, significant limitations on the effectiveness of loan guarantees in actually reallocating resources toward the targeted activity.

Unlike other subsidies, a loan guarantee against default has a perverse distributional effect on projects within the loan category because it is worth the most to the riskiest, worst-conceived projects.[24] In most cases government loan guarantees are defended as a means of encouraging a specific line of activity, such as mortgage credit or small business loans, not to encourage lenders to accept a higher rate of loan defaults.

Loan guarantees may also vary substantially in their effect on the demand for real resources. When risk insurance is available in the private sector, a guarantee program is equivalent to a simple reduction in interest costs equal to the annual cost of private insurance. The effect on resource use could be approximated from existing empirical studies of the effect of interest rates on expenditures.

Alternatively, if the private sector cannot provide risk insurance and a concern for risk causes private lenders to deny credit, the program could trigger real spending equal to or more than the subsidy and perhaps even more than the guaranteed loans. That situation, however, combines two separate issues: a market imperfection (the absence of loan insurance) that leads to credit rationing, and the subsidy element of a loan guarantee. The market imperfection itself does not require a subsidy.

Finally, the effect of loan guarantees and insurance is often limited by the common practice of restricting the total volume of guaranteed loans. Because the guarantee will be provided to the most creditworthy proposals first, the volume of the guarantee will probably be exhausted

24. The same potential problem exists with loan insurance, but if the qualifying criteria are too liberally drawn, low-risk borrowers will opt out of the program, driving up the fee for those who remain. No such self-correcting mechanism exists for loan guarantees.

before covering even all those loans that would have been extended in its absence. The main effect will be to substitute government-guaranteed credit for private credit.

In general, categorical loan guarantees would be more effective if they were converted to unsubsidized loan insurance programs. The government would have an incentive to define reasonable criteria for insurance coverage, as otherwise the low-risk borrowers would opt out of the program, increasing the cost to those who remain. Insurance programs are also more effective than loan guarantees in encouraging the development of private insurance institutions.

Small borrowers may constitute a special case for which a partial loan guarantee is appropriate. The administrative costs of gathering information about borrowers' financial conditions are greater in the case of small borrowers than in the case of large borrowers, and the benefits of collecting it cannot always be restricted to those who pay the costs—it has elements of a public good.[25] If so, a partial subsidy of loan insurance costs might be justified. By limiting the guarantee as a percentage of the loan, the government can ensure the lender's strong incentive to exercise care in approving and servicing the loan.

Special-Project Guarantees

The use of loan guarantees to facilitate the financing of specific investment projects, such as the synthetic fuels program, or to prevent the default of a private sector firm, such as guarantees for Lockheed and Chrysler, is a newly emerging area of government finance. In most cases these guarantees are not justified on the basis of capital market imperfections: the firms involved have access to capital markets, and the information available to the private markets allows them to evaluate the risk as well as or better than the government can. The problem lies with the high expectation of default rather than the uncertainty of potential outcomes. As a result, these programs include a much larger element of subsidy than normal and heighten concerns about how loan guarantees affect the behavior of borrowers.

Take the use of loan guarantees to encourage investment in synthetic fuel demonstration projects as an illustration. First, the existence of the

25. Many of the standard arguments about the optimality of unsubsidized markets do not apply if information is restricted or costly. See Stiglitz, "Information and Economic Analysis."

guarantee actually increases the probability investors will default and prematurely terminate a project. For example, an unguaranteed synthetic fuels project with operating costs of $8 a barrel (oil equivalent) and fixed capital costs averaging $10 a barrel over the life of the project will make a profit at any price over $18 a barrel. It will continue to operate, however, at any price above $8 a barrel because the revenues in excess of operating costs contribute to repayment of the fixed costs: the loss is minimized even if no profit is made. With a guarantee, the firm will default on a 100 percent debt-financed project at any price below $18 a barrel, pay off bondholders with the guarantee, and leave the government to operate the plant. Even if half of the capital costs are supplied by equity holders, the plant would close at a price of $13 a barrel.

The problem of premature shutdown is exacerbated by a consideration of the tax advantages that can be derived from a special project. For example, the combination of a 90 percent loan guarantee and a 10 percent investment tax credit will result in zero owner equity at the end of the construction phase. In future years rapid tax depreciation and depletion allowances will further reduce the owner's equity in the project. Still another reason to shut down early is that the construction phase and the first few years of operation provide the best opportunities to learn about the new technology.

As a result, many special-project guarantees have a high expectation of future default and thus a cost to the government. But the costs will appear in future, not current, budgets. In fact, in many cases an actual default will never occur because the potential embarrassment to the government and to the private parties creates pressure to extend subsidies in future years to prevent the default.[26]

A second problem arises from the common practice of limiting loan guarantees to the financing of capital as opposed to operating costs. By reducing the cost of capital financing, the guarantee distorts the choice of the most economic technology in choosing between capital-intensive (subsidized) and operating-cost-intensive (unsubsidized) projects.

In most cases the government becomes involved in the financing of new technologies not because of financial market problems, but because

---

26. For example, the threat of the collapse of the Chrysler Corporation was not a trivial influence in the decision to seek quotas on Japanese automobile imports in the early 1980s. Similarly, Congress has revised contracts on synfuel projects in the face of a threatened default by the operators.

of economic externalities. That is, the benefits—knowledge gained—cannot be captured by the initiators of the project but accrue to society as a whole. Potential future investors gain from simply observing the progress of the project without the need to participate in its operation. The situation is similar to that of infant industries, where those who follow benefit from the experience of those who go first. A case could be made for government intervention, but in most instances it should not be in the form of loan guarantees.

The previous example from the synthetic fuels demonstration program also illustrates how alternative forms of assistance can be more appropriate than loan guarantees. In a case in which the cost of the project may be known, but there is a major risk of future price declines, a loan guarantee would precipitate a premature shutdown of the plant if prices were to fall below total unit cost. A price guarantee, however, would enable the plant to continue to operate—and society to benefit—at any price above variable cost.[27]

In a case where the risk arises from uncertainty about future costs rather than prices, a loan guarantee could again cause the premature termination of the project. In this case, a price guarantee also would be ineffective in encouraging additional activity, and the government would have little choice except to participate in the project as a partner—sharing in the cost as well as the revenues.[28]

Finally, the chief expected benefits may be in the form of knowledge gained in the first few years of operation. Again, the distribution over time of benefits relative to costs creates an incentive for premature shutdown, and the government has little choice except to become an equity participant in the project or to provide an initial grant.

Loan guarantees may be appropriate in responding to situations of financial market imperfections, such as when the cost of gathering information about the borrowers' financial situation is high. Guarantees are designed to reduce the variance of potential outcomes, but they are not responsive to the problems raised by projects that have high real expectations of failure or by projects whose future benefits cannot be captured by the project sponsors. Furthermore, in freeing up resources to devote to such projects, there is little rationale for using the capital

---

27. A price guarantee should always include an option for government purchase of the plant in the event of a fall of market prices below the level of variable costs.

28. Such joint ventures were used by the Atomic Energy Commission to encourage nuclear-power projects in earlier decades, and they are a common practice in Europe.

market to squeeze out other interest-sensitive projects. A direct expenditure, financed by a tax on the potential beneficiaries, seems a better alternative.

A final problem that the government encounters with any effort to intervene to encourage high-risk investment projects is that the administrative machinery that replaces the market in sorting out alternative proposals is likely to be more risk-averse than the private market. Government administrators receive little credit if a project succeeds, but they are likely to catch most of the blame if an expensive project fails. On the other hand, private investors are likely to seek an equity position so that they share in the gains as well as the losses. As a result a government subsidy program may inadvertently tilt the balance in the direction of the least-innovative, lowest-risk projects.

Summary

The methodology outlined above for evaluating the economic effects of government credit programs requires a focus on the magnitude of the subsidy, not the volume of loan activity. Viewing federal credit agencies as equivalent to private financial intermediaries means that the costs of their lending activity, including administrative expenses and a reserve for expected default costs, can be fully identified. The amount of the subsidy can then be measured as the net cost to the government: all costs of furnishing the loan minus expected borrower payments. The subsidy value of a loan guarantee, for example, can be measured, just as it is in private institutions, as the cost of maintaining a reserve equal to expected default costs.

The impact of the subsidy on resource allocation can then be measured in terms of an equivalent reduction in the interest rate charged the borrower and the effect of that reduction on the price of, and thus the demand for, the targeted asset. Such information on loan costs is not now readily available for most credit programs. One object of subsequent chapters is to demonstrate that such information can be gathered and evaluated. The response of expenditures to a decline in the price of the targeted asset is crucial to the measurement of the effect of credit programs on resource allocation. If expenditures are not sensitive to price changes, a loan program will largely redistribute income. The basic difficulty with credit programs as a tool of resource reallocation is that the effect on expenditures is likely to be diluted severely as borrowers simply substitute government loans for private loans.

CHAPTER THREE

Credit for Housing

PROGRAMS DIRECTED AT the housing market are among the oldest of government credit activities. In terms of outstanding investments, they are the largest. Roughly 60 percent of total credit advanced to the public under federal auspices is directed at the residential mortgage market.[1] The reasons for such a government commitment are not hard to find: the importance of residential construction in the economy, the status accorded homeownership as a principal goal of national policy, and the peculiar financing problems associated with the mortgage instrument. Another reason may be the success of past programs: by reducing some of the costs associated with mortgage transactions and expanding the market, the credit programs are perceived to have been highly successful.

The History of Federal Involvement

The federal credit programs, created to rescue the housing market during the Great Depression, had an enormous influence on the development of a national mortgage market. Until the 1930s mortgage loans were similar to many other investments made by financial intermediaries. They were for short terms, they were held in the asset portfolios of the institutions that originated them, and they often required a large final payment at maturity. Savings and loan associations, the principal mortgage lenders during the 1920s, held half of the outstanding residential mortgage debt. The balance was in the portfolios of commercial banks and life insurance companies. Typical mortgage loans were written for

1. Includes outstanding direct and guaranteed loans and outstanding loans by government-sponsored enterprises. Authors' calculations based on *Special Analyses, Budget of the United States Government, Fiscal Year 1986*, pp. F-55–F-76.

less than 60 percent of the value of the property; down payments were 40 percent or more. Repayment was required over no more than eleven years, and some loans were due in six years or less.[2]

That system did little to overcome the inherent difficulties of financing the purchase of a house, the most costly and longest-lived asset purchased by individuals. While the builder or seller must be paid at the outset, the structure will provide shelter over a period of thirty years or more. Few buyers can quickly amass enough savings to buy a house outright.[3] Under the terms prevailing during the 1920s, few could accumulate the wealth necessary to make the down payment on a house before the later stages of life.

The financial crises of the early 1930s destroyed the existing housing finance system. Unemployed borrowers were unable to meet their monthly payments. Institutions that relied on income from such assets curtailed new lending and denied continued financing to homeowners whose short-term balloon loans were maturing, tipping those loans too into default.[4] By 1933 the mortgage market had effectively ceased to function. Between 1929 and 1933 the stock of mortgage loans declined 15 percent and housing construction dropped 80 percent.[5]

Drawn in to revive a market that had collapsed, the federal government took measures that permanently changed the structure of the market. Apart from emergency provisions, government reforms were designed to address four major concerns of housing lenders, then and now: default risk, the chance that the borrower will not make some or all of the scheduled repayments; high transactions costs associated with originating, servicing, and selling the mortgage; liquidity risk, the holding of long-term nonmarketable assets when funding sources may be of short-term maturity and unpredictable availability; and interest rate risk, the

---

2. Henry J. Aaron, *Shelter and Subsidies: Who Benefits from Federal Housing Policies?* (Brookings, 1972), pp. 76–77.

3. Housing finance systems in some other countries continue to require purchasers to save for a major down payment at the time of purchase. In the United States, extensive borrowing occurs at the time of purchase with the saving taking place afterwards as periodic mortgage payments are made.

4. A balloon loan requires a large repayment of the principal when the loan matures. Borrowers generally expected to refinance their loans when they matured. Thus they financed home purchases with a series of short-term loans. Today most mortgages are amortized, repaying interest and principal in fixed monthly installments.

5. *Economic Report of the President, February 1983,* p. 164; and U.S. Department of Commerce, Bureau of the Census, *Historical Statistics of the United States: Colonial Times to 1970* (Government Printing Office, 1975), pt. 2, p. 647.

uncertainty over the ultimate rate of return on a mortgage relative to alternative investments with different cash-flow characteristics.

Default Risk

Mortgage loans are secured by the purchased house and land, the value of which must, to protect the lender, exceed the balance due on the loan. Because houses have a long economic life, long-term loans for a substantial portion of their purchase price are generally safe investments. Yet the ultimate return on such a loan is not known until it is completely repaid, and before the depression-era reforms lenders were not eager to make mortgage loans.

Lenders have several means of addressing the risks of individual loans. One is by diversifying their portfolios, holding a large number of loans with varied and unrelated risk characteristics. The result is a pooling of the random risk elements of an individual default, similar to insurance.[6] But small, geographically limited lenders such as those characteristic of the early decades of this century cannot achieve this diversification on their own. Intermediaries and secondary markets must provide the mechanism to exchange and diversify assets.

Lenders can also shift some or all of the risk to an insurer or guarantor. Alternatively, lenders may decide to accept more risk if they can lessen the degree of uncertainty about the amount of risk through standardization of underwriting criteria or demonstration projects. Before the 1930s, neither option was available.

The Federal Home Loan Bank Act of 1932 and the Home Owners' Loan Act of 1933 addressed all aspects of default risk, primarily by establishing two federal agencies, the Federal Home Loan Bank System and the Home Owners' Loan Corporation, and by federally chartering savings and loan associations. From 1933 through 1936, mortgages in default were purchased from private lenders by the Home Owners' Loan Corporation and converted to long-term amortizing loans. The purchases injected new funds into the lending institutions, prevented owners from losing their homes through default, and demonstrated the soundness of the fully amortizing loan. Funds for the purchases were raised under government auspices, since the creditworthiness of the private lending

---

6. See chapter 2 for a more detailed discussion of the effects of portfolio diversification on risk.

institutions was in doubt. Savings and loans gained an additional means of attracting funds when federal deposit insurance was extended to them under the National Housing Act in 1934.

That act also established the Federal Housing Agency (FHA, now the Federal Housing Administration) to insure lenders against the risk of default on mortgage loans. A similar program targeted at lenders to veterans was established in the Veterans' Administration in 1944 under the Servicemen's Readjustment Act, the "G.I. Bill of Rights." Lenders were authorized to make long-term loans, up to twenty years and more, and to allow down payments as low as 20 percent or less. The loans were to be fully amortizing. This liberalization of credit terms reduced initial and subsequent monthly payments and thereby enabled more individuals to buy homes.

Transaction Costs

From the lender's point of view, a mortgage is an unwieldy instrument compared with other assets. Mortgages are small, and each is unique in terms of risk, loan-to-value ratio, interest rate, and maturity. By contrast, business and government entities borrow repeatedly and in large denominations. The multiplicity of borrowers, the frequency of payment (monthly), and the complexity of the amortization schedule mean that servicing mortgage loans is relatively costly. The continuing need for servicing may create further problems if the originator wishes to sell the loan. A prospective investor may be unwilling to take on the servicing burden, but separating the servicing and investment functions can create an adverse incentive structure because, to the servicer, the value of a payment collected is only the small percentage retained (usually less than 5 percent of the total payment).[7] Before government intervention in the mortgage market, the inability of loan originators to warrant the performance of the firms that service mortgage loans constituted a serious obstacle to trading in mortgage loans.

The multiplicity of lenders and borrowers also led, in the pre-depression market, to a lack of standardization that raised the cost of originating and holding mortgage loans. The absence of standardization meant that each lender had to search for and identify instruments that

7. This is also known as the "agency problem." The servicer, who acts as an agent for the ultimate holder of the mortgage loan, may not be as diligent as the investor in seeking to ensure repayment.

were sound. Nonstandard loans were not saleable except at a discount for the added costs of obtaining information.

The sheer volume of mortgages newly insured by the FHA and VA, however, set a standard for most conventional (non–federally insured) mortgages and encouraged other lenders to liberalize their loan terms. Standardization also permitted the eventual development of a secondary market—the buying and selling of loans. Even today the government credit programs encourage standardization. The largest purchasers of conventional loans, the Federal National Mortgage Association (FNMA, or Fannie Mae) and the Federal Home Loan Mortgage Corporation (FHLMC, or Freddie Mac), set the benchmarks for mortgage underwriting and loan terms and establish standards for mortgage servicers. Their licensing of approved servicers has essentially eliminated investor concerns about servicer performance.

Liquidity Risk

Because mortgage lenders cannot count on repayment before maturity, they can have no assurance that cash will be available to meet unexpected needs. The lender must therefore maintain liquid balances, at some sacrifice in rate of return, to hold the illiquid mortgage loan. Such opportunity costs will be passed on to the borrower unless alternative sources of liquidity are available or the mortgage loan can be sold, in which case the lender's need for precautionary balances will be reduced. Again, the mortgage market before the depression-era reforms offered neither solution.

Savings institutions, the largest group of mortgage lending institutions, were relatively small and were constrained to operate within a single state. Their vulnerability to local economic conditions and their periodic inability to raise cash impaired the extension of new credit for mortgage loans. Also, most had a mutual form of ownership, meaning that growth was dependent on deposits alone. The issuance of unsecured debt was largely foreclosed to them.

Opportunities for raising cash through the sale of assets were also limited. Mortgage loans were difficult to sell, for reasons discussed above. At certain times the problem has been regional imbalances in the demand for and supply of funds. After 1932, however, the Federal Home Loan Bank System became a major source of liquidity for savings institutions, lending large and small amounts for short and long terms against a wide variety of mortgage loan collateral.

Fannie Mae was established in 1938 to buy FHA, and later VA and conventional, loans from originators, primarily mortgage bankers, with funds raised from public bond sales. Much later, in 1970, Freddie Mac was established to provide similar services to savings institutions. Both institutions expanded the potential number of (indirect) investors in mortgages and established a basis for a secondary market for mortgages. The activities of Fannie Mae, and later Freddie Mac, allowed funds to be gathered from any place in the country with savings to invest. The resale mortgage market also allowed thrift institutions in regions with excess saving to begin purchasing mortgages from others in areas with an excess of loan demand.

In the 1970s and 1980s the federally sponsored agencies—Fannie Mae, Freddie Mac, and the Government National Mortgage Association (GNMA, or Ginnie Mae)—developed a market for mortgage pools by creating securities backed by mortgages that can be sold to private investors. The new securities greatly expanded the potential sources of funds for mortgage lenders and eliminated much of the risk involved in the origination of mortgages for their own accounts.

Interest Rate Risk

Rate of return, an important characteristic of any investment, can be difficult to predict in the case of a mortgage loan. More than on most assets, the return on a mortgage investment is affected by changes in future market interest rates. This risk has several dimensions.

MATURITY. The value of an asset with a fixed interest rate moves inversely with changes in market interest rates, and the magnitude of that price change increases with the duration of the asset. Residential mortgages, written for terms of fifteen to thirty years or more, have historically provided for a constant interest rate over the entire term. As with all such long-term investments, lenders demand a premium for accepting the risk associated with a possible rise in market interest rates during the term of the mortgage. Long-term assets generally provide higher returns than comparable short-term investments, giving rise to the normal upward-sloping shape of the yield curve.

REINVESTMENT RISK. The holder of a long-term fixed rate asset may also be concerned about a future decline in market interest rates. Unless the asset is a pure discount bond, wherein the principal is repaid and all interest is paid at maturity, the holder will receive some cash flow in advance of maturity. If interest rates have fallen from the levels obtaining at the time of the original investment, these proceeds will have to be reinvested at a rate lower than that on the original asset. The greater the cash flow during the term of the investment, the greater the reinvestment risk.

Corporate and government bonds usually pay interest semiannually and principal at maturity. In contrast, most mortgages are self-amortizing: they provide for monthly payments that comprise not only the interest due but also a portion of the principal. Both the monthly payment feature and the periodic repayments of principal increase the cash flow, and therefore the reinvestment risk, relative to bonds.

PREPAYMENTS. Most mortgages can be paid off in full at the option of the borrower at any time before final maturity. If market interest rates fall after a mortgage is written, the borrower may decide to pay off the old loan and refinance at a lower interest rate. This possibility substantially increases the reinvestment risk for the lender. Although some corporate bonds have such a "call" feature, they provide for substantial premiums to be paid in the event the option is exercised, compensating the holder for reinvestment risk. Prepayment penalties (in effect, call premiums) on mortgage loans, however, are strictly limited by laws and regulations and apply only if the loan is repaid within the first few years. This additional risk to the lender must therefore be recouped in the form of a higher interest rate on the loan.

MEANS OF ADDRESSING INTEREST RATE RISK. Contemporary financial intermediaries have a variety of means for reducing the riskiness of a long-term fixed rate portfolio, including futures and options contracts, interest rate swaps, and long-term financing. But until recently, mortgage lenders funded long-term lending through short-term borrowing from the public in the form of deposits or through sales of mortgages to investors. The market operated on the assumption that future interest rates would fluctuate over a narrow range.

For much of the postwar period, that assumption proved to be accurate. Monetary policy was often confined to supporting the government's financing of its own debt, and fiscal, not monetary, measures provided the dominant tool of stabilization policy. Over the business cycle, monetary policy leaned against the general cyclical pattern of the economy, but it was generally accommodative to the goals of fiscal policy.

All this began to change in the mid-1960s, when a more active monetary policy and a greater variability of inflation contributed to much larger swings in market interest rates. In addition, the rise in market rates during the 1970s imposed large capital losses on those who financed long-term asset portfolios with short-term liabilities. Interest rate risk became an issue of much greater concern for markets, such as that for mortgages, that emphasized long-term financial commitments. The practice of financing long-term loans with short-term deposits became untenable, and mortgage lenders were forced to move toward greater emphasis on matching the maturity structure of their assets and liabilities.[8]

Of all the risks associated with residential mortgage lending, interest rate uncertainty has proved the least susceptible to amelioration. The introduction of adjustable rate mortgages (ARMs), initially in California in the 1960s and nationwide by the early 1980s, has shifted some of the burden to homeowners. But even ARMs are not fully sensitive to movements in the short-term interest rates that determine lenders' cost of funds, and long-term fixed rate mortgages continue to be popular with borrowers.

Government activity aimed directly at interest rate risk has been modest. In fact, during the 1970s federal law prohibited federally chartered savings and loan associations from offering ARMs, and the law was changed only when those instruments had become widespread among state-chartered institutions. Ginnie Mae developed an ARM-backed pass-through security in 1984. Fannie Mae and Freddie Mac began purchasing ARMs once private institutions had developed the instruments but did little to assist in standardization. The Federal Home Loan Banks have offered long-term advances to their member thrift institutions to insulate them against market rate increases, but the prepayment penalties impose a burden in the event of an interest rate decline. In 1983 Freddie Mac issued the first collateralized mortgage obligation (CMO), an instrument designed to allocate more efficiently the cash-flow uncertainties surrounding mortgages; private issuers, however, had developed the concept independently and their issues

8. Between 1966 and the late 1970s, deposit rate ceilings at banks and savings institutions held down the cost of interest payments but induced depositors to withdraw their funds, drying up that source of mortgage money. Beginning in 1978, the elimination of rate ceilings improved the overall inflow of deposits, but the increased competition for deposits led to widespread insolvency in the industry; many firms were left with insufficient capital to take on new loans. This situation is discussed more fully in Andrew S. Carron, *The Plight of the Thrift Institutions* (Brookings, 1982).

reached the market soon after Freddie Mac's.[9] The agency offers partial protection against losses from a rising rate environment by guaranteeing that prepayments will not fall below a minimum rate on each CMO it has issued.

Summary

Borrowers, lenders, and speculators have different interests in the risks and costs of a home mortgage. The more flexibility the parties have to redistribute the risks and costs of the loan, the more efficient the operation of the market. Many of the federal housing credit programs are designed to facilitate the decomposition of a mortgage loan into its component parts (interest income, risk, and so forth) so that each can be marketed individually. By improving the efficiency of the market, the government may increase activity in the market and reduce costs.

Most of the reforms and programs established during the 1930s remain intact today. The development of long-term amortizing mortgages, default insurance, specialized lenders, and Fannie Mae are all important features of the mortgage markets of the mid-1980s. In effect, the modern mortgage market is a creation of government.

One question raised in the current debate over government involvement in credit markets generally is the appropriateness of continuing support for housing credit programs designed under the crisis conditions of a half century ago. A second pertains to more recently developed programs, particularly the rapid expansion of mortgage pools by government-sponsored agencies. The new mortgage-backed securities have dramatically broadened the sources of funds for the mortgage market but have raised concerns about unfair competition between the sponsored agencies and private financial intermediaries.

Finally, there is a concern that many housing credit programs are subsidized and that the subsidy may constitute either an undesirable degree of resource distortion or a source of competitive advantage over private financial institutions. Since those actions of government aimed at improving the efficiency of the mortgage market should not require a subsidy, the concern merits close attention.

9. The CMO established different classes of investors, who are repaid in sequence. The risk of unexpected prepayment is allocated to those investors who are most willing to bear it.

Figure 3-1. *Schematic Outline of the Mortgage Market*[a]

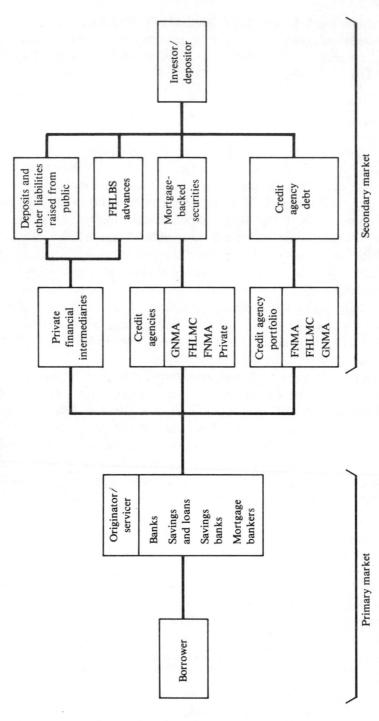

a. GNMA = Government National Mortgage Association; FHLMC = Federal Home Loan Mortgage Corporation; FNMA = Federal National Mortgage Association; FHLBS = Federal Home Loan Bank System.

Current Status of the Mortgage Market

Today's mortgage market has many participants and is substantially integrated into the capital market generally. Government agencies remain a part of the system, although private institutions often operate in parallel. Figure 3-1 illustrates the process by which funds flow from investors to mortgagors.

In what is known as the primary mortgage market, prospective borrowers arrange mortgage financing with a mortgage originator— usually a depository institution (a savings and loan association, savings bank, commercial bank) or a mortgage banker (a finance company specializing in housing loans). The originator advances the funds to the borrower and, during the term of the loan, services the loan by collecting the monthly payments due from the borrower.[10]

The subsequent sale or funding of mortgages involves transactions in the secondary mortgage market—a collection of institutions, financial instruments, and activities designed to channel funds from investors to mortgage originators. Financial intermediaries play a dominant role in both mortgage markets. Purchasing assets with one set of attributes and selling liabilities with a different set, they are a major vehicle by which funds are transmitted from savers to investors. They may purchase mortgages for their own accounts, financed by deposits and the issuance of their own bonds, or they may repackage the mortgages and simply sell shares in a mortgage pool to other investors—the secondary market. By specializing in this process, they relieve both borrowers and investors of the costs and time involved in matching the suppliers and users of funds. Intermediaries collect a fee for their services by paying, on average, somewhat less for the funds raised than is earned on the funds advanced.

The ultimate source of funds is investors, both individuals and institutions whose funds are channeled by intermediaries to mortgage originators. The overwhelming proportion of outstanding mortgages is held in the portfolios of the financial intermediaries themselves—savings and loan associations, savings banks, commercial banks, and life insur-

---

10. The originator normally continues to provide servicing. In some cases, however, the servicing contract may be sold with the underlying mortgage loan; in other cases, the servicing may be sold independently of the loan, since there is a secondary market in such servicing activities.

Table 3-1. *Ownership of Residential Mortgages, 1984*

| | Mortgage holdings | | Mortgage pools percent |
Holder	Billions of dollars	Percent of total	
Savings and loans	521.2	34.6	20.0
Mutual savings banks	84.7	5.6	6.0
Commercial banks	216.5	14.4	3.4
Insurance	44.7	3.0	10.6
Government	194.4	12.9	2.3
Mortgage pools	288.5	19.2	. . .
Other holders	155.4	10.3	57.7
Total	1,505.4	100.0	100.0

Source: Board of Governors of the Federal Reserve System, *Flow of Funds Accounts: Financial Assets and Liabilities, Year-End, 1962–85* (The Board, 1985), pp. 42–44; and U.S. Department of Housing and Urban Development, Office of Financial Management.

ance companies (see table 3-1). The development of mortgage pools has increased the participation of other investors, however.

In the primary market, origination and servicing are handled almost entirely by private firms; the government's role is limited to providing mortgage insurance and guarantees and a small number of direct loans. Government involvement is greater in the secondary market. Residential mortgage loans resold in 1984 equaled 62 percent of mortgage loans originated that year; 66 percent of the resold loans passed to or through the federal credit agencies, and the balance, directly to nonfederal investors.[11] In 1985 loan sales increased relative to originations by about 10 percentage points, all of the increase attributable to the agencies and mortgage pools.[12]

The major government-sponsored activities in the mortgage market are summarized in table 3-2. There is a considerable degree of overlap between the programs because insured mortgages are often involved in secondary market activities. The net credit column excludes insured and guaranteed loans from the secondary market activities when those mortgages are involved in an agency purchase or mortgage pool program. As the table shows, the major share of net loan activity is accounted for by the loan insurance and guarantee programs. Secondary market activities, however, have grown enormously during the 1980s because

11. U.S. Department of Housing and Urban Development, Office of Public Affairs, "Survey of Mortgage Lending Activity, 1984," *News Release*, HUD 85-65, May 3, 1985, table 3.

12. Estimate based on Department of Housing and Urban Development, Office of Public Affairs, "Survey of Mortgage Lending Activity, July 1985," *News Release*, HUD 85-193, December 17, 1985, tables 3, 5, 8, and 10.

Table 3-2. *Amounts Outstanding in Housing Programs,
September 30, 1984*
Billions of dollars

Category and program	Amount outstanding	
	Gross credit	Net credit[a]
Loan insurance and guarantees		
Farmers Home Administration, rural housing	1.0	1.0
Department of Housing and Urban Development, low-rent public housing	20.0	20.0
Federal Housing Administration, mortgage insurance	170.0	170.0
Veterans' Administration, mortgage guarantees	125.4	125.4
Secondary market activities		
Government National Mortgage Association, guarantees	176.5	0.0
Federal National Mortgage Association, programs	117.7	88.5
Federal Home Loan Bank System, advances	74.9	73.0
Federal Home Loan Mortgage Corporation, programs	73.5	72.6
Direct loans		
Farmers Home Administration, rural housing	27.2	27.2
Department of Housing and Urban Development		
Government National Mortgage Association, guarantees	2.4	2.4
Other	13.4	13.4
Veterans' Administration, programs	1.1	1.1
Total, housing programs	. . .	594.6
Total, all credit programs	. . .	930.1

Source: *Special Analyses, Budget of the United States Government, Fiscal Year 1986*, pp. F-55–F-75.
a. Excludes secondary guarantees on loans issued or guaranteed by another agency.

of the emergence of mortgage pools. Direct loan programs are relatively small except for the rural housing program of the Farmers Home Administration, which is discussed in chapter 5.

Primary Mortgage Loan Insurance and Guarantee Programs

The Federal Housing Administration and Veterans' Administration assist borrowers in primary mortgage markets by making the instruments more attractive to lenders through government insurance or guarantees. The agency pledges to repay the lender if the borrower defaults. As will be discussed in a later section, these programs also contribute to the development of the secondary market.

FHA MORTGAGE INSURANCE. The insurance of mortgages by the Federal Housing Administration is the largest of the credit programs.

There are four separate insurance funds, the largest and best known of which is the Mutual Mortgage Insurance Fund for single-family homes. The agency also operates insurance funds for multifamily dwellings, cooperatives, and high-risk borrowers. Outstanding FHA-insured loans total $190 billion.[13] Yet the impact of FHA-insured loans on resource use may be among the smallest of all government credit programs, because the program is largely run on a businesslike basis, free of any substantial subsidy.

The FHA charges an actuarially sound fee, currently 3.8 percent of the loan amount, for its loan insurance. As a result, the mutual fund program for single-family homes has operated with a surplus since its inception. In fiscal 1985, the latest period for which data are available, the Mutual Mortgage Fund registered a profit of $162 million, while the General Insurance and Special Risk Insurance funds showed losses. Overall the insurance programs had net revenues of only $9 million.[14] By the end of fiscal 1985, the FHA had, since its inception, insured 14.9 million mortgages totaling $342 billion on 19.1 million units. Of that total, unsubsidized single-family general purpose programs accounted for $237 billion, or 69 percent, while similar programs for multifamily units totaled $51 billion, or 15 percent. Special-purpose, high-risk, and subsidized programs made up the balance.[15]

Despite its financial soundness, the guarantee program does raise a concern about the cross-subsidy of high-risk borrowers by low-risk borrowers because both pay the same fee.[16] By policy, the FHA does not make distinctions among borrowers, even distinctions based on borrower characteristics shown to be useful predictors of default as a basis for charging differential premiums.[17]

If the low-risk borrowers were to avail themselves of private insurance, the cross-subsidies would disappear, but the FHA system could

13. Department of Housing and Urban Development, Office of Administration, *Summary of Mortgage Insurance Operations, Fiscal Year 1985* (HUD, 1985), p. 7.

14. Ibid., p. 1.

15. Ibid., pp. 4–7.

16. George M. von Furstenberg, "Risk Structures and the Distribution of Benefits within the FHA Home Mortgage Insurance Program," *Journal of Money, Credit and Banking*, vol. 2 (August 1970), pp. 303–22.

17. See, for example, the statistical evidence reported in James R. Barth, Joseph J. Cordes, and Anthony M. J. Yezer, "Federal Government Attempts to Influence the Allocation of Mortgage Credit: FHA Mortgage Insurance and Government Regulations," in Congressional Budget Office, *Conference on the Economics of Federal Credit Activity*, pt. 2: *Papers* (CBO, 1981), pp. 208–09.

Table 3-3. *Mortgage Insurance and Guarantees, Selected Years, 1950–84*

| | Percent of originations insured | | | |
| | Insured by Federal Housing Administration | Guaranteed by Veterans' Administration | Private insurance | Percent of originations not insured |
Year				
1950	19.5	26.0	. . .	55.3
1960	18.4	8.4	. . .	73.6
1970	24.6	10.8	3.3	61.3
1975	8.0	11.3	12.9	67.8
1980	11.2	9.0	14.2	65.5
1981	10.7	7.7	19.1	62.5
1982	11.8	7.9	19.3	61.0
1983	14.2	9.4	21.0	55.4
1984	8.1	6.0	31.4	54.5

Sources: Arnold H. Diamond, *Mortgage Loan Gross Flows,* U.S. Department of Housing and Urban Development (Government Printing Office, 1969), p. 45; HUD, Office of Public Affairs, "Survey of Mortgage Lending Activity," *News Release,* various issues; and HUD, Office of Public Affairs, "Private Mortgage Insurance Activity," various issues. Components may not add to 100 because of rounding of original data.

break down as it increasingly found itself insuring only the more risky borrowers for whom the uniform premium is too low. In fact, private mortgage insurers have entered the market, and many charge a lower fee than does the FHA.[18] As shown in table 3-3, private mortgage insurance has expanded since 1970 as a share of the market, although not all of its growth has been at the expense of the FHA program: the proportion of uninsured mortgages has also declined. In 1984 private insurance covered 31.4 percent of originations; government insurance and guarantees, 14.1 percent. The remaining 54.5 percent of originations were not covered by mortgage insurance.[19]

FHA insurance retains enough advantages, despite its higher price, to attract the low-risk borrowers. The eligibility of FHA mortgages for

18. Some of the growth in private insurance can be accounted for by the ceiling limit on the size of a mortgage that the FHA will insure.

19. The effect on the FHA program of the growth in private insurance may not yet be fully evident. If private insurance has skimmed off the low-risk borrowers, the historical default rates of the FHA program may be a poor guide to the future. In addition, high rates of home price inflation held down formal defaults in the 1970s. They may be more common in the 1980s, if inflation stays low. See David L. Kaserman, "An Econometric Analysis of the Decline in Federal Mortgage Default Insurance," in Robert M. Buckley, John A. Tuccillo, and Kevin E. Villani, eds., *Capital Markets and the Housing Sector: Perspectives on Financial Reform* (Cambridge, Mass.: Ballinger, 1977), pp. 363–79.

inclusion in Ginnie Mae pools is paramount among them. And there continue to be certain types of mortgage instruments, even of apparently low risk, that private firms will not insure because of unfamiliarity. The agency has taken the lead in offering to insure such alternative mortgage instruments.

Still, there is a question about the need for FHA insurance in the modern mortgage market. Much of the support for its continued operation springs from concern about discrimination. Public policy has sought to prevent the use of such borrower characteristics as sex, race, and home location to evaluate default risk, despite evidence that they are significant predictors of default. Because regulations to control their use by private insurers are difficult to enforce and because they increase the costs of private insurers, direct provision of the insurance by the public sector may be more effective.

The FHA's link to the government and its ability to draw on the Treasury in an emergency implies coverage both against the risk of a major economic collapse, in which losses would exceed the reserve provided by fee income, and against mismanagement of the fund of the sort suffered occasionally by private insurers, who simply go bankrupt. This greater degree of insurance is not reflected in the fees charged borrowers. However, the historical record of government bailout of large private enterprises implies that the fees charged by private insurers also fail to reflect these risks.[20]

Overall, the guarantee program, by covering the costs of its operations, meets the criteria of a self-financing insurance program and does not constitute a significant government subsidy. The existence of private insurance alternatives limits the significance of any cross-subsidy between high-risk and low-risk borrowers.

Two FHA insurance funds, both directed at high-risk, low-income borrowers and inner-city properties, require subsidies to cover their costs. The two funds had $18 billion in loan insurance outstanding in 1984, about 11 percent of the FHA total. Budget funds appropriated by Congress to cover their annual net losses during 1980–84 averaged 45 percent of their income.[21] Because these high-risk activities operate

20. These implicit guarantees in the event of extreme outcomes are not necessarily undesirable, because they contribute to greater stability of the entire financial system. It is not clear that it is desirable for the risk premium embedded in interest rates to reflect the risk of a major economic collapse.

21. Department of Housing and Urban Development, Office of Administration,

separately from the standard program, the degree of cross-subsidy is reduced, but the high loss rates of the special programs have nevertheless generated substantial controversy. High loss rates have also meant the failure of the program as an experiment to encourage private insurance of targeted borrowers. Continued operation of the program does not represent a response to capital market imperfections, but rather a subsidy to a particular class of borrower.[22]

VA MORTGAGE GUARANTEES. At the end of fiscal 1984, outstanding loans guaranteed by the Veterans' Administration totaled $125.4 billion.[23] Initially, no fee was charged for the guarantee, and no down payment was required on the loan. A one-half percent fee was imposed in the late 1960s. As a result of the Deficit Reduction Act of 1984, borrowers now pay a onetime fee of 1 percent upon initiation of a VA guarantee. The fee, however, still does not cover the cost of loan defaults, and the program does subsidize borrowers. In addition, VA-insured mortgages are assumable by a subsequent purchaser, allowing the value of the subsidy to be capitalized in the sale price.[24] Given the similarity of default costs between the FHA and VA programs, the amount of subsidy is roughly equal to the difference between the fees: 2.8 percent of the loan value. Given the existence of the FHA program, the VA guarantee cannot be viewed as a market-perfecting program.[25] It is simply a transfer payment to veterans conditional upon their ownership of a house.

The Secondary Market Programs

The greatest variety of government programs is found among those directed at the secondary market, where agencies operate much like private financial intermediaries. In some cases, the agency performs only administrative functions and has no portfolio of its own. In others it may operate much like a private bank or thrift institution, borrowing

Summary of Mortgage Insurance Operations, Fiscal Year 1984 (HUD, 1984), pp. 4–7; and *Budget of the United States Government—Appendix*, various years.

22. For a further discussion of the issues raised by these programs, see Barth and others, "Federal Government Attempts to Influence the Allocation of Mortgage Credit."

23. *Special Analyses, Budget of the United States Government, Fiscal Year 1986*, pp. F-70–F-71.

24. Aaron, *Shelter and Subsidies*, pp. 74–90.

25. The fact that loan size limits are higher for VA loans does not attenuate this argument.

for and lending from its portfolio according to its perception of market opportunities.

DIRECT SOURCES OF LIQUIDITY FOR THE MORTGAGE MARKET. The Federal Home Loan Bank System (FHLBS) borrows in the capital markets to relend to member savings and loan associations and mutual savings banks. The stated objectives of the system are to provide liquidity for unexpected withdrawal demands, to link mortgage markets to other capital markets, and to stabilize the flow of housing funds through member institutions when deposit inflows are reduced. In recent years, more than half of the savings and loan associations in the country have borrowed from the system.

The system operates through twelve regional Federal Home Loan Banks, each an instrumentality of the federal government but owned by member thrift institutions. Each member must hold capital stock in its district bank equal to 1 percent of the member's total loans outstanding, and members borrowing from the bank must hold stock equal to 5 percent of the principal balance owed. Borrowings must be secured by approved categories of assets, which include fixed rate and adjustable rate mortgage loans, mortgage-backed securities, and Treasury and agency debt. The system maintains a close match between the maturity of its assets and liabilities, thus avoiding any significant interest rate risk.

The twelve banks set the terms for advances to members, subject to general guidelines established by the Federal Home Loan Bank Board, to yield a profit over the cost of funds and administrative expenses. Retained earnings are divided between additions to reserves and dividend payments to members.

In many respects, the FHLBS operates much like a large commercial bank. It differs in three ways: debt issues, tax treatment, and lending policies.

Unlike the debt issued by commercial banks or thrifts, FHLBS consolidated obligations are legal investments for federally supervised fiduciary trusts and public funds and, in most states, for savings banks, insurance companies, trustees, and other fiduciaries subject to state supervision. They are not guaranteed by the federal government, however, although market participants accord them the highest credit rating. In addition, since 1971 the Federal Reserve System has bought and sold agency issues in the conduct of open market operations, and since 1975 it has been possible to issue FHLBS debt through the Federal Reserve wire system.

The Treasury Department is statutorily authorized to purchase FHLBS debt, another distinguishing characteristic. Until 1969 the limit was $1 billion and the intent was to provide support only in emergency situations. The 1969 amendments increased authorized purchases to $4 billion and broadened the range of permissible uses to include lending to members substantially impaired by monetary stringency or rapidly rising interest rates. The system has never used this source of borrowing. The problems encountered by the savings and loan industry in the 1980s, however, increase the probability that this or a similar form of government support may ultimately become necessary.

These aspects of FHLBS debt improve its marketability and therefore reduce the cost of funds to the system. For the 1969–84 period, the cost of funds to the FHLBS averaged about 30 basis points more than Treasury securities of comparable maturity on the issue date. This ratio was remarkably stable. The highest-rated corporations paid rates averaging 31 points above the ten-year comparable Treasury issues during 1976–84, with a peak yield spread of 50 basis points in the recession year of 1982.[26]

During 1985 some thrift industry representatives suggested that the FHLBS invest in a new corporation that would purchase and liquidate nonperforming real estate investments then owned by the Federal Savings and Loan Insurance Corporation. The proposal was taken under review by the Federal Home Loan Bank Board. Almost immediately the possibility of greater credit risk in the FHLBS asset portfolio raised quoted secondary market yields on FHLBS debt to as much as 100 basis points over Treasury issues of comparable maturity, even though no change in the bank system's agency status was contemplated. The jump in the cost of funds suggests that the system obtains little, if any, advantage in credit markets from its agency status.

Unlike private financial intermediaries performing a similar function, the Federal Home Loan Banks do not pay tax. Since dividends in recent years have accounted for 75–105 percent of the banks' net income, it is clear that application of the statutory corporate tax rate would have had a material effect on either the interest rate on advances or the return to stockholders. At the full corporate tax rate, federal income taxes would

26. Yield on medium-term AAA industrial bonds compared with ten-year Treasury securities. Data from Salomon Brothers, *Analytical Record of Yields and Yield Spreads,* 7th ed. (Salomon Brothers, 1986), pt. 2, table 9. Longer-term industrials have a higher yield spread, but FHLBS bonds do not generally exceed ten years.

have averaged approximately $300 million a year during the 1980–83 period—an annual average of 0.4 percent of assets. On the other hand, private financial institutions paid taxes on effective rates below the statutory rate—25 percent for commercial banks in 1983, the latest year for which data are available from the national income accounts.[27]

The FHLBS also acts as an emergency lender-of-last-resort for its member institutions—a function similar to that provided commercial banks by the discount window of the Federal Reserve System. Historically, the amount of subsidy, as measured by the discount below prevailing market rates, has been less than that provided by the Federal Reserve. On the other hand, advances are a far larger share of assets for savings and loans than for commercial banks, since such borrowing by savings and loans is not limited to liquidity needs alone.

During the 1970s FHLBS advances were an important source of financing for its members. In part, that is expected and is consistent with the objective of stabilizing the flow of funds to the mortgage market. The deposit institutions were especially vulnerable to fluctuations in market interest rates both because of deposit rate ceilings and because of the maturity imbalance of their assets and liabilities—long-term mortgages versus short-term deposits. The historical pattern of a significant inverse correlation between changes in advances and deposits at savings and loans, shown in figure 3-2, is consistent with the argument that the role has been fulfilled by the FHLBS. At the same time, there has been only a modest increase in the importance of advances in the overall liability structure of savings and loans. The ratio of advances to deposits rose from 7 to 9 percent between 1970 and 1974, declined to 5 percent in 1976, and reached a peak of 12 percent in 1981 before declining to 9 percent in 1984.

The effect of any subsidy on lending rates charged to FHLBS member institutions must be small. In recent years the larger thrift institutions have been able to tap the credit markets directly, with a variety of collateralized financing techniques, at costs equal to or lower than those offered by the Federal Home Loan Banks. For smaller institutions that require less than $50 million to $75 million in new funds at a time, the lower fixed costs of FHLBS advances offset the more favorable rates available through a direct borrowing.

27. Federal Home Loan Bank Board, *Annual Report, 1983: Revitalizing America's Savings Institutions*, pp. 78–84; and *Survey of Current Business*, vol. 66 (July 1986), p. 71.

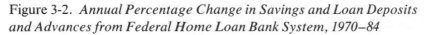

Figure 3-2. *Annual Percentage Change in Savings and Loan Deposits and Advances from Federal Home Loan Bank System, 1970–84*

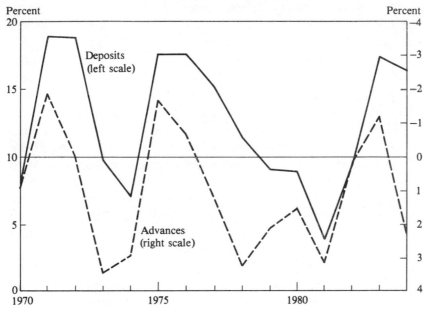

Source: Board of Governors of the Federal Reserve System, *Flow of Funds Accounts*, various issues. The change in advances is divided by the previous year's deposits.

MORTGAGE PURCHASE ACTIVITIES. The Federal National Mortgage Association (Fannie Mae) was established in 1938 to provide a resale market for FHA-insured and VA-guaranteed mortgage loans originated by other institutions. Since then it has shifted its orientation to conventional loans. The agency's mortgage portfolio was valued at $87.9 billion at the end of 1984, of which $34.1 billion was guaranteed by the FHA or the VA.[28]

Each day Fannie Mae sets the interest rate at which it is willing to purchase mortgages. It then commits itself to buy a specified quantity of mortgages from mortgage originators whom it has previously certified. Once the loans are delivered to Fannie Mae, the originator continues to collect monthly principal and interest as agent for Fannie Mae. For this service, the originator or servicer retains a fee. Most risk of default is borne by Fannie Mae as owner, although the risk is mitigated by the requirement for insurance on mortgages that exceed 80 percent of the appraised value of the property.

28. Federal National Mortgage Association, *1984 Annual Report*, p. 21.

Although Fannie Mae has certain ties to the federal government, it has been a private shareholder-owned corporation since 1968. Unlike the FHLBS, it is subject to federal income taxation. A few subsidized, low-income assistance programs once run by Fannie Mae were transferred to the Government National Mortgage Association (Ginnie Mae) in 1968. On the other hand, Fannie Mae's charter may be changed only by Congress, a third of its board of directors is composed of government appointees, it is subject to the general oversight of the Department of Housing and Urban Development, and it is authorized to borrow up to $2.25 billion from the Treasury.

Important problems arose during the 1980s because of Fannie Mae's failure to match the maturity structures of its assets and liabilities. With its mortgage portfolio financed largely with short-term debt, Fannie Mae had operated, in effect, through much of its history as an interest rate speculator, rather than simply as a secondary market link to the rest of the capital market. It did fairly well during the 1970s, but the cost of debt exceeded the yield on the mortgage portfolio from 1979 to 1984. In recent years Fannie Mae has made major efforts to redress this problem by lengthening the maturity of its bond issues, by acquiring shorter-term assets such as adjustable rate mortgages and fifteen-year fixed rate loans, and by selling many of its older fixed rate mortgages. Beginning in 1985 the agency's earnings were adversely affected by defaults on many loans, even as the problems brought on by high interest rates abated.

The cost of funds has reflected the market's increased awareness of the risk inherent in Fannie Mae's operations. From 1969 through 1979 the agency issued $75 billion in long-term debt at rates averaging 41 basis points over Treasury issues of comparable maturity. During that same period the agency also sold $68 billion in short-term discount notes at an effective yield 31 basis points above Treasury bills. These rates were somewhat lower than those of highly rated, fully private corporations.

In the 1980s, as Fannie Mae's earnings fell, investors raised the agency's premiums. For 1980–82, $39 billion in long-term Fannie Mae debt sold at an average of 72 basis points over government issues and $82 billion in discount notes at 87 basis points higher than comparable Treasury bills. As market interest rates declined after 1982, the interest premium charged Fannie Mae declined back to the level of the 1970s. Given the agency's earnings difficulties, however—it lost an average of $69 million a year on average annual revenues of $7.7 billion in the 1981–84 period—the retention of a relatively high credit rating would seem to reflect Fannie Mae's links to the government. It is also evident, however, from the changing size of the risk premium, that it is not viewed as a simple extension of the federal government.

The Federal Home Loan Mortgage Corporation (Freddie Mac) also purchases conventional mortgages for its portfolio, financed by the sale of debt. Freddie Mac is organized as a corporation controlled by member savings institutions, which directly and indirectly own all of its stock, and by the Federal Home Loan Bank Board, which constitutes Freddie Mac's board of directors. Its policies are subject to government approval. Its portfolio activities are now confined to home improvement loans and adjustable rate mortgages, instruments that have not yet achieved widespread acceptance in the secondary market. At the end of 1984, Freddie Mac held $10.4 billion in loans in its portfolio.[29] It has not encountered the same problems as Fannie Mae because it has been careful to avoid interest rate risk by maintaining a balance in the maturity of its assets and liabilities.

MORTGAGE-BACKED SECURITIES. The mortgage-related security is now an important link between the capital market and mortgagors. The most common is the mortgage-backed "pass-through" security. In its simplest form, a private lender, such as a bank, savings and loan, or mortgage banker, originates a number of mortgage loans. The originator or an agency to which the loans have been sold creates a security backed by the pool of mortgages and sells the security to capital market investors, either as a public offering or a private placement. The original lender retains the responsibility for servicing the loan. Borrowers' monthly payments of principal and interest are "passed through" to holders of the security on a pro rata basis, after deducting the servicing and guarantee fees.

The process is one of intermediation, transforming an asset (the mortgage) with one set of characteristics into a security that is more attractive to investors. The original mortgage has thus been changed in many respects: it is now diversified (a typical pool will contain from a few dozen to several hundred loans); it is typically available to the investor in units of $25,000; the investor is freed of concerns over servicing the loan; prompt payment is assured; and the instrument has been standardized to such an extent that it is easily marketable.

In 1965, 1 percent of outstanding mortgages were held in mortgage-

29. Federal Home Loan Mortgage Corporation, *1984 Annual Report*, p. 42.

Table 3-4. *Measures of Secondary Mortgage Market Activity,*
Selected Years, 1950–84
Percent

Year	Share of outstanding mortgages held in pools	Mortgage sales as share of originations[a]
1950	0.0	25.7
1955	0.0	28.7
1960	1.8	27.5
1965	1.0	30.7
1970	5.3	31.8
1975	11.6	26.5
1980	15.9	39.1
1982	20.7	85.1
1984	25.8	61.0

Sources: Diamond, *Mortgage Loan Gross Flows,* tables 4, 5, 10, 11; HUD, Office of Public Affairs, "Survey of Mortgage Lending Activity," various issues; and Board of Governors, *Flow of Funds Accounts,* various issues.
a. Data are for single-family and multifamily residential mortgages. Data for 1950–65 include construction loans, whereas 1970–84 tabulations are for long-term financing only. Loan sales are adjusted by subtracting sales by credit agencies and pools.

backed securities (see table 3-4). By 1984 more than 25 percent of outstanding mortgages were held in mortgage pools. The growth of these securities is largely a result of federal action.

Ginnie Mae helped to establish the market in 1970 by offering to insure timely payment of interest and principal on securities where the underlying mortgages were insured by the Federal Housing Administration or guaranteed by the Veterans' Administration or the Farmers Home Administration (FmHA). Ginnie Mae issues outstanding totaled $212.1 billion at the end of 1985.[30]

The agency never owns the underlying mortgages or the security, and the private mortgage originator is responsible for lining up both the borrowers and the investors. For an annual fee of 0.06 percent of the outstanding loan amount, Ginnie Mae stands ready to advance scheduled payments to security holders should the servicing agent fail to do so. Ginnie Mae is protected by the underlying federal insurance or guarantee. The GNMA mortgage-backed securities program had accumulated a surplus of $816 million from operations at the end of fiscal 1984.[31] Alone among the agencies operating in the mortgage market, Ginnie Mae

30. Data from First Boston Corporation, *Handbook of Securities of the United States Government and Federal Agencies,* 32d ed. (First Boston Corp., 1986), p. 116.
31. Department of Housing and Urban Development, Government National Mortgage Association, *Annual Report, 1984,* p. 6.

obligations are backed explicitly by the full faith and credit of the federal government.

Freddie Mac has operated a similar market for conventional mortgages since its inception in 1970. It purchases mortgages for inclusion in pools backing its pass-through securities, called participation certificates. Mortgage originators (primarily savings and loan associations) obtain mandatory delivery commitments from Freddie Mac at posted yields. The originator keeps as a servicing fee the difference between the rate on the underlying loans and Freddie Mac's net yield requirement. Freddie Mac pass-through securities outstanding amounted to $99.0 billion at the end of 1985.[32]

In 1981 Fannie Mae began to supplement its purchase program with pools that contain either FHA- or VA-guaranteed loans or conventional loans. By the end of 1985, its mortgage-backed securities outstanding totaled $55.0 billion.[33] Unlike its portfolio investments, these pass-through securities pose little risk to Fannie Mae as a result of adverse interest rate movements. Fannie Mae warrants the performance of the servicing agent, for which it receives a fee.

New programs initiated by Freddie Mac and Fannie Mae in late 1981 permit banks and savings institutions to exchange their mortgage loans for pass-through securities backed by those loans. The agency issues the securities at a yield slightly below the yield on the underlying mortgages, collecting a fee for guaranteeing payment to investors. For the diminution in yield, the originator gains a security that can be sold in the market or borrowed against. Thus the transformation improves the marketability of the institution's asset portfolio. In 1984 such swap operations accounted for 82 percent of Freddie Mac's mortgage participation certificate issues and 93 percent of Fannie Mae's mortgage-backed securities issues.[34] In 1985 the swap operations continued to grow, although they were a smaller share of the total market.

As mentioned above, a new type of mortgage-backed security, the collateralized mortgage obligation, was first issued by Freddie Mac in mid-1983. The CMO apportions the principal repayments on pools of mortgage loans to holders of "fast-pay" and "slow-pay" bonds, an innovation that has transformed the homogeneous mortgage into short-term, intermediate-term, and long-term bond-like instruments. Other

32. First Boston Corporation, *Handbook*, p. 101.
33. Ibid., p. 105.
34. Data supplied by the staffs of Ginnie Mae, Freddie Mac, and Fannie Mae.

issuers soon followed Freddie Mac, and at the end of 1985, $30 billion in CMOs had been issued.

The right-hand column of table 3-4 shows that the volume of secondary market activity has rapidly increased in recent years. The ratio of sales to originations prevailing in the 1950s and 1960s—25 to 30 percent—represents the activities of mortgage companies on behalf of specific life insurance companies. The more recent growth is linked with the advent of mortgage-backed securities facilitated by government-sponsored mortgage agencies.

Mortgage-backed securities have created such an effective link between the mortgage market and the rest of the capital market that it may no longer be necessary for the agencies to continue to purchase mortgages for their own account—particularly when they fail to hedge against interest rate risk. In chapter 2 we argued that such purchases have at best a transitory influence on mortgage interest costs to borrowers. Although the purchase programs could be operated as a countercyclical stabilizer, the effects would be small, and countercyclical purchases would expose the private owners and the government to significant interest risk.

The mortgage-backed securities programs, on the other hand, can be defended as self-financing, market-perfecting activities. They involve little or no subsidy and impose minimal risk on the government. The agencies have some advantage in providing these services because of economies of scale, their established position in the market, and, perhaps, an implicit government guarantee that they will be soundly managed.

Direct Loans

Direct loan programs represent a relatively small portion of government activities in the mortgage market. The largest, rural housing, is operated by the Farmers Home Administration and is discussed in chapter 5 with other agricultural credit programs. The other major direct loan programs are run by the Department of Housing and Urban Development for the benefit of low-income families, the elderly, and the handicapped. In addition, until 1983 Ginnie Mae purchased from private originators mortgages on low- and moderate-income property at or above market value. In 1984 HUD disbursed $2.8 billion in new loans; outstanding loans totaled $13.4 billion.[35] The housing loans for the elderly and handicapped are forty-year mortgages with an interest rate—9 percent in 1985—well below the government's costs. By providing the borrowers with a subsidy, the program aims to reduce rents for these target groups. The present discounted value of the program's subsidy is roughly 25 percent of the loan value.[36] The administration estimates the present value of subsidy costs for all 1984 housing loan obligations at $253 million.

Because these programs are intended as subsidies to specific groups rather than addressed to credit market concerns, they should be treated in the context of government assistance rather than in an analysis of credit programs.

Impact of Government Credit Programs on Mortgage Interest Rates

There have been dramatic changes in the structure of the mortgage market in recent decades, largely as a result of government involvement. Yet it is difficult to measure the effect the changes have had on the interest rate charged primary borrowers. The rate on conventional first mortgages during 1960–84 is shown in figure 3-3; its premium over ten-year government bonds, in figure 3-4. Despite a substantial rise in the overall level of all interest rates, the premium has remained quite stable. In fact, it increased during the late 1970s and early 1980s, when the market innovations were most rapid. As discussed in appendix A, much of the increase appears to be related to the breakdown of segmentation between capital markets: mortgage lenders can no longer draw on low-cost deposit funds.

Part of the difficulty in evaluating the effect of the government credit programs is due to the changing value of the call option to prepay the loan that is embedded in every mortgage. This option has a relatively high value when interest rate levels are perceived to be at a cyclical peak. When interest rates are stable, the option has little value. This may account for the widening of mortgage-Treasury spreads from the late 1970s to the early 1980s. Nevertheless, a general decline in the

35. See *Special Analyses, Budget of the United States Government, Fiscal Year 1986*, table F-19.

36. Ibid., p. F-33.

Figure 3-3. *Market Yields on Conventional Mortgages and Ten-Year Treasury Securities, 1960–84*

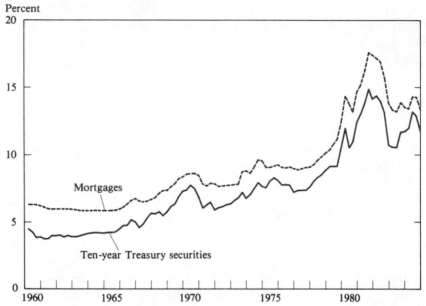

Source: Board of Governors, Statistical Release G. 13, "Selected Interest Rates," various issues. Mortgage yields are calculated by weighted averages of new and existing home mortgages as reported by the Department of Housing and Urban Development using weights of one-third and two-thirds.

spread after 1983 seems to indicate the impact of the mortgage-backed security in arbitraging away discrepancies between the two markets.[37]

The mortgage market actually had a preferred position in the early 1960s, when government banking regulations provided the major lending institutions a favored position in competing for deposit-type funds. The result was a lower mortgage rate than would exist in a fully open capital market. When the increased risk of interest rate fluctuations after the mid-1960s made a reliance on short-term financing untenable, deregulation forced mortgages to compete with a wider range of financial instruments. The innovations by the government-sponsored credit agencies—principally the mortgage-backed security—eased that transition

37. See Arthur J. Corazzini, Stephen H. Brooks, and Perry D. Quick, *Housing Finance and Secondary Mortgage Markets: Review of Recent Developments and Proposals for Change* (Washington, D.C.: Homebuilders Ad Hoc Policy Group, 1985), pp. 14–16, 53–54.

Figure 3-4. *Yield Differential between Conventional Mortgages and Ten-Year Treasury Securities, 1960–84*

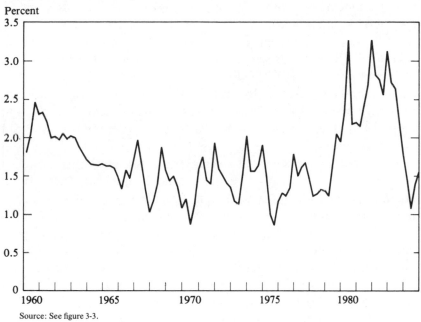

Percent

Source: See figure 3-3.

and allowed mortgages to become a competitive financial instrument in an open capital market.

Overview

Housing credit programs are often blamed for drawing too many resources away from other sectors of the economy: "Recent experience has shown that these programs preempt private sector investment resources, and this absorption has an inhibiting effect on productivity and economic growth."[38] However, while the full extent of reallocation of credit between business and household investment may be undesirable, it is largely a result of tax rather than credit subsidies. In general, the credit programs have concentrated on improving the efficiency of the mortgage market, and they do not incorporate large subsidies. Only a few programs have had explicit or implicit subsidy elements, and these

38. *Special Analyses, Budget of the United States Government, Fiscal Year 1984,* p. F-1.

have been declining in importance in recent years. The tax system, on the other hand, does provide a large subsidy for homeownership.

Government credit programs for housing achieve their objective by changing the attributes of the mortgage instrument as it makes its way from the borrower through a variety of intermediaries to the ultimate investor.[39] They are intended to give each party its desired mix of risk and return, with all that implies for liquidity, maturity, and denomination. The appropriate framework for analysis, therefore, is the type and degree of transformation that is effected. If each transformation is allowed to be priced by the market, then the existence of a federal role does not connote a subsidy.

At present, the agencies are focusing their efforts on mortgage-backed securities, where any subsidy element must be minimal. The costs of creating a Ginnie Mae, Fannie Mae, or Freddie Mac pass-through have heretofore been a bit less than those associated with a private pass-through. A pool of conventional loans carrying private mortgage insurance can be made into securities by Fannie Mae or Freddie Mac at an annual cost of 0.1 to 0.2 percent of the remaining loan balance. For a private intermediary to create an equivalent security would cost approximately 0.2 to 0.3 percent of the remaining balance annually.

The average difference of 0.1 percent in net yield is sufficient to shift virtually all of the eligible mortgage security business to the agencies, but it is doubtful that it significantly affects resource allocation. If passed through to the buyer, a 10-basis-point reduction in the interest rate on a typical mortgage would permit less than a 0.06 percent increase in the dollar value of the property financed, and the increase in real resources would be less than the increase in nominal value. Applying this estimate to the value of all loans securitized under the auspices of Ginnie Mae, Fannie Mae, and Freddie Mac in 1985 suggests that the agency's advantages could account for at most $400 million of the roughly $300 billion spent on new and existing housing.

It is apparent that the federally related mortgage credit agencies have enjoyed a number of advantages that reduced their operating costs— interest and dividend payments, administrative expenses, taxes, required capital—below those of private firms. It is also true that these advantages have diminished in recent years, as the agencies have taken

39. Patric H. Hendershott and Kevin E. Villani, "Residential Mortgage Markets and the Cost of Mortgage Funds," *American Real Estate and Urban Economics Association Journal*, vol. 8 (Spring 1980), pp. 50–76.

on more attributes of private corporations and as private market participants have become more adept. Private mortgage insurance is now
more prevalent than FHA and VA insurance. The Secondary Mortgage
Market Enhancement Act of 1984 removed some of the limitations on
private mortgage-backed securities and was intended to narrow any
remaining advantage of Fannie Mae and Freddie Mac. The two agencies
are now taxpayers, and their stock is more widely held than previously.[40]
In 1985, for example, a new class of Freddie Mac stock was created to
be held and traded by savings institutions. Fannie Mae has expanded its
sources of funds through debt offerings tailored to European and
Japanese investors. Because of substantial unrealized losses in Fannie
Mae's portfolio of low-yielding assets, however, government linkages
cannot be severed quickly. The competition between Fannie Mae and
Freddie Mac also means that further privatization must proceed in
tandem.

In its 1986 and 1987 federal budgets the administration proposed the
imposition of user fees on the housing agencies. If enacted by Congress,
the proposal would mean that the guarantee fee on Ginnie Mae securities
would rise from 0.06 percent to 0.15 percent annually and that higher
charges would be levied on Fannie Mae and Freddie Mac pass-through
issues. FHA mortgage insurance fees would go up more than 30 percent.
The charges are not necessary to cover costs; they are intended solely
to bring agency financing rates into line with those of the private market.[41]
Some of the proposals, such as a 0.5 percent fee on new debt issued by
Fannie Mae, are frank attempts to discourage certain activities alto-
gether, in this case Fannie Mae's mortgage purchase program.

Future Role

In resuscitating the mortgage market after the Great Depression, the
government initiated many of the institutional reforms that integrated
the mortgage market with the national financial system. The government
having paved the way, the private market now offers virtually as full a
range of services as the federally related agencies do. The question may

40. The FHLBS and Ginnie Mae remain exempt from taxation.
41. *Budget of the United States Government, Fiscal Year 1986*, pp. 5-59–5-61. A
proposal to increase VA guarantee fees would reduce or eliminate the subsidy that
exists in that program.

be asked, then, whether the continued involvement of the federal government is required. The answer is probably yes, for several reasons, mostly having to do with the government's unique ability to overcome market imperfections.

Government can be a source of innovation. A government agency can act in a less risk-averse fashion than private financial intermediaries to demonstrate the attributes of a new financial device. Private lenders may individually be too small to conduct a sufficiently large experiment. An agency can provide the scale required.

Once the experiment has been conducted, the results are visible to all lenders. Even if a private lender *could* conduct the experiment, it could not keep the benefits of the experiment to itself to compensate for the risk undertaken. The public nature of the benefits argues for a government role in the early stages of development. That argument, however, is for an ongoing role for the agency in developing new programs, not for its continuing to run a well-developed program.

Federal agencies can also facilitate private risk-taking. For example, private investors willing to take risks may be prevented from doing so by existing federal laws. Creation of a new agency program is one way of removing regulatory restrictions on the private sector. Inconsistency among state laws may also prevent the large national lenders best able to take risks from conducting an experiment. For example, until the 1980s, variations in state requirements for adjustable rate mortgage loans effectively prevented a common instrument from being used nationwide. A federal agency can override state laws.

Finally, the government-sponsored agencies are, on the whole, efficient institutions with significant economies of scale and specialization of knowledge. They have consistently tried to divorce their activities from dependency upon government and to allow purely private competitors to develop. As long as their operations are not subsidized by the government, they should not be a major cause of concern.

Credit subsidies for housing are limited to the FHA special assistance fund, veterans' mortgage guarantee programs, and the HUD direct loan programs for low-income, elderly, and handicapped renters. In recent years, the administration has so scaled back the volume of direct loans that they are a relatively small part of the overall supply of credit for housing. Despite the large share of government-related credit directed at housing, the total impact on resource allocation is relatively small.

CHAPTER FOUR

Credit for Business

GOVERNMENT CREDIT PROGRAMS do not assume the dominant role in the business finance markets that they play in the housing and agricultural credit markets. To a great degree the private business credit system matches the needs of borrowers and preferences of investors efficiently and offers few opportunities for the government to improve the market by performing a neglected or unprofitable intermediation function. Federal credit for business is limited to relatively small programs focused on specific problem areas, including small businesses, international trade, certain industries, and specific firms.

Most government credit programs for business were initiated for a combination of two reasons: to correct a perceived failure in some particular portion of the business credit market and to influence the behavior of, or give special advantages to, selected types of business activity. Although a credit program is likely to be the most efficient way of addressing the first type of problem, other forms of assistance could easily be used for the second. Similarly, a subsidy may or may not be required to achieve the first purpose, but it is clearly needed to achieve the second. Assessing existing business credit programs requires disentangling these two purposes.

Business Credit Markets and the Government

The market for business finance is characterized by a great range of credit instruments developed primarily as a response to differing concerns of borrowers, intermediaries, and investors about credit risk and loan maturity. The three main sources of debt finance are bonds, commercial mortgages, and bank loans. Bonds provide long-term fi-

Table 4-1. *Business Credit Programs of the Federal Government, Fiscal Year 1984*
Billions of dollars unless otherwise specified

Credit Program	Amount outstanding
Export-Import Bank	
Direct loans	17.5
Guarantees and insurance	5.7
Small Business Administration (SBA)	
Direct loans	4.6
Guaranteed loans	8.9
Rural Electrification Administration	
Direct loans	35.6
Loan guarantees	0.9
Ship-financing guarantees	7.0
Synthetic fuels program	1.3
SBA disaster loans	5.0
All other direct loans	1.9
All other loan guarantees	5.4
Total	93.8
Total business credit	1,930.5
Federal participation rate (percent)	5

Source: *Special Analyses, Budget of the United States Government, Fiscal Year 1986*, pp. F-55–F-73.

nancing for large firms with low default risk. Commercial mortgages are used by firms of all types and depend heavily on the future market value of the collateral rather than on the expected performance of the firm. Bank loans are a mixture of short- and medium-term loans, both secured and unsecured. Together, these three sources account for three-fourths of total business credit. The actual variety in business credit markets is even greater because of intracategory specialization and quasi-credit arrangements such as lease financing. Finally, equities, though distinct from credit, are a major potential source of financing. The basic components of this system have changed little during the past thirty years.

The government has played an important role in the development of these private markets. Federal legislation established the basic structure and operating rules for the lead institutions—investment banks and commercial banks. Public agencies like the Federal Deposit Insurance Corporation and the Securities and Exchange Commission help maintain investor confidence in the system. The government has not, however, been a major participant in business credit allocation. As shown in table 4-1, its credit activities are fragmented among different kinds of programs and amount to less than 5 percent of business financing. This chapter discusses two of the most important, the Small Business Administration (SBA) and the Export-Import Bank.

The Origins of Business Credit Programs

Like many other federal credit programs, the first business programs were a response to the financial crises of the Great Depression. In the thirties the volume of bank lending to businesses dropped far below the level it had reached during the previous decade. Between 1929 and 1932, loans made annually by commercial banks fell 44 percent and for the rest of the decade stayed below the already low 1932 level.[1] The federal government became an emergency source of finance.

The Reconstruction Finance Corporation (RFC) was the first agency to extend government credit to businesses. Beginning in 1932 the RFC lent large amounts to railroads. In 1934 it started a general business lending program, of which the current Small Business Administration programs are the direct descendents.

The RFC was given a broad mandate to "maintain and increase employment by making RFC loans available to solvent business enterprises unable to obtain credit through normal channels."[2] It was up to the agency to decide which channels were working. At first, few were. With commercial banks not lending actively, the RFC could be confident that most loans it made would not have been made by commercial banks. As the program continued and banks began to recover, the RFC rapidly moved through successive generations of new target groups and forms of credit, continually refocusing on areas still lacking adequate service. It concentrated more heavily than did private lenders on medium-sized firms and on manufacturing. It also lent disproportionately to the capital-poor but fast-growing southern and western regions of the country.[3] Perhaps the most important difference was that the RFC made loans with longer maturities than did commercial banks. Half of its loans had terms of five years or more. Its borrower selection shifted in response

1. Paul Studenski and Herman E. Krooss, *Financial History of the United States: Fiscal, Monetary, Banking, and Tariff, Including Financial Administration and State and Local Finance,* 2d ed. (McGraw-Hill, 1963), pp. 370, 400.

2. R. J. Saulnier, Harold G. Halcrow, and Neil H. Jacoby, *Federal Lending and Loan Insurance* (Princeton University Press, 1958), p. 422.

3. Ibid., pp. 439–42.

to the most pressing national needs: first relief, then recovery, then war production, and finally postwar reconversion. Throughout its lifetime the RFC subsidized borrowers with slightly below-market interest rates. About 10 percent of its business loans ended in default and foreclosure.[4]

The RFC experimented widely with lending strategies. It struggled with questions such as how much collateral a government agency should require, how it could determine whether a private bank would have provided credit in its absence, and what form joint participation with private lenders should take. As the RFC's successors, the Small Business Administration and the Export-Import Bank, show, these fundamental issues in government lending to business remain controversial.

Another of the New Deal credit programs was the Export-Import Bank, created by executive order in 1934 as a subsidiary of the RFC. To an even greater degree than the RFC, the Eximbank entered a financial market that was barely functioning. International trade and lending had fallen far below the average levels of the 1920s, and even during the twenties, medium- to long-term trade credits by U.S. commercial banks had been virtually nonexistent. The commercial banks supported the creation of Eximbank, whose activities were carefully crafted to complement their own. Eximbank was to avoid the types of loans that commercial banks already made, extend the long-term loans they could not make, and assume the political and commercial risk on the intermediate range of credits.[5]

Business Credit in the Postwar Period

After World War II the banking industry began to argue that the RFC was not needed to support general levels of lending, and in 1953 the corporation was closed. Its business lending functions were reborn in the Small Business Administration, which adopted many RFC practices. Small businesses were targeted for continued government assistance on the grounds that they faced special problems in obtaining credit and were essential to the competitive, entrepreneurial character of the American economy. The American Bankers Association opposed the creation of the SBA, but acquiesced once it was provided that the SBA would be

---

4. Jesse H. Jones with Edward Angly, *Fifty Billion Dollars: My Thirteen Years with the RFC, 1932–1945* (Macmillan, 1951), p. 184.

5. A third major federal credit program for business, the Rural Electrification Administration (REA), was also created during the depression as part of reconstruction of rural areas. That program is discussed in chapter 5.

allowed to lend only to borrowers who did not meet commercial bank credit standards.[6]

Although the postwar push toward less reliance on government credit was sufficient to transform the RFC into the SBA, it did not affect the Eximbank significantly, for the government did not compete so closely with private lenders in trade credit.

Few new business credit programs have been established in the postwar period. Those that have been include a program to guarantee long-term loans for construction of merchant marine and other vessels, programs by the Economic Development Administration and Farmers Home Administration for attracting businesses to distressed areas, and a loan program by the SBA for victims of natural disasters.

During the 1970s two new uses for federal credit attracted widespread notice. The first was for energy development. Established during the late 1970s, energy programs were justified under the premise that while initial attempts at commercialization of alternate fuel technologies might be too risky for private investors, they would provide information that would contribute to energy self-sufficiency for the United States. The companies that have received assistance have often been large, already profitable energy firms.[7]

Second, loan guarantees were extended to rescue the Lockheed and Chrysler corporations from bankruptcy. The problems of these two companies, though they resulted from poor investment and management decisions, took on a financial character as insolvency approached. It was believed that these firms would be profitable in the future if their productive assets could be freed from the burden of past debts. The use of loan guarantees here is perhaps best understood as a government-managed bankruptcy proceeding that allocated unavoidable losses among creditors and employees while providing a means of keeping the firm in operation.

Rationale for Business Credit Programs

The public or political justification for the creation of all business credit programs has been to assist some segment of the economy, from

6. See statements of Everett D. Reese and William Kelley, American Bankers Association, in *Creation of Small Business Administration*, Hearings before the House Committee on Banking and Currency, 83 Cong. 1 sess. (Government Printing Office, 1953), pp. 63–68.

7. Issues related to the guarantee of such loans are discussed in chapter 2.

small store owners to synfuels developers, not just because they were deserving, but because credit markets in the target sector were believed not to be efficient. In the economic climate of the 1930s, this was generally true. Over the years, however, credit markets have learned to perform some of the very tasks the programs were created to address, weakening the original rationales. For example, the maturities offered on bank loans have gradually increased, and geographical barriers to credit in the South and West have long since fallen. Yet the government credit programs continue apace. Once created, the political tenacity of the groups supporting the programs has kept federal aid flowing.

When private markets grow more capable and become potential competitors, credit programs can respond in three ways. They may preserve demand for their services by becoming more clearly subsidized; they may operate alongside private lenders, duplicating private activities and becoming, in effect, competing financial institutions; or they may redirect themselves to the market frontier. The route taken by most of the major business credit programs has been that of greater subsidies. The SBA's subsidies have grown as defaults have increased, and the Eximbank has developed a specific policy to subsidize loans in certain cases.

The third choice, that of moving to the new market frontier, is clearly the most desirable. If the credit markets have genuinely erred in judging the cost or risk of an activity, the government will be able to create its intended effect at low cost. Opportunities for a program to overcome a business credit market defect, however, are rare.

These alternatives make it clear that it is crucial to know how each government credit program has interacted with private financial institutions as they have grown in capacity. The next two sections examine such questions for the Small Business Administration and the Eximbank.

Small Business Administration Loan Guarantees

The Small Business Administration's section 7(a) loan guarantee program takes on the ambitious task of improving the performance of the capital market in an area in which private institutions already generate an enormous volume of activity—commercial and industrial term lending. It acts on the premise that small businesses needing intermediate- and long-term credit face disadvantages in competing for such financing, and it is aimed at extending the boundaries of commercial and industrial lending in the direction of longer maturities and more marginal firms.

Under the program the SBA guarantees repayment of up to 90 percent of the principal and accrued interest on loans that banks make for periods averaging seven to eight years to businesses unable to obtain such credit on their own. Banks are delegated primary responsibility for borrower selection and credit evaluation, along with liability for the remaining 10 percent of the loan. The guarantee is intended to encourage banks to lend more to marginal borrowers; the remaining risk, to induce them to select borrowers carefully and manage loans prudently. The success of the program depends heavily on the effect of such incentives on bank decisions.

Guarantees have been part of the SBA's business credit program since it was first established, as they were for the RFC before it. In its first two decades, however, the SBA relied mainly on direct loans and "immediate participations," loans where the SBA and the bank each disbursed portions of a single loan. Guarantees became the preferred form only in the 1970s. The government gradually withdrew from direct lending because guarantees appear to use fewer constrained federal resources. They add less to budget outlays than direct lending and save federal staff because of their reliance on administration by private lenders. By 1981 virtually all new SBA business lending took the form of loan guarantees.

In fiscal 1984 the SBA approved about 17,000 guaranteed loans averaging $150,000 under the 7(a) program. The loans totaled $2.5 billion and raised the SBA's portfolio of outstanding guaranteed loans to $10 billion.[8] The program is small in comparison with total private business bank loans of $643 billion at the end of 1984, but in the context of small (less than $500,000) commercial and industrial term loans it is a significant force. Among banks participating in the SBA program, the Government Accounting Office found the proportion of commercial long-term loans backed by the SBA to be as high as 30–40 percent.[9]

The loans receiving guarantees are fully amortizing, issued at interest rates up to a ceiling of 2.25 percent (or 2.75 percent for longer-term

8. *Budget of the United States Government, Fiscal Year 1986—Appendix*, p. I-W3; and U.S. Small Business Administration, Office of Computer Sciences, *Management Information Summary*, RCN 309 (SBA, 1984), p. ii.

9. General Accounting Office, *SBA's 7(a) Loan Guarantee Program: An Assessment of Its Role in the Financial Market*, GAO/RCED-83-96 (GAO, 1983), p. 31.

loans) above the prime rate, and secured by firm assets or personal assets of the owners. The average five- to ten-year maturities are longer than maturities available for most commercial loans.

Rationales for the SBA Program

Like all government business credit programs, the SBA loan guarantee program is justified on the basis of a general credit market problem: small businesses are disadvantaged in the competition for debt financing. A second justification is the extraordinary economic and social benefits small businesses are said to produce. Each rationale implies a different standard by which to judge program performance.

FINANCIAL MARKET FLAWS. It is claimed that financially sound small businesses are unable to obtain reasonably priced medium- and long-term credit for expansion. For large businesses, most such financing comes through equity and bond markets, from which small businesses are excluded by the high cost of underwriting relative to the amount of funds raised. Underwriting costs have a high fixed component. As the volume of funds raised in a single issue rises, the proportional cost of underwriting falls. A survey undertaken in the early 1970s found that for equity issues up to $500,000, the maximum SBA loan size, the administrative cost of issuance was 24 percent of the total funds raised, while for issues over $20 million it was as low as 5 percent.[10] Bond issues would exhibit a similar pattern. Such costs are prohibitive. The SBA has used size at which access to equity and bond markets disappears as a working definition of small business in their deliberations over SBA eligibility rules.[11] In addition, large firms are able to obtain bond financing on the basis of their general reputation as good credit risks, whereas bank loans normally require specific collateral.

Although small businesses can borrow from commercial banks, the banks are not able to furnish long-term loans to substitute for bond or equity finance. Maturities of three or five years are usually the longest available.[12] The banks' preference for shorter maturities comes in part

10. Reported in David L. Cohen, "Small Business Capital Formation," in Federal Reserve System, *Public Policy and Capital Formation* (Washington, D.C.: Board of Governors of the Federal Reserve System, 1981), p. 258.

11. Jack McCroskey, "Federal Credit Programs for Small Business," in Commission on Money and Credit, *Federal Credit Agencies* (Prentice-Hall, 1963), p. 436.

12. Commercial mortgages are an exception, as real estate retains its value as collateral for longer periods.

Table 4-2. *Distribution of Bank Loans to Small Business,*
by Maturity Period, 1982
Percent

Maturity period	Small Business Administration loans	Other loans
Under 1 year	2	52
1–5 years	24	33
6–10 years	59	11
Over 10 years	15	4
Total	100	100

Source: General Accounting Office, *SBA's 7(a) Loan Guarantee Program: An Assessment of Its Role in the Financial Market*, GAO/RCED-83-96 (GAO, 1983), p. 90.

from liquidity needs. Banks attempt to avoid a mismatch of maturities of their own assets against their mostly short-term liabilities.

The reliance banks place on collateral also reduces the amount and raises the price of credit that small businesses, especially new firms, can obtain. Collateral policies may also reduce maturities, if there is a mismatch between the useful physical lives of the assets and their shorter market or resale lives.

The SBA program addresses this problem by guaranteeing loans of longer maturity than commercial banks normally issue, by generating loans to more new firms, and by allowing larger loans to be made to firms than would otherwise be permissible. Asked by the General Accounting Office (GAO) why they participate in the SBA program, bankers cited these three reasons most often. The GAO survey, summarized in table 4-2, found that while 74 percent of SBA loans have maturities of more than five years, only 15 percent of private loans do so. About 25 percent of SBA loans (by dollar amount) are made to businesses less than one year old.[13]

ECONOMIC BENEFITS OF SMALL BUSINESS. The second justification for the SBA program is that small businesses generate social and economic benefits that are not captured in the lender-borrower transaction.[14] While such an argument acknowledges that small businesses may be riskier on the whole than large ones, it postulates that SBA loans

13. Information supplied by the staff of the Small Business Administration.
14. Examples of possible benefits are discussed in Richard Klein, "SBA's Business Loan Programs," *Atlanta Economic Review*, vol. 28 (September–October 1978), pp. 28–37.

Table 4-3. *Distribution of Small Businesses, by Industry, 1982*
Percent

Industry	All small business	Adjusted small business[a]	Small Business Administration borrowers
Wholesale trade	10	12	11
Retail trade	30	35	40
Services	22	26	19
Manufacturing	9	11	16
Finance	7	1	1
Transportation	4	5	3
Mining	1	1	1
Construction	14	6	6
Agriculture	3	3	3
Total	100	100	100

Source: Data were supplied by the Small Business Administration. Small business comprises firms with fewer than 100 employees. Figures are rounded.

a. The Small Business Administration is not permitted to make loans for certain types of business activities, such as real estate development, that are classified in finance and construction. Thus the percentages of all small business in these two industries are constrained to be the same as for SBA borrowers, and the distribution within other industries is recomputed to sum to 100.

induce or permit small firms to produce more of the desired benefits, such as increased competition, innovation, and jobs.

In evaluating economic benefit arguments, care must be taken to establish an appropriate baseline for comparison. In this case the proper comparison is between an SBA-funded firm and a firm that would have received private funding. It is not between the SBA-funded firm and zero. The SBA's target firms should be able to show that they are more productive of the desired benefits for each dollar invested than are the firms receiving private credit.

It is doubtful that they could. If SBA loans are to generate greater competition and product innovation, they must be targeted at industries believed to be deficient in competition or to be involved in creating new products. However, no policy directives or eligibility criteria direct the participating banks to lend in certain areas, to certain industries, or to certain types of firms. Three-fourths of SBA loans go to wholesale trade, retail trade, and nonfinancial services—all sectors where competition is very strong. In fact, the distribution of SBA borrowers across industrial sectors closely parallels the distribution of firms nationwide (see table 4-3). Nor are SBA borrowers the high-technology firms usually mentioned in connection with new products. The majority are firms serving local economies: stores, distributors, and restaurants.

Social and economic benefits, if they exist, are more likely to be found in the form of faster growth and employment creation. Yet one study of employment growth between 1978 and 1980 found that firms with fewer than 100 employees contributed to net employment gains in about the same proportion as their share of total employment. They created a somewhat larger share of new jobs but were also responsible for a larger share of job losses.[15]

DISTRIBUTIONAL MOTIVATIONS. The SBA's efforts to direct a portion of its guaranteed loans to firms owned by members of minority groups are clearly intended to promote greater social and economic equality, regardless of whether minority firms generate faster growth or additional jobs. In 1984 about 10 percent of all SBA loan guarantees went to minority-owned firms, although only some 5 percent of all firms are minority-owned.[16] As minority loans cover only a small portion of the portfolio, they can be taken as a special, but not central, aim of the program.

STABILIZATION GOAL. Although a commonly avowed aim of the program is to counter the effects of business slowdowns on small firms, it may actually make them worse.

Small businesses are often suspected of being squeezed out of credit markets during periods of credit restriction. Whether or not they are, however, the SBA's program does nothing to help. To do so, its lending levels would have to increase at times of high unemployment. Rather, as shown in figure 4-1, SBA lending levels fall as unemployment rises.

The only governmental attempts to regulate lending levels are annual limitations on the SBA's guarantee authority, which are set according to political rather than economic considerations. The actual volume of lending is then determined by borrower demand, which falls during business-cycle troughs. In 1982, for example, the volume of SBA lending fell 22 percent below that of the previous year because the combination of recession and high interest rates discouraged demand by borrowers. SBA administrators, implementing a program of tighter standards of creditworthiness, exerted further downward pressure.

Program Performance

The central rationales for the program are then basically two: that financial markets provide credit on too stringent terms to small busi-

15. Catherine Armington and Marjorie Odle, "Small Business—How Many Jobs?" *Brookings Review,* vol. 1 (Winter 1982), pp. 14–17.

16. Small Business Administration, Office of Computer Sciences, *Management Information Summary,* p. ii; and *The State of Small Business: A Report of the President* (GPO, 1983), p. 303. The estimate of 5 percent is based on data for 1977.

Figure 4-1. *Small Business Administration Lending Rates and the Unemployment Rate, 1973–84*

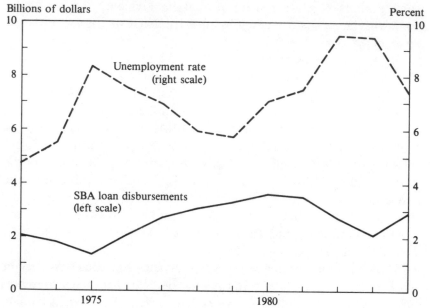

Sources: *Special Analyses, Budget of the United States Government, Fiscal Year 1986*, p. F-71, and earlier issues; and *Economic Report of the President, February 1985*, p. 271.

nesses despite their underlying solvency and that small firms offer social and economic returns greater than the minimum required to repay debt. The first rationale can be examined by asking whether the SBA's longer-term, more generous lending policy has proved to be profitable. The second is more difficult to examine without exhaustive information on the borrowers themselves, which is not available. However, by reviewing the financial returns from the program, it is possible to set minimum estimates on how large the benefits would have to be in order to exceed the costs.

The argument that the SBA program corrects a market failure to provide credit to small firms is seriously undermined by the high rate of default among loan guarantees. At the end of 1984, more than a fifth of all guaranteed loans were delinquent or in liquidation, necessitating purchase of the loan by the SBA from private lenders (see table 4-4). This experience stands in sharp contrast with other guarantee programs, such as FHA mortgage insurance, where the government appears to have been correct in judging that private standards of creditworthiness

Table 4-4. *Status of Outstanding Loan Guarantees of the Small Business Administration, Fiscal Year 1984*
Amounts in millions of dollars

Loan status	Bank loans		Purchased loans		Total	
	Amount	Percent	Amount	Percent	Amount	Percent
Current	6,383	89.1	221	12.7	6,604	74.2
Deferred	50	0.7	22	1.3	72	0.8
Past due (1–59 days)	297	4.1	33	1.9	330	3.7
Delinquent (more than 60 days)[a]	334	4.7	159	9.2	493	5.5
Liquidation[a]	101	1.4	1,300	74.9	1,401	15.7
Total	7,164	100.0	1,735	100.0	8,899	100.0

Source: U.S. Small Business Administration, Office of Computer Sciences, *Management Information Summary*, RCN 309 (SBA, 1984), p. 1b. Figures are rounded.

a. Eligible for purchase.

were too strict. More than ten times as many SBA loans default as do commercial bank loans. Banks, then, are basically correct in their judgment that small business loans are risky. A loan guarantee, which protects the lender, does little to reduce the risk. If there are failures in financial intermediation services for small business, the SBA program does not address them.

Absent market failure arguments, the burden of justification rests on the claim that SBA loans will enable borrowers to contribute economic benefits such as long-run employment generation or high growth above and beyond the financial return embodied in the loan transaction. The default rate is critical here, as well. The baseline for evaluation is the performance of privately financed firms that on average meet their financial obligations. If the SBA program is to break even from a social point of view, its firms must compensate for falling below the minimum financial standard of debt repayment by surpassing the performance of privately financed firms in other respects. The minimum value of the social benefits must equal the value of the financial losses the government sustains.

The remainder of this section describes the default behavior of SBA loans, calculates rates of loss for the SBA, and shows how large additional benefits should be in order to compensate for this loss. A similar calculation shows what would be required to place the program on an actuarially sound basis.

ESTIMATED FREQUENCY OF DEFAULT. Although the failure rate among SBA loans is of crucial importance in evaluating the program, default

Figure 4-2. *Probabilities of Default on Small Business Administration Loans, Various Maturities*

Percent probability

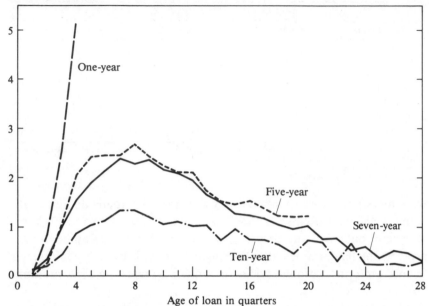

Age of loan in quarters

Source: Authors' calculations as explained in text.

rates (defined here as purchases by the SBA in response to guarantee claims by private lenders) and final loss rates (principal and interest charged off) are not published in public documents. The government budget and the SBA's annual report give loans purchased or charged off during the year as a proportion of currently outstanding loans—6.3 percent in 1984. If the SBA program were in a steady state, these would be accurate measures of long-run defaults. But, because the dollar size of the program has been growing over the past decade, such ratios understate the rate of default over the lifetimes of the loans.

LOSSES FROM 1973 TO 1983. An analysis of data supplied by the SBA covering 120,000 loans made between 1973 and 1983, most of the loans disbursed during this period, found the rate of default (loan purchase) to be 23.5 percent (by number of loans). Adjusted for recoveries and discounting losses back to the time of disbursement, that default rate translates into a 9.7 percent (by dollar volume) loss rate.

Figure 4-2 shows the default rate for loans of various maturities. During the first months after disbursement, while the business is spending

Figure 4-3. *Cumulative Probabilities of Default on Small Business Administration Loans, Various Maturities*

Percent probability

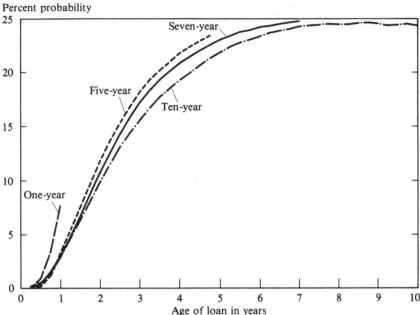

Age of loan in years

Source: Authors' calculations as explained in text.

the proceeds of the loan, the likelihood of default is small. For loans with a maturity beyond one year, default rates continue to rise during the second year, but turn down thereafter. For some purposes it is more useful to construct a cumulative index of default, as in figure 4-3, showing the proportion of loans that will default over their lifetimes. About 25 percent of multiyear loans end up in default.

After purchase a few loans eventually reestablish regular payments and are fully repaid. Eighty-three percent, however, are soon charged off. Repayments and liquidation of assets bring in few proceeds for the SBA. For a charged-off loan the average loss to the SBA is about 67 percent of the purchase amount. When these receipts and losses are accounted for, as they accrue over time, then discounted back to the time of disbursement and compared with the total amount of loans created, the figure of 9.7 percent of original principal results. This is the loss the SBA suffers. Losses that exceed the fees charged by the government to cover them constitute a subsidy that taxpayers bear. Because banks have paid an initial 1 percent guarantee fee, the net

Figure 4-4. *Default Rates on Small Business Administration Loans and Industrial Production, 1973–83*

Percent deviation from mean

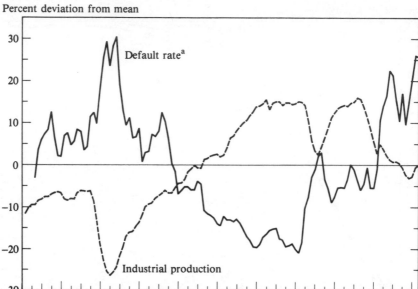

Sources: Authors' calculations; and *Economic Report of the President, February 1985*, p. 280, and previous issues.
a. Six-month average. Default probabilities are the likelihood that a loan will go into default, conditional on the loan having survived to that point.

subsidy is 8.7 percent. An 8.7 percent subsidy on the $2.8 billion in new guarantees the SBA extended in 1984 is $240 million—to say nothing of the SBA's administrative costs, which constitute an additional subsidy.

The rate of default on SBA loans is sensitive to economic conditions. As shown in figure 4-4, the default rate is highly correlated with cyclical changes in the index of industrial production. For example, from the beginning of 1974 through the third quarter of 1975, a period of recession, the propensity to default within the subsequent twelve months soared to 9.2 percent—far above the decade average of 5.9 percent. By contrast, during 1979, the last year of an economic expansion, the propensity to default within twelve months was 3.6 percent.

Implications of Loss Rates

The economic and social benefits of SBA loans over and above those of private borrower-lender transactions must be sufficient to compensate for the government's subsidy costs. Although such benefits are difficult to measure, it is possible to calculate the minimum economic benefit per loan that would be required to cover SBA loan losses. For the program to be thus justified SBA loans must induce borrowers to generate compensatory economic benefits totaling at least 8.7 percent of principal.

The only SBA loans that can do so could not have been made in the absence of SBA assistance. A loan that would have been made without the SBA's help cannot be ascribed to the SBA program, nor can the returns the firm generates be said to depend on the program. In addition, such loans must end in full repayment rather than default. Behind most loans that default are firms that are failing and therefore unlikely to produce unusually high levels of employment, productivity growth, or other benefits.

What proportion of all SBA loans fall into that category? Optimistically, all SBA loans to new and minority-owned firms might be assumed to be ineligible for private bank lending. New businesses receive about 25 percent of SBA loans and minority-owned firms 10 percent.

Among the remaining 65 percent of SBA loans, overlap with private credit may be substantial. In two recent surveys, commercial bankers have indicated that some one-fifth of SBA loan guarantees are made to already creditworthy borrowers.[17] Moreover, the bankers reported that SBA loans to existing businesses are generally used not for utterly uncreditworthy borrowers, but for borrowers whose equity or collateral is insufficient to justify the amount of loan desired or who seek an extended maturity loan. Thus only a portion of each loan is additional to what would have been forthcoming privately. Considering both total and partial overlap, an optimistic estimate would put the incremental volume of credit that the SBA induces for existing firms at two-thirds of the SBA-guaranteed amount.

The combination of loans for new and minority-owned businesses plus two-thirds of the remainder yields an optimistic estimate that 78 percent of SBA loans do not overlap with private bank lending. Of these nonduplicative loans, a substantial percentage default. If the 23.5 percent default rate for the whole portfolio is applied to the nonoverlapping loans, the proportion of SBA loans that can generate compensatory benefits is no more than 60 percent.

Since only 60 percent of the loans can produce the benefits, to break

17. GAO, *SBA's 7(a) Loan Guarantee Program,* p. 93; and Cynthia A. Glassman and Peter L. Struck, *Survey of Commercial Bank Lending to Small Business* (Washington, D.C.: Interagency Task Force on Small Business Finance, 1982), p. 88.

even from a projected overall loss rate of 8.7 percent, they must generate benefits equal to 14.5 percent of the loan amount (8.7 divided by 0.6). These required benefits are in excess of the receipts needed to repay the loan. Given that the distribution of SBA firms among industries so closely parallels that of all firms, and given that participating banks are not required to use social criteria in selecting borrowers, it is unlikely that SBA borrowers outperform other small businesses in generating social benefits. At best, the relative importance of the SBA in longer-term lending suggests that it may provide some extra benefit in the financing of small business expansion. When the lack of identifiable social benefit is weighed against the clear costs of loan defaults, the program's claim to effectiveness appears weak.

Conversion to Insurance Basis

A proposal that often surfaces is to put the SBA program onto an insurance basis by charging premiums to cover default losses. Such a proposal would convert the program into an actuarially sound financial intermediary, along the lines of FHA mortgage insurance. If successful it would show that long-term lending to new or expanding firms could be self-sustaining. But if defaults maintain their current levels, the initial premium would have to be at least 9.7 percent of the loan amount rather than the 1 percent fee currently required, and premiums of that magnitude would obviously discourage borrowers. Demand would drop and the most creditworthy of SBA borrowers would turn elsewhere. Whether the drop would be large enough to change the nature of the program cannot be foreseen without experiment.

Bank Incentives for Loan Management

A less radical reform would be to give banks greater incentive to select and manage loans efficiently. The current 90 percent guarantee level protects banks almost fully from the consequences of default.[18] A lower guarantee percentage would induce banks to take greater care, thus lowering the default rate.

There are two hypotheses about the response of banks to the high

18. Loans in excess of $100,000 may have guarantee rates below 90 percent, but the weighted average guarantee was 87 percent over 1973–83.

guarantee protection. One view is that the guarantee protects banks from default costs to such a degree that the loans become virtually equivalent to government securities. Yet banks receive interest at levels more than 2 percent above the prime rate. Under this hypothesis, banks retain this difference as profit and earn a higher return on SBA loans than on their normal activities. This would mean that banks absorb some of the subsidy meant for business. It would also mean that loans are not being allocated among individual credit markets so as to equalize the risk-adjusted net return.

The other hypothesis is that banks have targeted ranges for postdefault costs on their portfolios. Because the guarantee greatly reduces that cost for SBA loans, it allows banks to make loans that are far more default-prone than normal. Under this hypothesis the SBA default rate is a consequence not of poor creditworthiness inherent in its target group, but of the lack of bank incentive to select borrowers carefully.[19]

Evidence on the returns to banks from SBA loans during the past decade suggests that the second hypothesis is closer to the truth. Banks do not actually make a greater profit on SBA loans than on other loans. Defaults among SBA loans are more than ten times as high as among privately made small business loans. The 10 percent of losses that banks bear after exercising the guarantee yields about the same loss rate as banks suffer on their private portfolios. The remaining interest rate spread is taken up by administrative costs, which are as high as, or slightly above, those on other loans of equivalent size. Banks could make slightly greater profits on SBA loans than on their normal activities if they lent to more creditworthy borrowers, but they do not.

One reason they do not is that large changes in creditworthiness are required to make a small change in postguarantee return. Banks bear only 10 percent of the loss on loan defaults. By halving the loss rate, from 9.7 to 4.8 percent, banks would make a less than 1 percent increase in the present value to them of an SBA loan portfolio. Other strategies for increasing returns on SBA loans would show a greater return to banks. That is, while changes in bank administrative costs or interest rates would have a one-for-one impact on the banks' earnings (assuming they did not affect defaults), banks gain only 10 percent of the benefits of lower default rates. By contrast, the costs of the program to the government are highly sensitive to default rates and unaffected by

19. The effect of guarantees on lender behavior is also discussed in chapter 2.

changes in administrative costs and interest rates. If defaults were halved, the SBA's costs would drop from 8.7 percent of the original principal to 3.8 percent.

If the government were to guarantee a smaller percentage of the loan it would create incentives for banks that are more congruent with the concerns of the government. It would undoubtedly result in a lower default rate, and therefore a smaller subsidy, by causing banks to select borrowers more carefully. Some banks might be less interested in participating under these circumstances, but a case can be made that the SBA should seek to have its loans made by banks who are good at selecting borrowers and managing loans. An experiment with a 75 percent guarantee is now under way. Its effect on default rates and on the types of borrowers selected bears watching.

Trade Credit: The Export-Import Bank

The Export-Import Bank (Eximbank) attempts to serve U.S. business and economic interests by promoting exports. The bank is the dominant force in the specialized market for medium- and long-term export finance. It now holds more trade loans with maturities over five years than all other American banks combined. Through direct loans, loan guarantees, and insurance, the Eximbank participates in financing most export sales of commercial aircraft and a large portion of the export sales of power generating equipment and other capital goods. It is almost alone in providing or insuring trade credits of more than five years in maturity.[20] Its clients are a diverse mixture of governments, state-owned corporations, and private firms.

Supporters of the Eximbank justify government involvement in trade credit in two ways. First, they claim that the particular types of risk associated with international lending, especially to developing nations, tend to keep the private sector from extending credit, except for short terms. Second, they point out that other countries subsidize export credit for their own industries; unless the U.S. government steps in, American exporters will lose sales. In response to these two very different issues, the Eximbank has developed two distinct types of

20. Through project loans, which often have intermediate and long maturities, commercial banks do participate, albeit indirectly, in term financing of exports. The Eximbank's specialty is trade credit per se.

activities, insurance for private export loans and direct lending at below-market rates of interest. The principles behind these two forms of assistance are far different, even though they are often combined in individual transactions. Therefore, they are best discussed in turn.

The Problem of International Risk

Before the Eximbank began operations in 1934, private banks, even working in concert, had been unable to develop an insurance scheme to cover international lending risks. In particular, long-term loans were not made or insured. All long-term loans are risky because national economic conditions change as time goes on, but loans involving two countries are particularly subject to change, and the total risk may become quite large. Yet long-term finance is essential for the large capital goods that certain U.S. businesses seek to export. Financing is often unavailable from the importing countries because of the rudimentary state of credit markets in many developing nations.[21]

The Eximbank classifies the risks it handles under two headings: political and commercial. It bears all the political risk for its clients, but in certain cases turns the commercial risk over to private sources. One form of political risk is that a borrowing firm will be destroyed in social or political unrest or be expropriated by a new regime. Another, more frequent, is that a firm will be unable to obtain U.S. currency to repay its loans because of a national shortage or refusal by its nation's government to make funds available. Supporters of the Eximbank believe that the U.S. government has a comparative advantage over private financial institutions in coping with political risks. Private firms can cope with such risks only by pooling them across countries and charging premiums to cover the remainder. The government can help induce foreign governments to reduce the risk, particularly when the purchasers are those governments themselves or corporations closely linked to them. As an example of the unique leverage of the U.S. government, the Eximbank recovered more than $400 million in claims against Iran after the hostage crisis in 1980, in large part because of the government's hold over Iranian assets in the United States.

The Eximbank defines commercial risk to include the same elements

21. The special risk arguments for government loan insurance in export markets are evaluated in greater detail in David P. Baron, *The Export-Import Bank: An Economic Analysis* (Academic Press, 1983), pp. 59–73.

as domestic credit risk (for example, borrower insolvency), plus default risk due to unfavorable exchange rate movements.[22] Even the commercial side of international risk has a strong political link, which supports the case for government involvement. It is clear, for example, that exchange rate movements are related to policy decisions by governments. Beyond this, the basic creditworthiness of firms is heavily influenced by government decisions, particularly in developing countries.

At first the Eximbank assumed risks primarily through direct provision of loans.[23] Later it added guarantee and insurance programs. For loans with maturities of more than five years, the Eximbank guarantees the loans itself, while for short- and medium-term finance it works through the Foreign Credit Insurance Association (FCIA), a subsidiary that includes some private insurance company participation.

Some long-term guaranteed loans are extended as part of a package, with the Eximbank providing some financing through direct lending and covering part of the commercial bank portion with a guarantee. Other long-term guarantees cover loans made by the Private Export Funding Corporation (PEFCO), a private firm whose sole function is to make long-term loans with the Eximbank's guarantee. The Eximbank charges a 2 percent insurance fee at origination, with an annual 0.5 percent fee on the outstanding loan balance. The fees do not vary with the risk of the borrower.

The FCIA insures against commercial risks up to a certain total level of losses. Beyond this level, the Eximbank provides what might be termed catastrophic commercial insurance and full political insurance. FCIA insurance premiums vary according both to coverage and risk and to features such as deductibles. During the 1980s the participation of private insurers in the FCIA has decreased severely.

FINANCIAL PERFORMANCE. Most, but not all, observers of export financing agree with the Eximbank's premise that private lenders and insurers supply inadequate amounts of risk coverage for trade credit and that governments have a unique ability to minimize such risks. Counterarguments are based on judgments that the supply is adequate and that governments are more likely to be lenient with credit terms than are private lenders, prompting borrowers to repay private loans first. In either case, the absence of private insurance does not justify a subsidy.

22. If firms are allowed to engage in hedging in financial futures markets, they can avoid exchange rate risk. This option is not open to many third-world firms.

23. The Eximbank still assumes risk when it makes direct loans, but these loans have additional, unrelated purposes, as described below.

Table 4-5. *Revenues and Expenses on Risk-Assumption Activities of the Export-Import Bank, Fiscal Years 1982–84*
Millions of dollars

Item	1982	1983	1984	Average
Expenses				
Administrative costs	13.7	14.8	16.8	15.1
Losses (net of recoveries)				
On insurance	2.9	9.4	118.5	43.6
On guarantees	22.4	4.9	20.8	16.0
On direct loans	32.3	5.4	−20.5	5.7
Total	71.3	34.5	135.6	80.5
Fee income				
Insurance and guarantee fees	35.6	34.6	33.2	34.5
Direct loan fees	83.0	40.7	46.0	56.6
Total	118.6	75.3	79.2	91.0
Net revenue	47.3	40.8	−56.4	10.6
Addendum				
Interest not received on				
delinquent loans	59.7	37.0	92.1	62.9

Source: U.S. Export-Import Bank, *Annual Report, 1982* and *1984.*

The program's fees should cover all costs. If export credit insurance is simply too risky to be provided by the private sector, then the Export-Import Bank programs that carry out these functions would be expected to have a loss rate greater than those that private financial institutions could bear. If the government is able to reduce the risk by its special abilities, then one would expect losses no higher than those on commercial operations. But to the extent that losses occur, unless fees are collected from borrowers to cover them, an element of subsidy has been introduced. A brief assessment of the revenues and expenses of these programs shows that while write-offs shown in the Eximbank's financial statements do not exceed fees, actual losses in income due to nonperforming loans do exceed fees. Thus the Eximbank's risk-assumption activities contain some subsidy. The situation has deteriorated significantly during the 1980s, as the effects of the international debt crisis have shown up in the Eximbank's portfolio.

In 1982–84 the Eximbank paid an annual average of $44 million in insurance claims and $16 million on guaranteed loan claims, net of recoveries (see table 4-5). Net write-offs on direct loans averaged $6 million.[24] Such loss rates are better than for private firms. On a portfolio

24. Claims and write-offs vary greatly from year to year. Because of the small number of individual cases that occur each year, a single default can greatly influence

Table 4-6. *Loans at Risk in the Portfolio of the Export-Import Bank,
Fiscal Years 1982–84*
Millions of dollars

Item	1982	1983	1984
Installments delinquent			
Principal and interest on rescheduled direct loans	83	200	209
Principal and interest on purchased guaranteed loans	48	118	17
Other principal and interest	512	258	537
Total	643	576	763
Principal on loans at risk			
Delinquent loans			
Rescheduled direct loans	708	752	330
Purchased guaranteed loans	289	397	757
Other	381	755	1,620
Rescheduled loans, now current	470	442	1,216
Total	1,847	2,346	3,923
Default reserve	2,040	1,792	1,450
Less: Delinquent interest payments previously assigned to reserve	221	317	362
Adjusted reserve	1,819	1,475	1,088

Source: U.S. Export-Import Bank, *Annual Report, 1982* and *1984*.

averaging $31 billion in direct loans and contingent liabilities, the
Eximbank lost $65 million annually, a loss rate of 0.2 percent. In most
years the losses plus administrative expenses are well below related
annual fee income of $91 million.

The Eximbank's portfolio, however, is not as sound as its write-offs
would lead one to expect. A significant proportion of the loans in its
portfolio are of doubtful value. In 1984 loans totaling $3.9 billion, or 11.9
percent of the total exposure, were classified as at risk. As shown in
table 4-6, the loans at risk fall into three categories: guaranteed loans
that have been purchased because of nonperformance, direct loans that
have been rescheduled, and other delinquent direct loans. As of 1984
the Eximbank held $757 million in purchased loans, many of which
should be considered in irreversible default. Moreover, in many cases,
only delinquent installments have been bought. The Eximbank acknowledges a high probability that it will have to purchase significantly more
principal on partially purchased loans.

The Eximbank does not write off loans made to or guaranteed by
other governments. It records write-offs only on loans backed by private

the total. Thus we use a three-year average experience to estimate expected annual
losses.

firms, which are only about a fifth of the loans it makes. It holds delinquent loans to governments in its portfolio indefinitely, allowing interest charges to accumulate. Loans for which the delinquent installments of principal and interest are a high percentage of total principal outstanding would have been written off by private institutions. From 1982 to 1984, most of the Eximbank's delinquent loans fell further behind, and new delinquencies appeared. Some delinquent loans are rescheduled, though the majority of these soon become delinquent under the new schedule. Among $1.5 billion in rescheduled loans, delinquent installments totaled $209 million (see table 4-6).

Combining all the sources of current delinquencies, at the end of 1984 the Eximbank faced likely losses of $763 million from delinquent loan payments and a potential loss from outstanding principal on delinquent loans of $3.9 billion. If likely additional purchases of partially purchased loans are considered, the latter total would be greater. Historically the recovery from loan defaults has been small. Delinquent payments are 70 percent of the Eximbank's default reserve, and the delinquent loan principal is 360 percent.[25] In view of figures such as these, in 1984 the Comptroller General of the United States took issue with the Eximbank's method of allowing delinquencies to accumulate without being charged against the default reserve. In the auditor's report accompanying the bank's 1983 and 1984 financial statements, he stated that the reserve should be reduced by $1 billion to $1.5 billion to reflect the bank's expected losses accurately.[26] If that were done, there would be no reserve.

Delinquent loans are reflected on the Eximbank's current financial statements, in the form of interest not received. In 1984 this totaled $92 million (see table 4-5).

In short the Eximbank's risk-assumption activities are not self-sustaining, particularly given the events of the early 1980s. Moreover, the Eximbank's financial statements do not accurately portray the effects of those risk assumptions on its financial self-sufficiency.[27] The resulting subsidy element reveals that the government is not able to reduce

25. This is after adjustment for delinquent interest payments previously credited to the reserve.

26. See U.S. Export-Import Bank, *1984 Annual Report*, p. 45.

27. At a minimum, unpaid interest should be included as a cost of the guarantee and insurance program. If that is done, as in table 4-5, fees are not sufficient to cover program costs.

political risk as much as might sometimes be claimed. Granting that, it is nevertheless appropriate for the government to take on international trading risks. All that should change is that the Eximbank should admit the magnitude of cost required to assume such risk.

RISK SHARING WITH THE PRIVATE SECTOR. Private markets have grown more complex since the Eximbank's birth, and one might argue that they should now be able to take on many of the functions the bank provided at the start. Indeed, the Eximbank has turned over an increasing share of its activity to the private sector. The development of the two privately owned companies wholly dependent on the Eximbank, FCIA and PEFCO, are key examples, as is the fact that the bank rarely finances all of a transaction, but lends in tandem with commercial banks.

The view that these sharing arrangements represent a greater role for the private sector is only partially correct, however. While the Eximbank calls on the fund-raising capacities of private financial institutions, it has stretched their risk-bearing abilities only minimally. For a time the private sector did genuinely participate in the FCIA, though its liability was carefully constrained only to the level it could easily bear. PEFCO has always been fully protected from loss because all its loans are guaranteed by the Eximbank. A more accurate description of such arrangements is that the Eximbank uses private lenders or insurers to obtain the maximum possible export coverage from its limited resources.

Private participation in the FCIA took a step back as a result of the general international debt crisis in 1982 and 1983. Eximbank staff report that the capital contributed as a reserve by the private participants in the FCIA has been depleted by these events and that the proportion of risk the Eximbank is bearing on new FCIA policies has been greatly increased in order to retain private participation. At present, private insurers bear almost no risk in the FCIA. The events of the debt crisis throw doubt on the possibility that the private sector either alone or in participation with the Eximbank will be willing or able to bear in the foreseeable future the risks the Eximbank now bears.

Subsidy for Exports Facing Foreign Competition

Beginning in the mid-1960s the focus of the Eximbank's direct loan program turned toward helping U.S. exporters win sales over foreign competition. During the next decade the Eximbank and its rivals in other industrialized nations gradually increased the amount of help they gave,

Table 4-7. *Subsidy Costs of the Direct Loans of the Export-Import Bank, 1980–83*

Item	1980	1981	1982	1983
Average loan rate (percent)	8.9	10.5	11.0	10.7
Average maturity (years)	11.3	11.0	12.0	10.0
Corporate bond rate (percent)[a]	12.2	14.6	15.6	12.8
Amount authorized (millions of dollars)	5,495	5,431	3,516	845
Present value of subsidy (millions of dollars)	810	880	650	120
Value of exports financed (millions of dollars)	8,116	8,574	5,300	1,287
Subsidy as a percent of export value	10	10	12	9

Source: Authors' calculations based on data supplied by the Office of Management and Budget and the Export-Import Bank.

a. Average of AAA- and BAA-rated bonds.

so as not to allow their own exporters to be disadvantaged by the actions of foreign export agencies. Loan subsidies became a tool for international competition.

When the government takes on commercial and political risks, its purpose is to convince private lenders to join, at affordable rates, in a transaction that both buyer and seller want to proceed. By contrast, export subsidies are intended to alter the potential buyer's choices. The Eximbank's direct loan program was originally created primarily to overcome the reluctance of private lenders, but once established, it was easily transformed into a buyer-persuasion vehicle.

Eximbank direct loans have interest rates well below market rates. In 1982 the average Eximbank rate was 11 percent, compared with the average corporate bond rate of 14.6 percent. Rates are now set according to an arrangement among the member nations of the Organization for Economic Cooperation and Development, which bases them on government bond rates prevailing in the exporting country. The arrangement has reduced but not eliminated the subsidy in Eximbank interest rates relative to purely private ones. Official Eximbank statements stress that the direct loans are targeted to those transactions where subsidized foreign credit competition is most intense.[28]

The amount of subsidy, as calculated in table 4-7, in newly authorized Eximbank loans reached its peak in the early 1980s when bank lending was larger and the difference between corporate bond and Eximbank rates was great. In 1981 the Eximbank made commitments for $5.4 billion in new loans at an average interest rate of 10.5 percent. If the

28. See U.S. Export-Import Bank, *1984 Annual Report*, statement of Chairman Draper, p. 3.

corporate rate is used as a reference for long-term market rates, a rough estimate of the present value of the subsidy embedded in that single year's loans is $880 million.[29] The subsidy is equivalent to a discount of about 10 percent in the price of the exported goods. Subsidy levels have dropped recently, as the volume of direct lending has fallen and the Eximbank's lending rate has grown closer to market rates.

The subsidy of interest rates affects the Eximbank's annual income. Since 1981 it has been paying more in interest costs than it has received in interest income, more because of the low rates of interest that it charges than because of nonperforming loans. In 1984, for example, the Eximbank made interest payments, largely to the Federal Financing Bank, totaling 11.5 percent of average borrowings. It received interest payments of 8.5 percent of loans receivable. Even if delinquent interest payments were included, its receipts would have reached only 9.0 percent. This negative interest spread is largely responsible for negative profits since 1981.

Export subsidies are defended on the grounds that any sale that otherwise would not have been made is a direct addition to U.S. gross national product and that overall U.S. influence is enhanced by maintaining a strong export presence in certain markets.[30] The subsidies are criticized for keeping investment and employment resources from moving to more profitable uses.[31] That is, if a company is unable to attract customers without a subsidy, it is inefficient. In the long run it is more costly to keep an inefficient industry going through subsidy than to allow the shift in resource allocation to occur.

Apart from examining the merits of subsidizing exports, it is important to ask how effective Eximbank loans are at increasing them. The Eximbank has produced several "additionality" studies which estimate the proportion of Eximbank financing that leads to sales that would not otherwise have been made. They assign a probability that each direct loan leads to a new export, based largely on the strength of foreign competition. The Eximbank's estimates of the additional sales range

---

29. Alternative estimates of the subsidy are provided in Baron, *Export-Import Bank*, pp. 142–77. We used the corporate bond rate in this case because most of the loans are used to finance the exports of large, well-established companies, and we lacked the internal operation data.

30. Ibid., pp. 73–79.

31. Congressional Budget Office, *Reducing the Deficit: Spending and Revenue Options*, pt. 2 (CBO, 1985), p. 164.

from 51 percent, excluding aircraft sales, to 77 percent, including aircraft, in 1984.[32]

These studies are highly optimistic estimates of the net export gain to the United States because they ignore the response of other exporting countries. The trade credit program is a form of price discrimination that attempts to define marginal buyers and offer them a price concession not available to others. But when account is taken of similar actions by other exporters, it is very doubtful that the program is of net benefit to U.S. trade. The issue becomes one of negotiating agreements with other countries not to engage in such activities.

Conclusions

The Eximbank's first mission is in an area where the credit market failure is easily delineated. The Eximbank supplies a high proportion of U.S. medium- and long-term trade credit. It is intended to address two problems: the risk of moving funds from nation to nation regardless of the creditworthiness of the borrowing firm, and the risk concerning the future performance of foreign firms, especially in less developed countries. The political element in both offers a strong argument in favor of government assistance. However, the financial consequences of this activity should be fully recognized in financial statements.

The Eximbank has done a good job of defining its position relative to private lenders, and it has made some attempts to withdraw from various activities as it has become clear that private lenders or insurers can handle them. Its pitfall has been in confusing the expansion of the administrative and fund-raising activities of private groups with their greater assumption of final risks.

The Eximbank leaves the problems of credit markets behind, however, when it aims to help U.S. firms win sales in competition with products subsidized by foreign governments. When it has moved in this direction it has also moved into high costs for the federal budget. The dynamics of the bank's export subsidies can be fully understood by treating them as grants, which could, in fact, achieve the same objectives.

32. A critique of those estimates and a more pessimistic estimate of the additional exports created by Eximbank financing is provided in Baron, *Export-Import Bank*.

CHAPTER FIVE

Credit for Agriculture

SEVERE FINANCIAL problems in agriculture have drawn a great deal of public attention in recent years. Commodity prices and land values have collapsed, driving many farmers into bankruptcy and compelling foreclosure. The crisis has also highlighted the dominant role played by government in the market for agricultural credit.

The federal government provides a larger portion of the total credit for agriculture than for any other sector of the economy. The form of that credit is also much different from that channeled to the nonfarm economy. In contrast to the emphasis on loan insurance and secondary market activities that is common in other credit programs, the government and government-sponsored agencies emphasize direct lending to farmers, operating their own local loan offices. In addition, agricultural lending accounts for a large share of the subsidies provided through government credit programs.[1]

The government's agricultural loan programs originated in the period between the two world wars. Soon after World War I ended both agricultural prices and land values fell sharply. Farmers who had borrowed heavily during the war encountered severe debt repayment problems, and many rural banks failed. Furthermore, in the absence of a national credit system capable of diversifying the risks of agricultural loans, the supply of credit was unreliable and often available only at interest rates far surpassing those paid by other industries. The government responded to these problems by creating the Commodity Credit Corporation (CCC), the Farm Credit System (FCS) of cooperative banks,

---

1. The Office of Management and Budget has estimated that direct loans of the Agriculture Department accounted for $4.5 billion in subsidy costs out of a total of $8.3 billion for those loans evaluated by OMB in 1984. See *Special Analyses, Budget of the United States Government, Fiscal Year 1986*, pp. F-31–F-35.

and the programs currently administered by the Farmers Home Administration (FmHA). Finally, the Rural Electrification Administration (REA) was founded with the specific mission of underwriting credit for rural electrical cooperatives.

These programs have been successful in providing the farm sector with access to credit on terms at least as favorable as those available to other borrowers. Over the years, however, both the programs and the credit market environment in which they operate have evolved considerably. While the original purpose was to overcome perceived credit market failings by furnishing credit on terms *comparable* to those available elsewhere, the current programs are alleged to be providing large subsidies in the form of credit costs substantially *below* those paid by other sectors—a condition that, critics say, has contributed to an excessive inflation of land values. At the same time private markets, stimulated by the activities of the government agencies, have become more capable of serving the financial needs of agriculture.

Some of the concerns about the agricultural credit programs are highlighted by recent changes in the composition of farm debt (see table 5-1). Total farm debt grew rapidly in the 1970s (12.3 percent annually, compared with a 5.7 percent average in the previous three decades), but because land values appreciated even faster, the debt-asset ratio did not increase. By contrast, farmers have encountered more serious problems in the 1980s when their debt obligations have not contracted in the face of falling land values.

More significantly, the government agencies' share of the debt, which declined between 1940 and 1960, has risen sharply since then. Today the government-assisted agencies hold about half of the outstanding debt and supply an even larger share of each year's new financing.[2] Such a pattern of increasing market dominance would not be expected if the programs were directed at offsetting capital market imperfections and if those imperfections were declining over time. It is more suggestive of an increased magnitude of subsidy in the loan programs.

The basic concerns about farm credit are illustrated by examining three major programs: the Farm Credit System, the Farmers Home Administration, and the Rural Electrification Administration.[3]

2. Most of that debt is held by the Farm Credit System, a government-sponsored but privately owned institution, and does not represent a direct liability of the government.

3. The Commodity Credit Corporation is not discussed here because its rules of operation change frequently and its subsidy costs depend on the gap between the market

Table 5-1. *Outstanding Farm Credit, by Type and Holder, Selected Years, 1940–85*[a]

Year	Total debt (billions of dollars)	Percent of total assets	Percent share Farm Credit System	Percent share Farmers Home Administration	Percent share Private market
			Real estate debt		
1940	6.6	12.5	42.7	0.5	56.8
1950	5.6	4.2	17.3	3.6	79.1
1960	12.1	5.8	19.3	5.6	75.1
1970	29.2	9.3	22.9	7.8	69.3
1980	85.4	8.4	34.7	8.3	57.0
1985	110.9	11.6	43.7	9.0	47.3
			Non–real estate debt		
1940	3.0	5.7	6.2	13.9	79.9
1950	5.2	3.9	8.5	6.7	84.8
1960	11.5	5.5	12.6	3.5	84.0
1970	21.2	6.7	22.3	3.7	74.0
1980	75.3	7.4	24.8	11.9	63.3
1985	93.0	9.7	20.4	16.4	63.2

Sources: U.S. Department of Agriculture, Economic Research Service, *Agricultural Finance Statistics, 1960–83*, Statistical Bulletin 706 (April 1984), pp. 1–3; Economic Research Service, *Agricultural Finance: Outlook and Situation Report* (USDA, 1984), pp. 20, 23–24; and Economic Research Service, *Economic Indicators of the Farm Sector: National Financial Summary, 1984* (USDA, 1986), p. 57.

a. As of January 1. The table excludes credit supplied by the Commodity Credit Corporation, the Rural Electrification Administration, and the nonfarm programs of the Farmers Home Administration.

The Farm Credit System

The Farm Credit System (FCS) encompasses three types of farmer-owned cooperatives: federal land banks and associations, which provide long-term real estate loans; federal intermediate credit banks and production credit associations, which provide short-term credit; and banks for cooperatives, which finance the activities of purchasing and marketing cooperatives. These three types of lending agencies are grouped into twelve regional banks. Originally capitalized by the government, today the system is privately owned and operates as a government-sponsored enterprise similar to the Federal National Mortgage Association and the Student Loan Marketing Association. The cooperatives are funded out of a consolidated pool of system bond issues, and they share in loan losses. The system is the largest private source of financing for agriculture, exceeding commercial banks in the volume of loans.

price of a commodity and an administratively determined support price. It is more accurately viewed as part of the price support system than as a source of credit.

Farming is heavily dependent on credit financing for several reasons. It is highly capital intensive—the capital-output ratio is roughly 10:1, compared with 1.5:1 for nonfarm business. In addition, farm income is highly volatile from year to year, yet farmers are limited in their ability to avoid risks through diversification.[4]

The FCS was designed to improve the credit system in three ways. First, it sought to give farmers credit on terms more suitable to their particular needs by providing long-term real estate credit and commercial loans with a maturity of a full crop year and sometimes longer. Before the FCS was established, real estate loans were limited to seven years or less, and bank credit was usually available for a maximum of ninety days.

Second, the FCS was designed to provide agriculture with a more dependable source of credit by linking it to national credit markets. Previously, farmers were dependent on local banks, which often found their own supply of funds shrinking at precisely the time of their borrowers' greatest need. National lenders, such as life insurance companies, were reluctant to become involved in agriculture because they lacked the local offices and expertise required to evaluate loan applications. Large interest rate differentials among regions of the country reflected this segmented nature of the market.

Third, the FCS sought to reduce the cost of credit to farmers. Farmers complained that the interest rates charged by merchants and trade sources were high compared with rates charged in other economic sectors, the result of a lack of competition in the market for agricultural loans.[5]

To a large extent the FCS has achieved these goals. The system provides a means of pooling the risks of individual farm loans, and the sharing of loan losses among regions of the country reduces the FCS's vulnerability to fluctuations in individual agricultural markets. Long-term real estate loans and annual production credit are now readily available. In sum, the FCS integrates the financing of a highly specialized economic sector, where local conditions are of primary importance, into a national financial system.

4. The futures markets provide a short-term means of hedging against price fluctuations, but insurance against variations in production is limited.

5. A discussion of the development of the FCS is provided in D. Gale Johnson, "The Credit Programs Supervised by the Farm Credit Administration," in Commission on Money and Credit, *Federal Credit Agencies* (Prentice-Hall, 1963), pp. 259–318.

As demonstrated by the farm crisis of the 1980s, however, the FCS cannot ensure against industry risk. Unlike large commercial banks, it does not hold a loan portfolio diversified across industries. Moreover, all of the system's equity is held by its borrowers; it has no publicly traded stock. If the structure of the system were changed to allow equity issues, as with most other government-sponsored agencies, risk could be dispersed outside agriculture.

The sheer magnitude of the 1980s collapse has put much of the FCS loan portfolio at risk. Land prices soared during the 1970s under the influence of booming export markets, high inflation, low interest rates, and sharp increases in government price supports. Agricultural land was viewed as an attractive hedge against inflation by both farmers and nonfarmers. Even after adjustment for general inflation, the price of farmland rose 7.1 percent annually between 1970 and 1980, compared with a rate of 2.5 percent during the previous twenty years. The bubble burst in the 1980s, and real land values fell an estimated 37 percent in 1980–84, pushing many farmers into insolvency (see figure 5-1).[6] The real value of farm real estate has fallen back to the levels of the early 1970s.

Paralleling the collapse of land prices, the average income of farm proprietors fell 40 percent in 1980–85 relative to the average of the 1970s (see figure 5-1). Because the government chose to combat inflation in the 1980s with an economic policy of extreme monetary restraint combined with fiscal expansion, agriculture bore the brunt of the adjustment costs. Sharply higher interest rates were costly to a capital-intensive industry, and the rise in the foreign exchange rate limited the export market. Both of these problems can be traced to government policy decisions.

Most of the 1980–84 loss in asset value ($370 billion in 1984 prices) has been absorbed by farmers. However, even under optimistic economic assumptions for future years, farmers are unlikely to pay off interest and principal on about 20 percent of the debt.[7] The write-off of farm debt is likely to be in the range of $10 billion to $20 billion, much of which must be absorbed by the FCS. In mid-1985 roughly 15 percent of

6. The real value of farm land is computed by dividing the nominal value of farm real estate by the consumer expenditure price deflator of the national income accounts.

7. See R. W. Jolly and D. G. Doye, "Farm Income and the Financial Condition of United States Agriculture: Executive Summary" (Iowa State University, April 1985), table 9.

Figure 5-1. *The Value of Farm Real Estate and Proprietor Income,
1960–85*

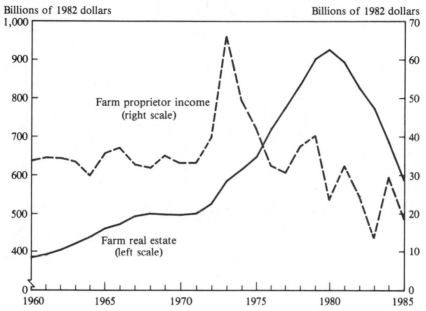

Billions of 1982 dollars   Billions of 1982 dollars

Sources: U.S. Department of Agriculture, Economic Research Service, *Economic Indicators of the Farm Sector:
National Financial Summary, 1984* (USDA, 1986), p. 60; National Income and Product Accounts of the United States;
and authors' calculations. Current dollar values are deflated by the fixed-weight price deflator for personal consumption
expenditures.

its loan portfolio—$11 billion—was projected to be uncollectible,[8] and
at the end of that year the system was holding a third of all farm debt.
Production credit association losses in 1983 and 1984 exceeded the
combined losses of the previous fifty years.[9] Similar problems are
expected to be faced by the federal land banks in future years. The
concentration of losses in the central part of the country has also created
dissatisfaction among member associations in other regions, which are
required to share in the losses.

Although the agricultural depression of the 1980s was not primarily
the fault of the credit system, the FCS did contribute in a small way to
the crisis through its loan policies. In retrospect, it should have been
more cautious in accepting the inflated land values of the 1970s as

8. Charles F. McCoy, *Wall Street Journal*, September 4, 1985.
9. Mark Drabenstott and Marvin Duncan, "Farm Credit Problems: The Policy
Choices," *Economic Review of the Federal Reserve Bank of Kansas City*, vol. 70
(March 1985), p. 8.

adequate collateral for its loans.[10] In addition, member banks base their loan rates on the current average interest rate of outstanding FCS debt, rather than the cost of raising additional funds. As a result, FCS loan rates lag behind those of other lenders during periods of rising interest rates, encouraging excessive borrowing demands on the FCS. Moreover, the federal land banks reduced the average maturity of their debt to less than that of their loan portfolio in an effort to obtain lower borrowing costs, but the mismatch of maturities made the system vulnerable to fluctuations in market interest rates. Finally, the FCS increasingly supplied credit to large borrowers driven to the system by limits on the size of individual loans at commercial banks.

Lending practices of the FCS, however, cannot be assigned a major role in the agricultural crisis. Nor is a vulnerability to severe economic disruption affecting an entire industry unique to those who finance agriculture. The same problems have arisen recently for institutions that made loans to less developed countries and to the domestic energy industry. In general, lenders do diversify away from excessive reliance on a single borrower, but diversification against industry-specific risk is often incomplete.

The main policy issue raised by the FCS is that its special relationship with the federal government constitutes a subsidy of farm credit. Agency status does provide some obvious competitive advantages. Interest on FCS securities is exempt from state and local (but not federal) taxation. The income of the banks, except for production credit associations, is exempt from taxation. The system is also not subject to the same federal and state regulations that apply to other financial institutions. On the other hand, the banks do not have deposit or check-writing functions and thus are not covered by deposit insurance. Removal of agency status would result in some increase in financing costs to farmers. A 1982 study by the Department of Agriculture estimated that taxing interest on FCS securities and taxing the banks' income would add about 0.5 percentage point to loan rates.[11]

---

10. There was an awareness in the mid-1970s among agricultural policymakers of the problems posed by rising land values. The government resisted pressure from farm groups to include land costs in the determination of crop price support levels and attempted to maintain a focus on variable costs of production as the appropriate basis for adjusting minimum price guarantees. Even the most conservative lending policy would have had difficulty, however, in anticipating a possible collapse in land values of the magnitude that has occurred.

11. U.S. Department of Agriculture, Economic Research Service, "A Study of the Farm Credit System," Report to the Secretary of Agriculture (July 1982), pp. 70–82.

Opponents of agency status cite the belief in financial markets that the debt issues of the sponsored enterprises carry an implicit federal guarantee against default, providing the FCS with an interest rate advantage relative to private financial institutions of comparable risk. For example, before the farm crisis FCS debt costs were about 90 basis points below rates paid by commercial banks on certificates of deposit. Yet the assumed guarantee cannot be viewed as absolute, since the financing costs of the FCS jumped sharply in 1985 with public reports of its financial problems. The interest rate charged on six-month issues increased from a premium of about 15 basis points over the comparable rate on Treasury issues before 1985 to a premium above 80 basis points in the fall of 1985. The system was also forced to suspend long-term bond issues.

It is unclear how removal of agency status would affect this situation, because it seems certain that the government would intervene in the event of a major financial crisis in agriculture, as it has for other sectors of the economy. Indeed, in late 1985 Congress furnished a direct line of credit from the Treasury to the FCS and created a separate warehousing facility to purchase and hold the system's bad debt.[12] These bailout measures are similar to those provided to the Continental Illinois Corporation, measures that also went beyond the requirements of existing legislation.

Overall, the combination of factors gives the FCS an advantage in its loan costs equal to about 0.5 to 1.0 percentage point on its loan rates. These costs must be balanced against the benefits that the system has bestowed in broadening the market for agricultural credit. Some of this subsidy could be reduced by gradually eliminating the special tax provisions, as is being done for other sponsored agencies. In addition, the ability of the system to diversify risk would be improved by changing its ownership structure to allow equity issues to a broader range of investors.

The Farmers Home Administration

The programs administered by the Farmers Home Administration (FmHA) were set up to provide credit assistance for the rural poor. They

---

12. Albert R. Karr, "Congress Approves Farm-Subsidy Bill, Clears Measure to Aid Credit System," *Wall Street Journal*, December 19, 1985.

differ from those of the Farm Credit System in that they are directed toward more marginal borrowers, and the loans are heavily subsidized. The focus is on assisting a specific group as opposed to correcting credit market imperfections. From the beginning the programs had the stated objective of promoting operator ownership and capital-intensive, technology-intensive production methods.

Over the last several decades the eligible group has grown to include farmers with holdings of all sizes and at all income levels. In addition, there has been a large expansion beyond farm credit to rural housing and community development programs.

The farm ownership and operating loans were intended to serve small farmers who could not easily obtain credit elsewhere. Those programs for limited-resource borrowers have been maintained, but the Farmers Home Administration has also become a significant supplier of credit to large commercial farms as a result of the tremendous growth of its emergency loan programs. Both the farm ownership and operating loan programs charge loan rates based on government borrowing costs (ignoring administrative and default costs), but the emergency loans are generally far below market rates—a 5 percent loan rate in 1984.[13]

When the programs began in 1961, housing loans for rural nonfarm residents were limited to communities of fewer than 2,500 people. By 1976 that limit had been raised to cover communities with populations as large as 20,000. In addition, both the homeownership and rental housing programs incorporate large interest rate subsidies. Interest rates on home loans can be reduced to as low as 3 percent in order to keep the monthly payment from exceeding 20 percent of the borrower's income. Loans on low-income rental housing are made at a 1 percent interest rate.

Programs to assist rural development have also expanded substantially. The agency makes loans to communities for water and waste treatment and other facilities at interest rates comparable to those on tax-exempt state and local government obligations. Furthermore, the agency guarantees loans of commercial lenders to business in communities of fewer than 50,000.[14]

13. The farm ownership and operating loan programs do have room for administrative discretion in setting rates. As a result, the loan rates change in step with market rates, but, on average, they are significantly less than Treasury borrowing rates of comparable loan maturities.

14. Further details on the programs are provided in Department of Agriculture,

The diversity of functions performed by FmHA programs can be seen in the 1984 distribution of its outstanding loans by major program areas: farm ownership, $6.9 billion; farm operating, $4.1 billion; farm emergency, $10.0 billion; economic emergency, $4.3 billion; homeownership, $22.1 billion; rental housing, $5.7 billion; and water and waste disposal, $6.1 billion. Not only have agency programs spread into new areas, they have also swollen tremendously in volume in recent decades. The outstanding loan volume totaled only $2 billion in fiscal 1963, rose to $11.2 billion in fiscal 1973, and reached $61.5 billion by the end of fiscal 1984.[15] Assistance under the emergency loan programs has grown to match lending under the original farm ownership and operating loan programs, and the rural housing programs exceed all farm programs in the volume of outstanding credit.

The principal programs of the FmHA are administered out of three revolving loan funds: agricultural credit, rural housing, and rural development. New loans are financed out of the repayment of old loans, sales of existing loans to the U.S. Treasury's Federal Financing Bank, direct Treasury borrowing, and budget funds appropriated by Congress. Each year's budget appropriation reflects the losses incurred on the outstanding loan portfolio two years earlier, but bears no relation to the cost of that year's loan disbursements or the expenditure the loans were intended to finance.

A simple perspective on the financial condition of the revolving funds is gained by noting that in fiscal 1984 they earned $3 billion on their loan portfolio (a 5 percent rate of return) while paying out $7 billion in interest on their debt (a 12 percent cost of funds). This deficit, or gap between interest income and expenses, will continue for many years even if they should cease to make new loans. If the agency is assumed to have matched the maturity structure of its liabilities and assets and if default costs are ignored, the present discounted value of the future deficit on the existing loan portfolio is more than $25 billion.

Subsidy Costs of FmHA Loans

The FmHA programs incorporate a wide variety of different provisions with respect to loan terms. The interest rates charged on farm

---

Farmers Home Administration, *A Brief History of Farmers Home Administration* (USDA, 1985).

15. Ibid., pp. 20, 27.

ownership and operating loans are tied to Treasury borrowing rates, but other programs incorporate much larger subsidies.

A recent study by the General Accounting Office illustrates how program subsidy costs can be computed. The GAO collected data on the administrative and default costs of FmHA loans by major program area and allocated those costs over the lives of the loans. The difference between the interest rate charged the borrower and the lender's costs, including the Treasury cost of borrowing for a bond of comparable maturity, provided a means of estimating the future interest subsidy costs. If the Treasury borrowing rate is used to discount those future costs, the present value of the subsidy can be computed as a percentage of the original loan amount.[16] This percentage is the subsidy rate.

The GAO data were updated and used to compute the subsidy costs of FmHA loans made in fiscal 1984. A summary of those calculations is shown in table 5-2.[17] The subsidy rates vary widely among the programs, ranging from a high of 100 percent of the loan disbursements for rental housing loans to a low of 7.8 percent for business and industrial guaranteed loans. The subsidy costs are dominated by the interest rate component for those loan programs that charge below-market rates. In most cases the administrative costs and the default guarantee are a small part of the total subsidy. In fiscal 1984 FmHA loans totaled $7.7 billion. On the basis of the subsidy rates shown in table 5-2, those loans committed the government to subsidize costs with a present discounted value of $2.3 billion—an average 30 percent of the loan amount.

The default costs used in the computations are suspect, however. The FmHA programs are driven by strong political pressures, which make it difficult to foreclose on loans. And unlike private financial institutions, government agencies are not subject to independent audits that can force the reclassification of delinquent loans and the establishment of adequate loss reserves. Consequently, government agencies can refinance prob-

16. See Comptroller General of the United States, *Long-Term Cost Implications of Farmers Home Administration Subsidized and Guaranteed Loan Program*, PAD-79-15 (General Accounting Office, 1979).

17. Estimates of average loan rates were obtained from the FmHA, and the ten-year Treasury bond rate, plus 50 basis points, was used as an estimate of the cost of funds. Administration and default costs were taken from the GAO study. The subsidy rates for the homeownership and rental housing programs were taken from the Congressional Budget Office, *Rural Housing Programs: Long-Term Costs and Their Treatment in the Federal Budget* (CBO, 1982), pp. 12, 14. Alternative estimates, based on the concept of benefits to the borrower, are provided in *Special Analyses, Fiscal Year 1986*, p. F-33.

Table 5-2. *Subsidy Costs of the Farmers Home Administration Loan Programs, Fiscal Year 1984*

Program	Average loan rate (percent)	Average maturity (years)	Loan volume (millions of dollars)	Present value of subsidy	
				Percent of loan amount	Millions of dollars
Farm ownership	10.5	40	701	22	155
Farm operating	10.5	7	2,071	12	240
Emergency loans[a]	5.0	7	1,651	27	360
Homeownership	3.4	14	1,851	29	535
Rental housing	1.0	40	919	100	920
Community facilities	9.0	20	130	24	30
Water and waste disposal	9.0	40	270	30	80
Business and industrial	n.a.	10	124	8	10
Total	...	...	7,717	30	2,330

Source: Authors' calculations as explained in the text.
n.a. Not available.
a. The reported subsidy rate applies to physical disaster loans. Economic emergency loans are assumed to have a subsidy rate equal to that for operating loans in computing the dollar amount of subsidy.

lem loans and carry delinquent borrowers for an extended time. For example, in 1984 the delinquency rates of FmHA loans reached as high as 43 percent for economic emergency loans and 31 percent for farm operating loans, while actual write-offs were only 0.3 and 1.2 percent, respectively.[18]

Most subsidy costs of FmHA loans are concentrated in the newer programs developed during the last two decades. Housing credit, which began to expand rapidly after 1970, represented 62 percent of the subsidy costs in 1984, but only 36 percent of loan volume. Farm emergency loans, a program that exploded in the 1970s, accounted for about half of the subsidy costs of all farm loans.

Economic Effects

There are few empirical studies that can be used to measure the increase in expenditure, as opposed to a simple substitution for private loans, of the FmHA loan programs. One is a recent study by LeBlanc and Hrubovcak, which examined the effects of tax policy on agricultural investment. Since they used a statistical model that included borrowing costs, their results can be extended to cover interest rate subsidies for

18. Farmers Home Administration, *Brief History*, pp. 20, 33.

farm loans.[19] They postulated that the demand for capital to invest in agriculture is inversely related to the annual cost of using it—the cost of capital. In the simplest case, a unit of capital must earn a return sufficient to cover interest and depreciation charges. A reduction in the interest rate increases the amount of capital that can meet that test. The actual measure used by LeBlanc and Hrubovcak is considerably more complex, because they included the effects of taxes and inflation.

LeBlanc and Hrubovcak found that agricultural investment was sensitive to changes in the cost of capital. A 1 percent reduction in the cost of capital increases the stock of equipment by about 0.4 percent, the stock of structures by 0.15 percent, and the demand for land by 0.03 percent.

How much interest rate changes affect the annual cost of capital depends heavily on the life of the asset, because depreciation becomes a progressively smaller part of the cost for longer-lived assets. Also, farmers can deduct interest expenses in computing their income taxes, diluting the effect of interest changes on after-tax rates of return. If new investments are assumed to be financed in equal proportions by debt and equity, a 1 percentage point reduction in the interest rate, working through changes in the cost of capital, increases the demand for both equipment and structures about 1 percent and the demand for land nearly 2 percent.

The implications of their study are that loan subsidies are a fairly inefficient means of promoting capital investment in agriculture and that farm loan subsidies should be seen primarily as income transfers. Because the supply of agricultural land is relatively fixed, the subsidy component of farm ownership loans will have its major impact on land prices, with the benefits of the subsidy largely going to existing landowners rather than borrowers.

The loan subsidies for rural housing may affect resource use more than subsidies for farming do, simply because the value of the subsidy is so great. The FmHA homeownership program issues mortgages with a maturity of up to thirty-three years. While the loans are written with a mortgage rate equal to the cost of borrowing from the Federal Financing Bank, the effective interest rate is reduced to ensure that borrowers do not spend more than 20 percent of their income on principal, interest, taxes, and insurance. Borrowers' incomes are recertified every two

19. Michael LeBlanc and James Hrubovcak, "The Effects of Tax Policy on Aggregate Agricultural Investment," Department of Agriculture, Economic Research Service (1984).

years so that, as their incomes rise, the effective mortgage interest rate approaches the cost of borrowing. Even then no charge is included for default or administrative costs. Borrowers are required to repay a portion of the subsidy when they sell the property if it has appreciated in value.

Loans for rental housing normally carry an interest rate of 1 percent. A minimum rent is established on the basis of construction and maintenance costs, and tenants are required to pay the higher of the minimum rent or 25 percent of their income. The FmHA collects any excess over the minimum rent standard as an offset to its interest costs. Information is not available on the extent of these offsetting collections.

These subsidies greatly reduce the effective price of housing for the loan recipients. Because housing investments are long-lived, the importance of depreciation is reduced and that of interest rates is increased as components of the annual cost of capital. In addition, the interest rate subsidy is directed toward individuals in low tax brackets for whom the tax deductibility of interest expenses is unimportant.

For example, at mid-1980s rates of interest and inflation, the unsubsidized annual cost of capital for housing in a typical case would be 10 percent of the purchase price.[20] A subsidized interest rate of 5 percent (the average FmHA rate in 1983) would reduce the cost of capital to 3 percent—a 70 percent drop. Plausible estimates of the price elasticity of the demand for housing range between -0.5 and -1.0. Even with an elasticity of -0.5, the FmHA housing loan programs in this example would have increased recipients' demand for housing about 35 percent.

The community development programs under the FmHA probably have a limited impact on resource use because many of the recipients have alternative access to tax-exempt bond financing. Many program loans were made only because they were tied into the environmental grants for waste and water treatment. The business and industrial loans are similar to the loan programs of the Small Business Administration discussed in chapter 4.

The Rural Electrification Administration

The Rural Electrification Administration (REA) is charged with ensuring access to financing for cooperatively owned public utilities in

20. This example assumes that the low-income homeowner does not file an itemized tax return, mortgage interest rates are 12 percent, expected home price inflation is 6 percent, property taxes are 2 percent of the home value, and depreciation is 2 percent annually.

rural areas. Historically, that objective has been achieved by providing direct loans to rural electrical cooperatives and by guaranteeing loans obtained elsewhere. At first the interest rate on direct loans was set slightly above the government's cost of funds, but a legislated fixed rate of 2 percent was adopted in 1944. The later upward drift of market rates created a growing degree of government subsidy.

In 1973 Congress acted to establish a higher but still fixed interest rate of 5 percent—about equal to market rates at the time—and converted the program to an off-budget revolving fund where new loans could be financed out of repayments of old loans.[21] The off-budget status meant that the loan activities of REA would not be reflected in the unified budget. Congress also lent the fund $7.9 billion, interest free, with repayment to begin in 1993. Furthermore, the REA was empowered to pool its loan assets and use them as collateral for thirty-year loans from the Federal Financing Bank. Finally, borrowers could use their REA guarantee to go directly to the Federal Financing Bank to obtain loans at the same rate charged the REA—the Treasury borrowing rate plus one-eighth of a percent.

The REA has continued since 1973 to make direct loans (averaging about $1 billion annually) at the 5 percent rate, financing about 60 percent of the credit out of loan repayments and borrowing from the Federal Financing Bank at an average rate of about 11.5 percent for the remaining 40 percent. In effect, the agency has been losing a substantial amount on each loan, but covering the cash-flow deficit by borrowing from the bank. The funds required to finance the interest subsidy have been raised by selling off existing assets rather than appropriating budget funds. As long as market rates remain above 5 percent, this is not a sustainable situation, and the REA is headed toward insolvency. At that time the government will have to write off its loan of $7.9 billion and provide an additional appropriation to cover the annual interest subsidy on the existing portfolio.

A recent study by the General Accounting Office contained an estimate of the market value of the current loan portfolio.[22] The 1983 loan portfolio

---

21. Utilities that are experiencing severe financial difficulties can obtain loans at 2 percent. The qualifying criteria for those loans were considerably tightened after 1981, and they are not now a major source of financing. See Department of Agriculture, Rural Electrification Administration, *A Brief History of the Rural Electric and Telephone Programs* (USDA, 1983).

22. Statement of John Luke in *Rural Electrification and Telephone Revolving Fund*

of the REA, with a book value of $13.3 billion, will generate a cumulative future cash flow (repayments plus interest) of $26.2 billion. At a 1983 interest rate of 11 percent for government borrowing, that cash flow had a current market value of $8.6 billion. Against those assets were borrowings from the Federal Financing Bank, valued at $6 billion, and the Treasury loan of $7.9 billion. Thus the fund had a net negative value of $5.3 billion in 1983.[23] That estimate is slightly optimistic in that it excludes all future administrative costs and assumes no defaults.

Subsidy Costs of REA Loans

The subsidy costs of each year's loans are chiefly a function of the spread between the 5 percent loan rate and the Treasury borrowing rate: administrative costs of the loans are low, and loan defaults have been extremely uncommon. The fact that private utility bonds trade in the market at an interest rate premium over the government rate of only 0.5–1.0 percentage point also suggests that default risk is not a principal factor.

A historical comparison of the interest rate on new REA loans and the Treasury's cost of borrowing is shown in figure 5-2.[24] As can be seen, a subsidy was not originally a major feature of the program. In the early years the loan rate typically exceeded the Treasury borrowing rate, and it was not until the 1960s that a significant interest subsidy began to appear. The magnitude of the subsidy widened considerably during the 1970s, and in the 1980s the 5 percent interest rate has been consistently less than half the Treasury borrowing rate.

Self-Sufficiency Act of 1983, Hearings before the Subcommittee on Agricultural Credit and Rural Electrification of the Senate Committee on Agriculture, Nutrition, and Forestry, 98 Cong. 2 sess. (GPO, 1984), p. 277. The GAO reported the net asset position slightly differently. Because the Treasury loan does not have to be repaid until after 1993, the GAO assigned a present discounted value of $1 billion to that obligation and then added the forgone interest on the loan, valued at $9.8 billion, as a subsidy cost—resulting in a net negative value of $8.2 billion. In the above calculation the net value of the fund is included on the basis of liquidation in 1983.

23. The negative net worth position reflects both a subsidy of below-market-rate loans in previous years and the fact that the government, like private lenders, did not anticipate the rise in market interest rates during the last two decades. The latter source of loss should not be identified as a subsidy since it would exist even if the loans had been originally made at market rates.

24. The twenty-year bond rate is used as the measure of the cost of borrowing because it approximates the average maturity of a thirty-five-year amortized loan.

Figure 5-2. *Average Interest Rates on Rural Electrification Administration Loans and Treasury Twenty-Year Bond Issues, 1936–84*

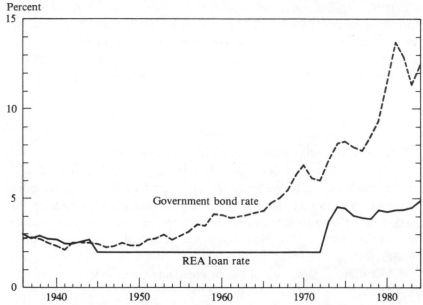

Sources: The loan rate data are from the Rural Electrification Administration; the twenty-year bond rate is from the Board of Governors of the Federal Reserve. The bond rate is extended back before 1954 by linking it to the average yield on long-term bonds for earlier years.

Each year's loans commit the government to a stream of subsidy costs that extend over the lives of the loans. Although the costs seem modest on an annual basis, the cumulative subsidy is a large proportion of the original loan. The present discounted value of the estimated subsidy costs associated with REA loans in each year since 1973 is shown in table 5-3. The subsidy is computed using a discount rate equal to the twenty-year Treasury bond rate plus 0.5 percentage point as a minimal allowance for the administrative costs of the REA and the Federal Financing Bank. In addition, all the loans are assumed to be amortized over a thirty-five-year period with a 5 percent interest rate—a simplifying assumption that understates the subsidy costs. The subsidy is the present value of the expenditures that taxpayers will pay over the life of the loan, assuming that market interest rates are correctly anticipated. Thus in fiscal 1983 loans of $856 million obligated taxpayers to make future payments with a present value of $430 million, or 50

Table 5-3. *Subsidy Costs of the Loan Program of the Rural Electrification and Telephone Revolving Fund, Fiscal Years 1973–83*

| Year | Loan disbursements (millions of dollars) | Present value of subsidy | | Discount rate (percent) |
		Amount (millions of dollars)	Percent of loan disbursements	
1973	92	23	25	7.5
1974	802	260	32	8.5
1975	855	276	32	8.5
1976	1,028	332	32	8.5
1977	875	252	29	8.0
1978	881	313	36	9.0
1979	1,105	454	41	10.0
1980	1,207	605	50	12.0
1981	1,204	684	57	14.0
1982	1,048	580	55	13.5
1983	856	430	50	12.0

Sources: Department of Agriculture, Rural Electrification Administration, *A Brief History of the Rural Electric and Telephone Programs* (USDA, 1983), p. 29; and authors' calculations as explained in the text. The subsidy is the present discounted value of the future interest costs.

percent of the loan disbursement. That compares with reported budget outlays (administrative costs) of only $27 million.

Economic Effects

It is possible to calculate the impact of the interest subsidy on the price of the capital equipment purchased by rural electric cooperatives. Because they are exempt from corporate income taxation, the annual cost of capital (c) is simply the rate of interest (i) plus depreciation (d) minus the expected rate of inflation for capital good prices ($\dot{P}$):

$$c = i + d - \dot{P}.$$

The Treasury estimates that the capital owned by utilities has a rate of depreciation of about 5 percent annually. Thus if the expected inflation rate is estimated at 5 percent and a utility borrowed all its funds in 1983 at the market interest rate of 12 percent (table 5-3), the cost of capital would be 12 percent (12 + 5 − 5). If, instead, it obtained 50 percent of its financing from the REA at 5 percent, its annual cost of capital would be reduced to 8.5 percent—a 30 percent subsidy of capital purchases.[25]

25. Those borrowers who used the REA obtained 63 percent of their total financing from the REA in fiscal 1983. See Rural Electrification Administration, *Brief History*, p. 19.

The subsidy could affect the behavior of the utilities that receive it in two ways. First, it might lead to an increased demand for capital because it induces utility cooperatives to choose more capital-intensive methods of supplying power to their customers.

Alternatively, utilities may choose to pass the savings on to their customers in the form of lower utility rates. This second outcome might be expected to dominate in the case of cooperatively owned utilities that feel pressured to provide tangible benefits to their owners. A recent study by Kiefer examined the effect of the subsidy on electric utility rates.[26] He concluded that, at the market interest rates in effect in 1981, elimination of the REA financial subsidy would result in a 23 percent increase in the capital costs for the average cooperatively owned utility.[27] Capital costs are in turn about 25 percent of utility costs. Thus the subsidy provides for about a 6 percent reduction in rates.[28] Kiefer's results seem roughly consistent with the observed trend of utility rates. Rates charged by REA borrowers were 25 percent above private utility rates in 1950, declined to equality by 1960, and were 10 percent lower in 1982.[29]

The current REA program is in serious difficulty. Taxpayers have already accumulated an unpaid liability of $5.3 billion from past operations. Since the REA is continuing to lend at a rate of about $1 billion annually, those costs will rise rapidly in future years. If market interest rates remain near 10 percent, the funding device being used to avoid entering the program's cost in the budget (sale of its assets to the Federal Financing Bank) will be exhausted in the 1990s. That day of reckoning can be delayed, but not eliminated, by converting the Treasury loan to a gift, as some of the program's proponents have suggested. In the longer term the program can be financed only by appropriating budget funds to pay for it.

26. Donald W. Kiefer, "Investor-Owned Electric Utilities versus Rural Electric Cooperatives: A Comparison of Tax and Financial Subsidies," Library of Congress, Congressional Research Service (November 1982).

27. Ibid., p. 30.

28. Rural Electrification Administration, *Brief History*, p. 47.

29. Ibid., p. 41; and U.S. Department of Commerce, Bureau of the Census, *Statistical Abstract of the United States, 1984* (GPO, 1983), p. 586, and previous issues.

CHAPTER SIX

Student Loans

FROM AN ECONOMIC perspective the guaranteed student loan (GSL) program is one of the most interesting of the government credit activities. The loans are directed toward a segment of the population that is frequently alleged to be a victim of credit market failures. Unlike loans for homes or cars, education loans are secured by an asset, the student's future income, that cannot be repossessed and sold by the lender. The potential of default, together with the high cost of evaluating loan applicants, deters private lending. The program is also large enough that evidence of its success in reaching its major objective—increasing enrollment in postsecondary education—should be readily observable.

The student loan program has undergone numerous modifications since its inception in 1965. The current program guarantees private loans to undergraduate students up to $2,500 ($5,000 for graduate students) annually, with a cumulative limit of $12,500 ($25,000 for graduate students). More important, the program includes a large interest rate subsidy: the interest rate paid by the student is fixed at 8 percent of the outstanding balance.[1] Also, the government pays all interest costs during the period that the student is in school. Repayment begins six months after the student leaves school and generally extends over five to ten years. And the lender receives a special allowance from the government sufficient to guarantee a return of 3.5 percent above the yield on ninety-one-day Treasury bills. These special allowance payments are adjusted on a quarterly basis over the life of the loan. If the Treasury bill rate is 10 percent, lenders receive 13.5 percent, students pay 8 percent, and the government pays the difference.[2]

1. Seven percent for those students who first borrowed before 1981. Loan rates were 9 percent for first-time borrowers during 1983 and 1984.
2. Further details and a legislative history of the program are provided in National

Table 6-1. *Financial Aid for Postsecondary Students, Selected Academic Years, 1963–84*
Billions of dollars unless otherwise specified

Program	1963–64	1970–71	1975–76	1977–78	1980–81	1982–83[a]	1983–84[a]
Tuition costs	2.0	5.5	9.4	11.5	15.9	21.0	23.0
Federally supported programs							
Need-based grants[b]	...	0.4	1.5	2.4	3.5	3.5	3.9
Benefit programs[c]	0.1	1.7	5.4	4.1	3.8	2.3	1.5
Loans[d]	0.1	1.3	1.7	2.4	6.9	7.2	8.4
Total	0.2	3.3	8.6	8.8	14.2	13.0	13.8
State and institutional programs	0.4	1.2	1.9	2.3	2.9	3.4	3.6
Total, all programs	0.5	4.5	10.5	11.1	17.1	16.4	17.5
Percent of tuition	27	81	111	96	108	78	76

Sources: Tuition data for higher education are authors' calculations based on W. Vance Grant and Thomas D. Snyder, *Digest of Education Statistics, 1983–84*, U.S. Department of Education, National Center for Education Statistics (Government Printing Office, 1984), p. 141. Tuition costs of vocational schools are estimated by the authors by using a tuition rate twice that for public institutions of higher education. Data on financial aid are from Donald A. Gillespie and Nancy Carlson, *Trends in Student Aid: 1963 to 1983* (Washington, D.C.: College Board, 1983), p. 5, and subsequent updates. Figures are rounded.

a. Estimated.
b. Primarily Pell grants to low- and moderate-income students.
c. Primarily social security and veterans' benefits.
d. Guaranteed student loans and national direct student loans.

The GSL program has been part of a revolutionary change in the financing of postsecondary education. Overall financial assistance to students increased from 27 percent of postsecondary tuition costs in 1963–64 to 111 percent in 1975–76, then declined to about 76 percent in 1983–84 (see table 6-1).[3] The composition of the assistance has also shifted. Much of the initial growth was fueled by veterans' programs and social security student payments. The 1970s saw a large expansion in grants to low-income students. The loan program did not begin to grow rapidly until the late 1970s, when the family-income limit was temporarily eliminated.

In the 1980s growth in the grant programs has slowed, and loans have come to account for more than half of federally supported student assistance. Students receiving federal loans rose from an average of 1 million annually in 1970–78 to more than 3 million in 1983, or about 30 percent of all students in postsecondary education. In 1984 the average loan was about $2,300, compared with tuition costs of about $900 at public institutions and $5,000 at private schools.[4]

The Rationales for Student Loans

The evolution of the loan programs into a position of dominance in student financial assistance reflects major shifts in the public debate over the financing of postsecondary education. Before the mid-1950s, the only aid available was furnished by states that subsidized tuition costs at public institutions, and by private institutions that offered a limited number of scholarships, some of them based on need, to superior students. Since then, Congress has sought politically viable means of helping families to pay for higher education.

Commission on Student Financial Assistance, *Guaranteed Student Loans: A Background Paper*, Report 1 (Washington, D.C., 1982).

3. GSL and other federal aid can be obtained for vocational programs also, but there are no reliable tuition data for vocational schools. The table includes the estimate of such costs, based on tuition payments per student twice that of public higher education. Student aid would be a smaller percentage if costs other than tuition were included.

4. Data are from the College Board, *Trends in Student Aid: 1980 to 1984* (Washington, D.C.: College Board, 1984); and W. Vance Grant and Thomas D. Snyder, *Digest of Education Statistics, 1983–84,* U.S. Department of Education, National Center for Education Statistics (Government Printing Office, 1984), p. 141.

The breakthroughs in federal aid to students occurred under the impetus of the National Defense Education Act (NDEA) in 1958 and the War on Poverty in the mid-1960s. Based on a national defense rationale, NDEA loans and fellowships answered a perceived need to promote science and technology in competition with the Soviet Union. With the War on Poverty, equality of opportunity became the justification for aid to low-income students. Increased education and training were seen as the means by which the poor would earn their way out of poverty. Student aid won out over institutional aid because it seemed to foster the principle of equality of opportunity more directly, and because it avoided the constitutional conflict over government aid to private institutions.

Loan programs had a limited role in the initial growth of government assistance. The GSL program was created in 1965, but only to head off a confrontation over tuition tax credits. By reverting to the notion that individuals should pay for their education, loan programs conflicted with the long-term goal of free education held by many supporters of financial aid in general.

Once in place, however, the student loan program expanded rapidly; the low initial capital costs made loans seem an inexpensive response to the pressure from middle-income constituencies to capture for themselves benefits originally aimed at the poor. As the program evolved, it became increasingly costly: the government was forced to guarantee a high return to the banks and state agencies to secure their participation, and the design of the program made it vulnerable to changes in market interest rates. Even in the 1980s, when efforts to cut budget outlays have devastated direct grants for students, the loan programs have emerged relatively unscathed because budget savings are small in the initial few years following a reduction in loans.[5]

Arguments based on imperfections in the capital market were not often heard during the development and growth of the student loan program. Yet severe barriers to a private market do exist. A student loan is a perfect example of the type of loan that private lenders find costly: the loan is for a small amount, there is no marketable asset that can provide collateral, and the highly mobile borrower generally has no

5. The history of the student aid programs is covered in more detail by several authors in Joseph Froomkin, ed., *The Crisis in Higher Education* (New York: Academy of Political Science, 1983).

credit history. Before the GSL program, there existed no private system of loan insurance, and the large-scale operation required to support a national collection system was an outstanding barrier to entry. In practice, private education loans are virtually unavailable unless they are based on the income and financial position of the parents.[6]

A further problem, discussed by Milton Friedman, is that the future return from education is risky: the average expected return is high but subject to wide variance. In the financing of physical capital this problem is handled by a combination of equity financing plus limited liability for firms. Friedman suggested that the counterpart for education would be an income-contingent loan under which the borrower pays the lender an agreed proportion of his or her future earnings.[7]

In the absence of government intervention, these market imperfections would lead to underinvestment in education. One remedy is to provide a general subsidy to educational institutions. But that course of action allows higher-income groups to receive most of the benefits. The more efficient solution to the problem of underinvestment is to operate a loan program that responds directly to the credit market imperfections. Credit market imperfections do not, however, constitute a rationale for subsidized loans.

A loan subsidy must be based on an argument that higher education confers benefits to society in excess of the benefits that accrue to the individual. The War on Poverty, for example, argued that educational aid for the poor, by creating a means of working their way out of poverty, was superior to general welfare grants. But why should a low-income student be required to take out a loan as a precondition for receiving an education grant? Similarly, while arguments might be made that higher education provides social benefits comparable to those for elementary and secondary education, such as a better-informed citizenry, they do not provide a rationale for making the subsidy contingent on a loan.

In point of fact, however, the student loan program is heavily subsidized. In the next section we attempt to evaluate the magnitude of

6. For an early discussion of capital market imperfections for education loans, see Milton Friedman, "The Role of Government in Education," in Robert A. Solo, ed., *Economics and the Public Interest* (Rutgers University Press, 1955), pp. 123–44; revised and reprinted as chapter 6 in Milton Friedman, *Capitalism and Freedom* (University of Chicago Press, 1962).

7. Ibid.

Table 6-2. *Illustrative Subsidy Cost of a $1,000 Guaranteed Student Loan*
Amounts in dollars

| | In-school period (year) | | | Repayment period (year) | | | | | | |
Item	1	2	3	4	5	6	7	8	9	10
General repayment information[a]										
Principal (beginning of period)	1,000	987	943	926	888	750	606	452	291	122
Default claims	13	44	17	10	7	4	4	3	3	3
Payments on principal	0	0	0	28	132	141	149	158	166	118
Student costs[a]										
Origination fee	50	...	...	...	...	...	...	...	...	...
Interest payments	0	0	0	73	66	54	42	30	17	5
Insurance premium	30	...	...	...	...	...	...	...	...	...
Government costs[a]										
In-school interest payments	29	77	75	...	...	...	...	...	...	...
Administrative costs	2	2	2	2	3	2	2	1	0	0
Net default costs	13	43	16	8	5	2	2	1	2	2
Default, death, disability costs	13	44	17	10	7	4	4	3	3	3
Collections on defaults	0	1	1	2	2	2	2	2	1	1
Special allowance										
At 4 percent Treasury bill rate	0	0	0	0	0	0	0	0	0	0
At 9 percent Treasury bill rate	45	43	42	41	37	31	24	17	9	3
At 12 percent Treasury bill rate	75	72	70	68	61	51	40	28	15	5
Total government costs[b]										
At 4 percent Treasury bill rate	44	122	93	10	8	4	4	2	2	2
At 9 percent Treasury bill rate	89	166	135	51	45	35	28	19	11	5
At 12 percent Treasury bill rate	119	195	163	78	69	55	44	30	18	7
Present value of government subsidy costs[b]										
At 4 percent discount rate	264	...								
At 9 percent discount rate	443	...								
At 12 percent discount rate	535	...								

Source: Authors' calculations based on data provided in Touche Ross, *Study of the Cost and Flows of Capital in the Guaranteed Student Loan Program*, report prepared for the National Commission on Student Financial Assistance (Washington, D.C., 1983).
a. Assumes an 8 percent interest rate to student. Interest payment to lender reduced by amount of origination fee in the first year.
b. Net of origination fee.

the subsidy and its impact on college enrollment decisions. In a later section we return to the issue of the appropriate role of loans in the overall structure of student financial aid.

Student Loans and Enrollment Decisions

The chief objective of the student aid programs has been to increase college enrollment rates—particularly of middle- and low-income students. However, the evaluation of the linkage between the growth of the loan programs and college enrollments is complicated by simultaneous changes in other determinants of the net cost of a college education—tuition and other sources of financing—and the determinants of demand.

Following the discussion of chapter 2, the impact of student loans on college enrollments is evaluated in several steps: measuring the subsidy element, evaluating the effect of loan subsidies and other forms of student aid on the costs of college attendance, and evaluating the influence of costs on enrollment decisions. These calculations allow us to estimate the probable impact of the student loan program on college enrollment trends in the United States and to compare those estimates with actual developments over the last two decades.

Subsidy Costs of Student Loans

The subsidy costs for an illustrative student loan of $1,000 are shown in table 6-2. The data are based on costs of the current program, and the example is for the average student who continues in school for three additional years after receiving the loan and repays it over a seven-year period. While in school, the student pays a 5 percent origination fee and a portion of the insurance premium equal to 1 percent of the loan amount multiplied by the number of years in school ($30 in the example).

The main costs to the government are (1) interest payments while the student is in school, (2) the special allowance to the lender that guarantees a return of 3.5 percent above the yield on ninety-one-day Treasury bills (the cost of which depends upon market rates of interest over the life of the loan), and (3) default costs.[8] Net default costs currently represent

8. Under the present program, with an 8 percent minimum student interest payment, the special interest allowance is eliminated only if the Treasury bill rate should decline

Table 6-3. *Trends in Average Education Costs and Student Financial Aid for a Full-Time College Student, Selected Academic Years, 1963–84*

Item	1963–64	1970–71	1975–76	1977–78	1980–81	1982–83	1983–84
				Current dollars			
Annual education costs[a]	1,585	2,430	3,290	3,825	4,930	5,715	6,060
Less: Average grants	115	440	995	975	1,110	930	855
Less: Average loans	30	195	210	285	795	785	850
Net cost of education	1,440	1,795	2,085	2,565	3,025	4,000	4,355
Percent of income per capita	67	53	41	43	38	43	44
				1984 dollars			
Annual education costs[a]	4,560	5,580	5,550	5,780	5,720	5,900	6,060
Less: Average grants	335	1,015	1,675	1,475	1,290	960	855
Less: Average loans	90	440	350	430	925	810	850
Net cost of education	4,135	4,125	3,525	3,875	3,505	4,130	4,355
Addenda							
Adjusted net cost of education (1984 dollars)[b]	4,200	4,425	3,710	4,095	3,905	4,545	4,755
Percent of income per capita	69	57	43	45	41	47	48

Sources: Gillespie and Carlson, *Trends in Student Aid: 1963 to 1983*, pp. 35–36, and subsequent updates; Grant and Snyder, *Digest of Education Statistics, 1983–84*, p. 141; and National Income and Product Accounts of the United States, relevant years.
a. Tuition plus forgone earnings.
b. Student loans are revalued to include only the present value of the subsidy.

about 8 to 9 percent of the loan portfolio and occur most frequently in the early years of the loan. The government has succeeded in reducing default rates in recent years but only with substantial increases in collection expenses.

As under other government loan programs, only a small portion of the long-term cost to the government of GSL loans is evident in the year in which the loan is made. At market interest rates of 9 percent, the government's subsidy costs will be 8.9 percent of the loan volume in the first year, but they will total 60 percent over the life of the loan, and nearly 80 percent of the loan volume at a 12 percent market interest rate. If future costs are discounted back to the year in which the loan is made (as is done at the bottom of table 6-2), a $1,000 loan at a 9 percent market interest rate is equivalent in its budget cost to a cash grant of $443. The subsidy costs increase at higher market interest rates, and all the risk of future fluctuations in market interest rates falls on the government. The public focus on the problem of loan defaults notwithstanding, the interest subsidy accounts for the largest share of program expenses. Default costs are, however, far in excess of the insurance premium paid by the student.[9]

Loan Subsidies and Education Costs

A student's cost of education consists of tuition and fees; room and board; and forgone earnings during attendance. These costs are not additive, however, because most of the room and board costs would exist in any case. Although public discussions often focus on the sum of tuition and room and board to measure college costs, we believe that the combination of tuition and forgone earnings more precisely reflects the actual economic costs.

Table 6-3 shows historical trends in the annual cost of a college education. Data on average tuition costs at higher educational institutions were combined with an estimate of forgone earnings to measure

---

below 4.5 percent. Before 1981 students paid 7 percent and the government continued to pay a subsidy for market rates as low as 3.5 percent. In the example, there are some default costs during the in-school period because the estimates provided by Touche Ross included students who failed to complete their education.

9. Similar estimates of the subsidy costs are reported in Arthur Hauptman, "Federal Costs for Student Loans: Is There a Role for Institution-Based Lending?" (Washington, D.C.: American Council on Education, June 1985).

total costs for the average student (row 1).[10] Comparable measures of financial aid (rows 2 and 3) are obtained by dividing the expenditures shown in table 6-1 by full-time equivalent students.[11] The net cost of education, total costs minus financial aid, is shown in row 4.

The total cost of obtaining a college education rose nearly fourfold between the 1964 and 1984 academic years. After adjustment for general inflation, the cost increase was 33 percent—from $4,560 to $6,060 in 1984 dollars.

On the other hand, the expansion of the financial aid programs more than offset these cost increases. Thus, adjusted for inflation, the net cost of attending college declined throughout the 1960s and 1970s—from $4,135 in 1964 to $3,505 in 1981. The declining cost of education is even more dramatic if measured against a growing level of income per capita.

Since 1981, however, the net cost has increased substantially, rising 24 percent by 1984. In part, this has been the result of a faster rate of increase in tuition costs, but the greater impact has come from the reduction in available government financial aid.

A loan, however, is not equivalent to a grant. If capital markets were perfect, the value of the loan to the student would be roughly equal to the present discounted value of the subsidy.[12] On the other hand, if the student is constrained by borrowing restrictions, the value of the loan would be much greater than the amount of the subsidy. We have used

10. A measure of forgone earnings equal to $400 a month in 1972 (obtained from the Manski-Wise study, as discussed in the following section) was adjusted to year-to-year changes in average wage rates and converted to a nine-month academic year. The value of forgone earnings was cut in half and added to a weighted average of tuition costs at public and private colleges. Forgone earnings were reduced by one-half to reflect the finding of Manski-Wise that their effect on enrollments was only half that of tuition. The tuition weights were 0.75 and 0.25 for public and private institutions, respectively. The costs of room and board are excluded since they would occur even if the individual were not attending school. Alternatively, room and board costs could be included and forgone earnings excluded. Such a change would have little net effect on the reported trends in enrollment costs.

11. The amount of financial aid is slightly overstated because of the lack of information on enrollment in vocational schools, but it should have a minimal influence on the trend over time. The data include funds provided by federal and state governments plus institutional aid, and they refer to both undergraduate and graduate students (see table 6-1).

12. For reasons discussed in chapter 2, we have used the government's cost of funds to discount further subsidy payments. Since that probably understates the student's discount rate, the value of the subsidy to the borrower may be overstated.

the face value of the loan as an upper estimate on the loan value and the present discounted value of the subsidy as a minimal value.

An adjusted measure of net education cost including only the present discounted value of the loan subsidy is shown at the bottom of table 6-3. On that basis the real net cost of higher education, adjusted for inflation, declined from $4,200 in 1964 to a low of $3,710 in 1976, but it has been rising rapidly since then. By 1984 costs had increased 28 percent relative to the price of other consumption goods, with most of that increase occurring after 1981. However, relative to income, education costs are still much lower than in the 1960s.

In 1984 federal loans to students alone were responsible for reducing the cost of a college education by an average of 16 percent if the full value of a loan is included as financial assistance, and by 8 percent if the value of the loan is restricted to the present discounted value of its subsidy component.[13]

The Demand for a College Education

The sensitivity of college enrollment decisions to the cost of attendance has been a frequent subject of empirical studies. A summary of their conclusions can be found in an article by McPherson.[14] Although those studies' estimates of quantitative effects vary greatly, they do agree that costs significantly influence the decision to attend college. McPherson averaged the results of several studies to conclude that a $100 reduction in tuition costs (1974 dollars) would increase national enrollment rates for 18- to 24-year-olds by about 1 percentage point.

A more recent study by Manski and Wise looked specifically at the influence of student financial aid.[15] They concluded that direct grants did have a strong impact on enrollment, particularly at two-year colleges,

13. This assumes that colleges did not raise tuition rates because they knew students could get subsidized loans. Such an argument has been made by some observers, but the pattern of tuition increase shown in table 6-3—a slow rise in the 1970s and rapid increases since—does not support such an interpretation. In addition, the correlation between annual changes in tuition rates and student financial assistance is statistically insignificant.

14. Michael S. McPherson, "The Demand for Higher Education," in David W. Breneman and Chester E. Finn, Jr., eds., *Public Policy and Private Higher Education* (Brookings, 1978), pp. 180–83.

15. Charles F. Manski and David A. Wise, *College Choice in America* (Harvard University Press, 1983), pp. 118–28.

and that the magnitude of the effect was equivalent to an equal reduction in tuition. Also, they estimated that forgone earnings—the income lost by a student who is enrolled—of about $400 a month (1972 dollars) had an effect on enrollment half as large as that for changes in tuition. Overall, this study implied that a $100 drop in education costs would increase enrollment rates by 0.4 to 1.5 percentage points—a conclusion comparable to the results reported by McPherson.[16] In percentage terms, these studies imply that a 1 percent reduction in net education cost—tuition plus forgone earnings minus fellowship aid—would increase national enrollment rates by 0.1 to 0.3 percentage point.[17]

The combination of these results with the previous estimate of the effective reduction in enrollment costs contributed by federal lending suggests that the existence of student loans raised overall enrollment 1 to 5 percentage points, or by 0.3 million to 1.4 million students, in 1984. By contrast, 3.3 million students received loans in the 1984 academic year. Thus a large portion of the subsidy was paid to students who would have attended college in any case.

The wide range of estimated enrollment changes—0.3 million to 1.4 million—results from uncertainties about both the extent of capital market constraints on private student loans and the magnitude of the price coefficient. The upper limit of the range corresponds to a valuation of loans at their face value (that is, it assumes significant capital market barriers) and a large effect of price on enrollment decisions (the larger value reported by Manski and Wise). The bottom limit includes only the present discounted value of the loan subsidy (that is, it assumes no private credit market constraints), and it uses a low price elasticity for enrollment decisions (the lower bound of the Manski-Wise study).[18]

16. The estimated enrollment effect had a wide range because the regression analyses used in the Manski-Wise study yielded a coefficient on scholarship aid for two-year schools that was much larger in absolute value than that for tuition costs. The lower bound results from an alternative regression that constrained the two coefficients to be of equal value though opposite in sign. If the second version is accepted as more reasonable, it is about half as large as a typical result reported in the survey by McPherson. The Basic Education Opportunity Grants, which Manski and Wise evaluated, provided an average of $1,073 for each recipient in 1984–85 and covered about 30 percent of full-time equivalent student enrollment ($350 for each full-time student). See College Board, *Trends in Student Aid: 1980 to 1984*, p. 8.

17. This calculation translates the 1972–74 dollar magnitudes to a percentage change concept by assuming a net education cost of $1,800 in the 1972–74 period. See table 6-3.

18. This method of estimating the enrollment effects ignores a large number of

Trends in School Enrollment Rates

It is useful to supplement the above estimate of enrollment effects of student loans with an examination of the trends in actual enrollments. Figure 6-1 shows enrollment rates for the population of 18- to 24-year-olds, disaggregated by sex and race. Rates for both black men and women increased substantially from 1961 to the mid-1970s, but since then the rate for men has declined, while the rate for women has remained unchanged. This pattern of change roughly coincides with the change in net education cost—the net cost fell until 1976 and rose thereafter. During the same period, the enrollment rate of white women has grown steadily, while that for white men seems to be dominated by efforts to avoid the military draft during the Vietnam War.

These conclusions can be checked by estimating statistical regressions that relate changes in enrollment rates to the proportion of the male population drafted into the armed forces, the net cost of attending college (total costs minus the subsidy component of loans), and per capita disposable income (see table 6-4). For the 1962–84 period enrollment rates of both white men and women show no statistically significant correlation with either education cost or income. The white male enrollment rate is heavily influenced by the military draft variable, and a simple time trend dominates the regression for the female enrollment rate. After adjusting for the draft, there is no significant evidence of either a positive or negative trend in the white male enrollment rate.

On the other hand, there is some statistical evidence that the economic variables influence the enrollment rates of blacks. For black women a decrease in net education cost of 1 percent or an increase in income of 1 percent is estimated to raise enrollment rates 0.2 percentage point. For black males the cost of education had a negative, but statistically insignificant, coefficient, while a 1 percent increase in income raises enrollment rates 0.6 percentage point. There also appears to be a significant negative trend in black male enrollment rates, given income. There is no evidence that college enrollment was used by black males to avoid the draft.

While an analysis using aggregate time-series data cannot be given too much weight, only the results for black students support the detailed

potential complexities in the response of individuals to changes in the cost of attending college. It is at best only suggestive of the magnitude involved. Still, the implication that at least 75 percent of student loan funds go to inframarginal borrowers is noteworthy.

Figure 6-1. *School Enrollment Rates, by Sex and Race, Ages 18–24, 1961–82*

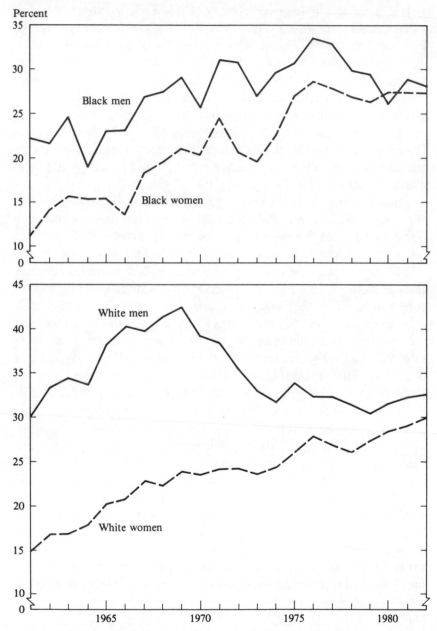

Source: U.S. Bureau of the Census, *Current Population Reports,* series P-20, "School Enrollment: Social and Economic Characteristics of Students," relevant years.

Table 6-4. *Regression Results for College Enrollment Rates, by Race and Sex, 1964–82*

Enrollment rate of race/sex group	Independent variables[a]				Constant	$\bar{R}^2$
	Armed forces draft	Net education cost	Per capita disposable income	Time trend		
White men						
A	0.2	−2.6	9.6	−0.3	43.3	0.75
	(4.1)	(−0.2)	(0.6)	(−0.8)	(0.5)	...
B	0.2	...	...	...	32.5	0.78
	(8.1)	...	...	...	(61.2)	...
White women						
A	...	−3.1	2.9	0.4	38.0	0.91
	...	(−0.6)	(0.3)	(2.2)	(0.9)	...
B	...	...	...	0.5	17.3	0.92
	...	...	...	(14.0)	(30.4)	...
Black men						
A	0.1	−23.1	64.2	−1.2	129.6	0.51
	(0.6)	(−1.6)	(2.8)	(−2.3)	(1.1)	...
B	...	−19.6	62.0	−1.2	107.1	0.53
	...	(−1.5)	(2.8)	(−2.3)	(1.0)	...
Black women						
A	...	−19.3	16.9	0.2	140.6	0.82
	...	(−1.7)	(0.9)	(0.5)	(1.6)	...
B	...	−20.3	25.4	...	140.0	0.83
	...	(−1.9)	(4.6)	...	(1.6)	...

Sources: Underlying data calculated by authors from table 6-3, and from U.S. Department of Defense, Directorate for Information, Operations and Reports, *Selected Manpower Statistics*, relevant years, table P27.3.

a. Enrollment rates are expressed as percentages of the population aged 18–24; net education cost and income per capita are expressed as logarithms; and the military draft is expressed as a percentage of the male population 18–24 years of age. The numbers in parentheses are *t*-statistics.

studies reported by McPherson, and overall they correspond most closely to the bottom range of the results reported by Manski and Wise.

Other Aspects

Several other dimensions of the relationship between the financial aid programs and college attendance are not addressed by analyzing overall enrollment rates. One is family income level. As conceived, the programs were intended to equalize educational opportunities across income classes by targeting the grant and loan programs on students from low-income families. But targeting was reduced during the 1970s, and today students from upper-income families often circumvent income limitations by claiming to be financially independent of their parents.[19]

A study by Hansen and Lampman reported that during the 1970s enrollment rates for college-age students from families with below-median incomes did not rise relative to those from above-median income families.[20] Instead, they concluded the student aid programs led to increases in the number of students claiming independent financial status and the number of low-income students attending private colleges.

For example, between 1969 and 1981, while the overall college participation rate of women increased 5 percentage points, the rate for female students from families with incomes of less than $12,000 showed little change, whereas there was a large increase in the participation of women from families with incomes in excess of $25,000.[21] And between 1978 and 1982, enrollment rates actually fell for men and women from families with incomes of less than $20,000 and rose for those from families with incomes of more than $20,000. Furthermore, the entire 1978–82 enrollment rate increase was accounted for by white students claiming independent financial status; enrollment rates dropped for the minority population claiming independent financial status and for all dependent individuals aged 18–24.[22]

Second, the assistance programs are alleged to strongly affect the choice between public and private institutions. The formulas used to

19. See Applied Systems Institute, "Changes in College Participation Rates and Student Financial Assistance: 1969, 1974, 1981," prepared for the National Commission on Student Financial Assistance (Washington, D.C., January 1983); and Lawrence E. Gladieux, "The Costs of the Guaranteed Student Loan Program and Implications for Federal Student Aid Policy," testimony before the National Commission on Student Financial Assistance (Washington, D.C., April 4, 1983). The changes in the targeting of financial assistance on low-income students implies that the average data of table 6-3 understate for low-income students the decline in education costs up to the mid-1970s and the increase thereafter.

20. W. Lee Hansen and Robert J. Lampman, "Good Intentions and Mixed Results: An Update on the Basic Educational Opportunity Grants," Discussion Paper 705-82 (University of Wisconsin–Madison, Institute for Research on Poverty, July 1982).

21. Applied Systems Institute, "Rates of College Participation, 1969, 1974, and 1981," Policy Brief, American Council on Education (Washington, D.C., April 1984). It is difficult to analyze the enrollment rates for males during the 1970s because of the strong influence of the military draft.

22. Applied Systems Institute, "Student Aid and Minority Enrollment in Higher Education," prepared for the American Association of State Colleges and Universities (Washington, D.C., January 1985).

calculate financial need create an incentive for aid recipients to enroll at more expensive schools. Under some circumstances the amount of aid will be adjusted to cover any cost differences among the schools that a student might attend. In effect, the student aid programs may have become an indirect, but important, source of government support for the private college system.

The Student Loan Marketing Association

The federal government has attempted to create a secondary market for student loans, much as it did in earlier decades for home mortgages. The existence of a resale market was expected to increase the attractiveness of student loans to private lenders by making the assets more liquid. In 1972 the Student Loan Marketing Association (Sallie Mae), a privately owned, government-sponsored enterprise, was established to purchase student loans from private lenders. It finances its activities by the sale of debt in capital markets.[23]

Although an active resale market has yet to develop, Sallie Mae has been a highly profitable operation from a business perspective, earning an average rate of return on equity of 31 percent in 1983–84, substantially more than that of other private lenders. Table 6-5 summarizes its financial operations for 1983–84. In 1984 it held $5.1 billion in fully guaranteed student loans for which the government provides a gross yield equal to the Treasury bill rate plus 3.5 percentage points. It also had $3.7 billion in advances, loans to primary lenders, on which it charged about 1.0 percentage point over the Treasury rate. Directly held loans of Sallie Mae represented about 42 percent of all student loans in repayment status.[24]

The corporation maintains a maturity structure of its debt that closely duplicates the short-term interest rate structures of its assets. The highly indexed yield on both assets and liabilities is reflected in the stability of the interest rate differentials shown at the bottom of table 6-5. Because of the guarantee and the matching of the maturity structures of its assets

23. In its early years Sallie Mae relied on the Federal Financing Bank. It has been issuing its own debt since 1981.
24. Goldman Sachs, Investment Research Division, "Student Loan Marketing Association" (New York, April 9, 1985), p. 3.

Table 6-5. *Selected Financial Data of the Student Loan Marketing Association, 1983, 1984*

Item	1983	1984
Average asset earnings (millions of dollars)		
Student loans	3,943	5,110
Advances	3,060	3,738
Other investments	975	1,036
Total assets	7,978	9,884
Debt (millions of dollars)	7,663	9,407
Average asset yields (percent)		
Student loans[a]	11.55	12.53
Advances	10.08	10.99
Other investment[b]	9.92	10.78
All assets	10.78	11.73
Debt costs (percent of debt outstanding)	9.28	10.22
Administrative costs (percent of assets)	0.36	0.32
Earnings (percent of assets)		
Pretax income	1.51	1.86
Income after taxes	0.83	1.00
Treasury bill rate (percent)	8.97	9.96
Yield spreads over Treasury bill rate (percent)		
Student loans	2.58	2.57
Advances	1.11	0.94
Other investments	0.95	0.82
All assets	1.81	1.77
Debt (percent)	0.31	0.26

Source: Computed by the authors from data supplied by the Student Loan Marketing Association.
a. Net of servicing costs and deferred income totaling 1.11 percent in 1983 and 1.07 percent in 1984.
b. Includes a small amount of noninterest income.

and its liabilities, the activities of Sallie Mae are practically devoid of any credit risk or interest rate risk.

Sallie Mae enjoys high profits because a high return to lenders is built into the GSL program; the agency's cost of funds is low; the agency efficiently controls its own administrative costs; and effective competition is lacking.

First, GSLs have a guaranteed yield of 3.5 percentage points above the Treasury bill rate, yet loan servicing costs have averaged only about 1.1 percent of the loan portfolio in recent years. Sallie Mae both operates its own national network for collecting loan payments and contracts with several private servicing organizations. Net of servicing costs, loans provide a yield about 2.6 percentage points above the Treasury bill rate, and the overall yield on all assets is 1.8 percentage points above the bill rate (see table 6.5).

Second, Sallie Mae is able to borrow at a rate about 0.3 percentage point over the Treasury bill rate. This low debt cost can be attributed both to the low risk of its asset portfolio and to the implicit guarantee associated with agency status. (Substantial controversy surrounds the issue of which of these two factors is of greater importance, as is discussed below. Here, it is sufficient to note the highly favorable spread between asset yields and debt costs.)

Finally, Sallie Mae maintains a very low level of general administrative costs, averaging between 0.3 and 0.4 percent of assets in recent years. It saves some costs because it is not subject to the same regulatory restrictions on its bond issues as fully private institutions, but the amount of money involved appears to be small. It is exempt from state and local, but not from federal, income taxes. Earnings in 1984 totaled 1.86 percent of assets on a pretax basis and 1.0 percent after tax. The return on equity is about twice that for private institutions.

The financial success of Sallie Mae raises some basic questions. Are its high profits attributable to the high guaranteed yield on its assets— the GSL program—or to the effect of its status as a federal credit agency on borrowing costs? And does the recent reduction in the cost of servicing GSL loans justify a reduction in the size of the special allowance?

The high profit rate earned by Sallie Mae, if it results from the yield on GSLs, should lead private competitors to enter the market. This increased competition should be reflected in a rise in the secondary market price for GSLs. After all, private investors have the same access to the national network of third-party loan servicing agencies. Alternatively, agency status may simply give Sallie Mae a competitive advantage over private lenders by allowing it to borrow at low rates. In that case, Sallie Mae would be preventing the development of an effective secondary market, earning profits through its subsidized position in the market.

There is evidence of increased entry into the market by several large banks, and whereas secondary market sales once required a discount, they are now negotiated at par.[25] Several factors, however, have slowed the pace of private entry. First, the fall in loan servicing costs is a relatively recent phenomenon. Second, regulation often limits the pur-

25. Primary lenders typically hold the loans until they enter repayment status (requiring an outlay for servicing).

chase of loans on a national scale by private institutions, restricting their market to their own states. Third, private entrants, having encountered difficulties in their dealings with state guarantor agencies, are not fully confident of success in collecting the guarantee on a loan in default.[26] Sallie Mae is in a stronger position to deal with the state guarantor agencies. Fourth, frequent changes in the GSL program's rules of operation have left a legacy of distrust in the private sector. Finally and most important, the GSL legislation prevents the establishment of a fully private institution, competing with Sallie Mae, that focuses exclusively on student loans.[27] Thus it is not really feasible to establish a private firm with the same lack of risk on the asset side.

It is hard to argue that federal credit agency status per se confers significant benefits. Even without such status the financing cost of Sallie Mae should be close to that of the Treasury, given its risk-free portfolio. Several factors prevent its financing costs from being quite that low. First, there is a political risk that Congress will change the rules of the game, either by shrinking the special allowance or by altering Sallie Mae's charter. For example, in the event of the failure of Sallie Mae, the government accepts a creditor status equal to that of other lenders, but the provision must be renewed by Congress every three years. Also, Sallie Mae issues some long-term debt with a floating rate tied to the yield on Treasury bills. Since the market is thin, there is some risk to bondholders if they need to sell. The average interest cost of Sallie Mae debt has been 5 to 10 basis points below AAA-rated private issues—a yield differential that is not surprising in view of the low asset risk.[28]

The whole effort to develop a secondary market has had few benefits for the government, in the form of lower costs, or for students, through a lower loan rate. Under the structure of the GSL program, there is no means by which increased efficiencies can be translated into a lower rate

26. The primary guarantor agency is a state agency. The federal government plays a secondary backup role to the state agency.

27. Higher Education Act of 1965, 20 U.S.C. 1085(g)(1)(A)(ii) and subsequent interpretations by the Department of Education.

28. Congressional Budget Office, *Government-Sponsored Enterprises and Their Implicit Federal Subsidy: The Case of Sallie Mae* (CBO, 1985), p. 14. In general, the CBO report places much greater emphasis on agency status as a contributing factor to Sallie Mae's profits. See, for example, pp. 21–35 of the report. The CBO made one comparison that suggested that agency status was worth 0.2 to 0.5 percentage point on the interest rate charged Sallie Mae in recent years. We believe the CBO places too little weight on the low-risk nature of the portfolio in deriving the appropriate cost of financing.

to the student or to the government. Both the rate charged the borrower and that paid to the lender are fixed by legislation. Thus to the extent that the subsidy to lenders is excessive, it is simply reflected as excess profits of either primary market lenders or Sallie Mae in the secondary market.

The guaranteed payment to lenders seems excessive while the student is in school, because there are few if any loan-servicing costs. During the repayment period, however, a reduction in the guaranteed payment, though justified by Sallie Mae's earnings, would slow the pace of entry of private firms into the secondary market. The GSL program grants Sallie Mae a favored position in the market by virtue of its ability to concentrate on student loans and its strong administrative position with the state guarantor agencies. A yield that is sufficient to maintain a secondary market price of par provides a windfall to Sallie Mae.

Proposals for Reform

Most dissatisfaction with the current program stems from the large subsidy embedded in it—a conflict between the desire to offer many students the opportunity to borrow funds to finance their education versus the large budget costs that any such program imposes. On one side are those who emphasize the need for financial assistance to low-income students, and who thus seek to maintain or increase the size of the subsidy but impose tighter income limitations—perhaps a reduction in the family income ceiling, now set at $30,000. Such restrictions quickly lead to reduced political support for the program by middle- and upper-income families. The program is also inherently hard to target because the subsidy for each dollar of loan varies with future market interest rates, not family income.

On the other side are those who propose to divorce the issue of capital market imperfections from the issue of subsidies for low-income students. They suggest two separate programs: a generally available *unsubsidized* student loan program, and a program of education grants to assist low-income students. The loan program would eliminate all income restrictions and establish a loan insurance fund, but impose a market rate of interest on the borrowers. Supporters argue such a self-financing system would ensure that an inability to borrow did not restrict education decisions.[29] Capital market imperfections are a problem faced by middle-income as well as low-income students. The proposed program would shift the focus in enrollment decisions from a comparison of parents' income with attendance costs to a comparison of education costs with future income prospects.

Lengthening the repayment period beyond the current five to ten years has been advocated as one way of obtaining a better match with the borrower's ability to pay. It has been suggested that the problem of risk in educational investments could be resolved by relating the loan repayments to a percentage of future earned income. In effect, the government would become an equity participant—sharing in the gains and losses of the educational investment.[30]

Thus far, Sallie Mae has not succeeded in creating an active secondary market for student loans, and the effort to involve the private sector has proved very costly. It may be time to abandon the current system in favor of providing GSL loans directly through the educational institutions. The federal government could continue to rely on the private network of collection agencies but provide funding to the GSL program directly, thus eliminating Sallie Mae. Alternatively, the government might convert the National Direct Student Loan Program, a new, small, institution-based program, to an unsubsidized program on an experimental basis. If it succeeded, the GSL program could be phased out.[31]

On a more modest scale, the cost of the current program might be reduced. First, a program that provides a 100 percent guarantee and fixes the interest rate to both the borrower and the lender, eliminating any market incentives, is bound to be abused. Greater diligence by private lenders to prevent defaults could be achieved by cutting the guarantee to 90 percent or below, as in other loan programs, such as FHA mortgage insurance. Second, either the rate paid by the borrower or that received by the lender could be removed from control and allowed to be set by the market. The current practice of guaranteeing a return to the lender 3.5 percentage points above the Treasury bill rate seems

29. For a discussion of the issues raised by one version of this proposal, the Student Loan Bank, see Robert Hartman, "The National Bank Approach to Solutions," in Lois D. Rice, ed., *Student Loans: Problems and Policy Alternatives* (New York: College Entrance Examination Board, 1977), pp. 74–89.

30. Milton Friedman, *Capitalism and Freedom*, pp. 104–07.

31. A suggestion along this line is contained in Arthur Hauptman, "Federal Costs for Student Loans."

excessive, given the evidence from Sallie Mae that servicing costs are about 1.0 percentage point.

Conclusion

Although the public has heard much about student loan defaults, it is less aware of the steep interest subsidy costs involved—roughly 50 percent of the loan amount. Yet the basic argument for government-supplied loans—private market limits on student borrowing—does not require subsidies as a remedy. Our evaluation suggests that the student loan program does encourage college enrollments, but that at least 75 percent of the subsidies go to students who would have attended college without the program. Thus it has become an expensive way of promoting education.

The most effective means of resolving the conflict between the spiraling costs of the current loan program and the failure of private markets to provide an alternative would be to convert GSL into an unsubsidized loan program, while dropping all income restrictions. That would remove parents' income as a limitation on college attendance and allow students to make such decisions on the basis of future benefits. The result would be to free budget funds for direct grant programs, which can more effectively target disadvantaged groups.

CHAPTER SEVEN

Accounting and Budgeting for Credit Programs

MUCH OF THE CONTROVERSY surrounding the federal credit programs stems from a lack of pertinent information: the government's current accounting and budget system does not provide the data needed to evaluate program performance. Consequently, too often debate rages over the single point of whether the volume of loans should be included in the unified budget, when other budgetary accounting and control issues are of equal or greater weight.

To be useful as a basis for public policy decisions a budget must provide a means of comparing the costs of alternative decisions. The current federal budget does that for expenditure programs, because all parties agree that the dollar volume of outlays is a valid common yardstick for considering different programs: a $1 billion outlay on defense is equivalent to a $1 billion outlay on food stamps, and the dollar amount is a fair measure of the costs to taxpayers.

Credit programs do not fit easily into this budgetary framework because there is no simple measure of their cost to taxpayers.[1] Most people would agree that a $1 billion loan is not equivalent to a $1 billion expenditure on defense, either in terms of its cost to taxpayers or its economic impact—loans are repaid. From this perspective the suggestion that the volume of loans be included in the budget on an equal footing with expenditures is wrong. Taxpayers should not be satisfied with a budget process that treats a $1 billion reduction in loans as equivalent to a $1 billion reduction in expenditures.[2]

---

1. Alice M. Rivlin and Robert W. Hartman, "Control of Federal Credit," in Albert T. Sommers, ed., *Reconstructing the Federal Budget : A Trillion Dollar Quandary* (New York: Praeger, 1984), p. 218.

2. This problem is particularly severe in the context of the Gramm-Rudman-Hollings law, which calls for a phased reduction in the budget deficit. Several groups, including

150

What is desired is a measure of the cost to taxpayers of a dollar of loan activity.[3] The subsidy component of the loan, used in earlier chapters to identify the economic impact, provides precisely that measure. If they were made at competitive market rates (including all costs of administration and potential default costs), government loans would substitute fully for loans of private lenders and would cost the taxpayers nothing. But many government direct and guaranteed loan programs do embody a subsidy, since the public earns less on the loan portfolio than it would if the resources were invested in assets earning the market rate of interest. That differential is one aspect of the cost of a dollar of loan activity.

The subsidy component of a government loan is a recurring expense. Yet most of the loan's impact on the use of resources occurs shortly after it is disbursed, when the borrower spends the funds.[4] As a result, both the cost to taxpayers and the economic impact are more accurately measured if the full cost of the future subsidy expense is recognized at the time the loan is made. That can be done by estimating the present discounted value of the future subsidy costs. In a perfect capital market, the present discounted value of the subsidy is equivalent to an outright grant that the borrower would accept in lieu of the loan. It is a unit of measurement by which loans and direct expenditures can be compared because it incorporates the long-term cost of subsidization.

As discussed in preceding chapters, the cash-flow accounting system now used by the government contributes to the problems of the credit agencies. They are overly concerned with minimizing budget appropriations of the current period at the expense of a mounting unfunded liability in the future.

Underlying the basic problems with the evaluation and reporting of government credit activity is a misplaced emphasis on the volume of credit rather than the amount of subsidy embedded in the transaction.

---

the administration, have suggested that these goals can be met simply by selling off existing government assets. Such a practice cannot be sustained, and the sale of financial assets will have no impact on the real economic problems that the deficit causes.

3. Rivlin and Hartman, "Control of Federal Credit," p. 221.

4. In normal budgeting for multiyear construction projects (particularly in defense), Congress handles this timing feature through the authorization process, granting the executive agency authority to enter into obligations equal to the full construction cost, exclusive of future operating and maintenance expenses. Loan subsidies differ in that they extend over a major portion of the asset's life, not just the construction phase. The subsidy costs of a government loan are spread out over the life of the loan because interest earned on the loan is less than the government's costs.

In fact, the programs are operated and reported to the public in a way that obfuscates the subsidy. If the income-expense accounting of private financial institutions were applied to government credit operations, it would highlight the subsidy element, for the reason that such accounting aims to measure profit or loss, a loss being the same as a subsidy in our context. And private institutions report financial transactions—asset exchanges—in a separate listing of assets, liabilities, and net worth that must balance. The federal government, however, combines income, expenses, and asset exchanges in a simple statement of cash flow that fails to identify the net costs of programs.

Current Practice

The unified budget, which is basically a cash-flow budget, is poorly suited for the reporting of loan activity.[5] First, the loan programs report only their *net* cash requirements. Although new loans require a cash outlay, they are offset by loan repayments, a negative outlay. Thus old loan programs, with high repayment flows, may appear to impose little or no net costs. Interest on old loans is recorded as a separate negative outlay, but since it is aggregated over all loans, the income from any specific group of loans cannot be separated out and compared with similar private market activities. Furthermore, some loan agencies have the authority to "sell" their loan assets, under a repurchase agreement, to the Federal Financing Bank, until fiscal 1987 an off-budget agency. Because these loan sales are also recorded as negative outlays, the budget does not even provide a measure of the net increase in outstanding loans to the private sector.

Second, critics often argue that the unified budget does not include the costs of government loan programs. If one means by costs the subsidy payments made by the government, that criticism is not accurate—those costs do increase budget outlays. The costs, however, often appear in other, seemingly unrelated, budget categories. The interest receipts from loans are reported as offsetting negative outlays in the expenditure

5. The cash-flow budget has other shortcomings; for example, it does not distinguish between consumption and investment. In most cases, the shortcomings are minor compared with the benefit of including all expenditures within a single comprehensive system. In the case of the credit programs, however, the inaccuracy of a cash-flow system is too great to go uncorrected.

category of net interest payments by government. Thus the amount of any interest subsidy is only implicit in the budget: the negative outlay for interest (that is, interest income) is not as large as it would be if the the loan assets earned a market rate of interest.[6]

More important, the costs that are reported cannot be related to current loan activity. An interest rate subsidy imposes costs over the life of the loan, and those cash payments are recorded only as they occur: the current year's budget largely reflects the costs of old loans. Finally, in a cash-flow budget loan guarantees impose zero cost until a default actually occurs. As a result Congress does not receive accurate reports of the costs of a loan or a loan guarantee at the time it is made. Instead, the costs of the loans accrue down the road and are lumped together and often referred to as "uncontrollables." Administrative expenses are often lumped in with the administrative costs of the parent agency.

Third, most loan agencies engage in accounting practices that understate the costs of default. When borrowers cannot repay, they may be allowed to refinance: a new loan is issued to cover the unpaid balance of the old loan. The old loan is then considered repaid, and the new loan is no longer in default. By such means loan defaults can be carried forward for several years. Moreover, if an agency is required to pay a private lender in the event of a default, it may record the transaction as the purchase of the loan asset. In effect, the agency transforms a loan guarantee into a direct loan and holds it in its own portfolio without writing down the loan's estimated recovery value.

These practices stand in sharp contrast to those of private lending institutions. To begin with, private lenders establish a cost basis for their loan activities. Those costs include the interest paid to raise funds to finance their loans and all administrative costs of loan origination and servicing. Furthermore, private lenders establish reserve funds to cover prospective costs of default and include additions to those reserves in the cost base. If actual losses exceed the anticipated level, the income statement is adjusted to show that fact. Government regulators also require private lenders to write down the reported asset value of loans that are experiencing repayment difficulties and insist that the costs of such write-downs be included in the income statement.

6. In this sense interest rate subsidies are like "tax expenditures." The cost of a tax preference is also only implicit: tax receipts are lower than they would otherwise be, increasing the tax that must be paid by others.

Private financial reporting is not perfect. In particular, institutions normally report the face value of their assets and liabilities, not their current market value—a significant misstatement of net value during periods of large swings in market interest rates. Also, an accounting system cannot prevent bad decisions. But it does provide a measure of the profit or loss on existing loans, and it can be easily adjusted to provide a cost basis for new loans.

The Federal Financing Bank

In 1973 the administrative structure of government credit programs was greatly altered by the creation of the Federal Financing Bank (FFB). The bank's primary purpose is to consolidate and reduce the cost of credit agency borrowing. Before then several agencies, the largest of which was the Farmers Home Administration, had financed their own lending by selling pooled loan assets, known as Certificates of Beneficial Ownership, to the public. Despite full government backing, these securities required high interest rates in credit markets because of their small volume and unfamiliarity to investors.

The FFB was established to purchase all such securities, using funds it borrows from the Treasury. The bank charges its client agencies the Treasury borrowing rate plus one-eighth of a percentage point to cover administrative expenses. It also extends loans directly to private borrowers if the loans are guaranteed by other government agencies. About fifteen programs use this service, the largest being the foreign military sales programs and the Rural Electrification Administration. Furthermore, the bank lends funds directly to the credit agencies, avoiding the need for an agency to find a private supplier of funds. Table 7-1 shows the relative importance of the three types of activity.

Although consolidation of credit agency borrowing in the Federal Financing Bank has reduced borrowing costs, the bank has stirred controversy because of the budgetary implications of its activities. Before passage of the Gramm-Rudman-Hollings deficit reduction act in 1985, FFB borrowing was not included in the unified budget.[7] When an on-budget credit agency obtained funds from the bank, the transaction was recorded as a negative outlay—the sale of the agency's assets, its loans. For example, when the Farmers Home Administration made a $1

7. The Balanced Budget and Emergency Deficit Control Act of 1985, P.L. 99-177.

Table 7-1. *Assets of the Federal Financing Bank, by Type of Activity, Fiscal Year 1984*
Billions of dollars

Activity	Amount
Purchases of loan assets	
Agricultural Credit Insurance Fund	25.5
Rural Housing Insurance Fund	26.8
Rural Development Insurance Fund	7.2
Rural Electrification Administration	3.5
Other	0.3
Subtotal	63.3
Direct loans to guaranteed borrowers	
Foreign military sales	17.1
Rural Electrification Administration	20.6
Student Loan Marketing Association	5.0
Energy	2.9
Low-rent housing	2.2
Other	3.0
Subtotal	50.8
Lending to agencies	
Export-Import Bank	15.7
Tennessee Valley Authority	13.5
Postal Service	1.1
Other	0.3
Subtotal	30.6
Total	144.7

Source: *Special Analyses, Budget of the United States Government, Fiscal Year 1986*, table F-22.

million loan and used it as collateral to borrow $1 million from the bank, the net outlay of the FmHA was recorded as zero in the budget.[8]

Under Gramm-Rudman-Hollings the bank's accumulation of loan assets and subsequent need for Treasury financing is reported in the budget. The outlay costs of FFB borrowing are attributed back to the credit agency responsible for the transaction. Thus the sale of assets to the bank no longer reduces net lending of the loan agencies. Such a change gives greater prominence to the loan programs. It is largely cosmetic, however, because it does not address the fundamental problems of accounting for loan activity. The basic problem lies with the lack of effective control of the original lending agencies, not the accounting conventions of the bank.

8. The costs of the loan programs (administrative expenses, interest subsidies, and default costs) are reported in the budget, but because they are accrued on loans of previous years, they bear little relationship to current loan activity.

The Credit Budget

In 1980 concern about the rapid growth of the federal credit programs led the Carter administration to initiate a credit budget, separate but parallel in structure to the regular unified budget. Credit activity is measured by new loan commitments, rather than net of repayments, and the loan programs are allocated by the same functional classifications (national defense, agriculture, transportation, and so forth) used in the unified budget. The process of congressional review and authorization of the credit budget is similar to that for the unified budget, resulting in a set of ceiling limitations on new loans for about half of total lending. The credit budget has been continued and emphasized by the Reagan administration.

The credit budget has achieved one major objective: to provide more complete information on the cash requirements that the credit programs place on financial markets. The process of congressional review has also focused greater attention on the credit programs.

Nevertheless, the credit budget suffers from some serious deficiencies. First, the focus on loan volume still obscures the basic issue of program costs. Loans with small subsidies are reported as equivalent to those with large subsidies.

Second, Congress tends to be generous in setting the loan ceilings well above any realistic projection of lending activity.[9] Thus for some programs the credit budget does not impose a meaningful constraint. In part, this may reflect a concern with the distortions, discussed below, that quantity restrictions impose. It is more likely that, because the credit budget does not identify the costs (interest subsidies and defaults), Congress is not as concerned with loans as with direct expenditures. In that sense credit subsidies, like tax subsidies, are popular because their costs are less visible than direct expenditures.

Third, the establishment of limits on loan volume rather than the rate of subsidy can, as discussed in chapter 2, substantially reduce the benefits, if any, of the program. The lending agencies have no mechanism for allocating loans or guarantees when demand exceeds supply. Consider, for example, a government program to expand the effort to develop synthetic fuels. If the demand for loan guarantees exceeds the limit set

9. For examples see the Congressional Budget Office, *An Analysis of the President's Credit Budget for Fiscal Year 1985* (CBO, 1984), pp. 8–10.

by Congress, the federal credit agency may allocate the available guarantees among potential borrowers on the basis of the merit of their projects. In that case the agency may exhaust its guarantee authority without ever getting to projects that could not be financed without the guarantee. Alternatively, it may allocate the available guarantees on the basis of need, denying assistance to those who can obtain credit in the private market. But in that case it is providing a subsidy, and thus a competitive advantage, to the least-promising projects. In general, the use of quantity restrictions, rather than prices, is an inefficient means of allocating any good or service—including government credit assistance.

Proposals for Change

There have been many suggestions for reforming the budgetary treatment of the federal credit programs. A publication of the Congressional Budget Office evaluated the major proposals.[10] They reflect two competing strategies for incorporating federal credit programs into the budgeting process. The first would continue the current focus on the volume of loan activity and seek to increase the comprehensiveness of the measures of loan activity in the unified budget. The second would shift the emphasis to the subsidy cost as the primary control.

The key reform of those who wish to emphasize loan volume is to include the transactions of the off-budget federal credit agencies in the unified budget. This action was formally proposed by the Reagan administration in 1984 and adopted in the Gramm-Rudman-Hollings deficit reduction act. From a financing perspective this change is desirable because the unified budget should be a comprehensive measure of the government's cash requirements. The previous mixed treatment, whereby loans of agencies that used the Federal Financing Bank were excluded while the loans of those who did not were included, makes little sense. However, the change will have no effect on loan guarantee programs, where an outlay would still be recorded only when a default occurred. Furthermore, the new treatment continues the fiction that a loan is equivalent to an expenditure and encourages Congress to ignore the issue of subsidy costs.

The change also increases the opportunities to manipulate budget

10. CBO, *New Approaches to the Budgetary Treatment of Federal Credit Assistance* (CBO, 1984).

numbers to reduce the reported deficit. For example, the sale of existing government financial assets reduces reported outlays and thus the deficit. Yet the sale of an asset is simply a substitute for issuing debt.[11] Such a transaction does not affect the economy. Even the reduction of the deficit is only a timing adjustment because the government loses future revenue from repayments.

For purposes of evaluating the economic impact of the federal budget, the inclusion of loans in the unified budget will simply cause economists to rely more on the budget measures in the national income accounts, which exclude all loan transactions. The national income accounts concept of the budget, by excluding all financial transactions, is already a better yardstick of the fiscal effect of the budget than the unified budget is, and under these proposals, it would become more so. If forced to choose, economists will prefer the assumption that the aggregate demand impact of a loan is zero over the assumption that it is equal to that of an expenditure.[12]

Alternative proposals highlight the subsidy element as opposed to loan volume. One proposal, known as the market plan, is appealing because of its conceptual simplicity.[13] It recommends that all direct loans of the government be sold in the private market, and that the government reinsure all loan guarantees by purchasing insurance in the private market. The plan produces a direct measure of the subsidy cost: the gap between the face value of a loan and its market value. Within the unified budget the original loan would be recorded as an outlay, but one immediately offset by the sale of the asset. The residual outlay cost is the market value of the subsidy. This proposal would also place an explicit value on the cost of a loan guarantee because, with reinsurance, any government liability would vanish, leaving only the government's premium payment to the reinsurers. The result is a budget treatment that focuses on subsidy costs, and moreover, the costs are completely paid

11. Such a program was proposed in the administration's budget for fiscal 1987, and asset sales constitute a significant portion of the reductions that they propose to meet the Gramm-Rudman-Hollings deficit targets.

12. The national income accounts measure of the federal budget does reflect the effects of loan subsidies—higher net interest payments by government than would otherwise be the case—but it does not identify the subsidy as a specific element of outlays. In addition, the subsidy costs are included only as they accrue, not when the loan is made. Payments on loan defaults are excluded.

13. CBO, *New Approaches*.

in the years in which the loans are made. The market plan meets all our objectives with respect to reporting the true costs of credit assistance at the time it is provided.

Despite the appeal of simplicity, the market plan would encounter serious practical difficulties. The government originally became involved in specific credit markets because market imperfections prevented private lenders from servicing some types of borrowers. In some instances the government has improved the functioning of the market, either through a demonstration effect or by creating an active resale market, and a private demand for those assets now exists. For example, the resale of mortgages through mortgage pools has been highly successful and has largely eliminated the need for the government or the government-assisted agencies to hold the assets directly. In its direct loan programs, however, the government has done much less to standardize the loan instrument or to give private investors a means of evaluating the quality of the loan instrument—investors would be buying a pig in a poke. If the government attempted to sell such assets or obtain private insurance, it would pay a price far greater than its own future costs of continuing to service the loans. In effect, no private market exists for such ill-defined instruments as agriculture disaster loans.

It is equally hard to foresee private insurance for student loans. Collecting information to evaluate the prospective creditworthiness of students is extremely costly. And most students do not possess readily attachable assets for use as collateral, even when the borrower can be expected to stay within one legal jurisdiction. Institutions are willing to lend to parents on the basis of their tangible assets, but that is a backward-looking rather than a forward-looking decision. Student loans, backed by government insurance, can be sold to private investors, but a private insurance market will take more time to become established.

The market plan denies the existence of significant capital market imperfections and assumes the true rationale for federal credit programs is an effort to redirect resources or redistribute income. In light of the arguments of previous chapters that loan assistance is an inefficient route to either of these goals, some market plan supporters might see the elimination of all government credit assistance as a logical next step.

Recent experience with private deposit insurance illustrates another problem. Neither the investor nor the private insurer behave as though they believe the government's claim of no liability. Implicitly, there is an assumption that the government will step in should markets suffer severe disruption. In the states where private insurance funds collapsed in the 1980s, the government did, in fact, step in.

Some of the current appeal of the market plan in Congress reflects its promise as a way out of budget deficit difficulties. By selling off loan assets and recording them as negative outlays, Congress cuts the deficit. But those reductions are simply a financial gimmick that glosses over the longer-term economic issues. Furthermore, when faced with the low private market value attached to a pool of loans, the government might be tempted to offer some form of a guarantee as a device for raising the value of the pool, undermining the whole principle of the market plan.

What is needed is a system that duplicates the focus of the market plan on subsidy costs, but without going so far as to attempt to sell every asset to a private market that might not be receptive. That is the objective of the proposal outlined in the next section.

Administrative Reform of Federal Credit

In recent years the budgetary control of federal credit programs has drawn more attention than accounting within agencies. Yet in a well-functioning system those two activities should be integrated. The internal agency accounting should produce one or several bottom lines for each program that then form the basis for budgetary choices about expenditures across programs. Even more important, the information needed to evaluate and reform the way the individual programs operate should be made accessible. Without changes in internal accounting, for example, it is hard to assess the size of past and projected subsidies in most programs. In previous sections we argued that many of the problems of evaluating credit programs can be traced to a misplaced emphasis on the amount rather than the cost of credit. That emphasis, in turn, results from the use of cash accounting.

Fortunately, an accounting and control system more suited to the credit programs is readily available from private financial institutions. Our basic recommendation is that government credit programs be operated more like private banks: they should be required to maintain a balance sheet statement of assets and liabilities, and to use income-expense accounting.[14] That accounting system produces a straight-forward measure of the subsidy part of a loan, and the present discounted value of the subsidy provides the appropriate link between the credit programs and the unified budget.

Credit programs differ from most direct expenditure programs in the timing and the uncertainty of their costs. When the federal government makes a loan, it commits itself to a future stream of subsidy expenses, and because of default and interest rate risks, their final value cannot be known for sure until the ultimate disposition of the loan. Private accounting practices are designed to deal with both of these features. A discount rate is used to arrive at the present value of future subsidy costs, and reserve funds are established to take account of future contingencies (such as default). Both the balance sheet and the income statement would force an agency to distinguish between purely financial transactions (loan disbursements and repayments) and the gap between income and expenses, their net profit or loss. The net loss on the income statement would be the measure of the subsidy needed to sustain the agency's operations.

A reserve for defaults, reflecting the riskiness of the loan portfolio, would be a key element of such an accounting framework. In a private institution the allowance for loan losses is maintained as a proportion of the loan portfolio, with the proportion tied to estimated risk. Increments to the reserve are charged as an expense on the income statement, just like administrative expenses. The cost of defaults is thus anticipated and reflected in the cost of current lending, rather than being delayed until a default actually occurs.

Income-Expense Accounting

The basic principles of income-expense accounting for loan programs are illustrated in table 7-2 for a hypothetical loan of $100. The borrower pays a subsidized rate of 8 percent, while the government agency's cost of funds is 10 percent. It is an amortized loan paid off in equal annual installments over five years. The loan history and the division of the annual payment between interest and principal repayment are shown at the top of the table.

---

14. Some elements of our proposed reform are discussed under "The Appropriations Plan" in CBO, *New Approaches*, pp. 52–56. The two approaches are not identical, but they have much in common.

Table 7-2. *Illustrative Calculation of the Income and Expense on a Subsidized Loan*[a]
Dollars

Item	Year				
	1	2	3	4	5
Loan balance	100.00	82.95	64.55	44.66	23.19
Annual repayment	25.05	25.05	25.05	25.05	25.05
Interest	8.00	6.64	5.16	3.57	1.86
Principal	17.05	18.41	19.88	21.47	23.19
Income					
Interest	8.00	6.64	5.16	3.57	1.86
Expenses					
Administrative costs	1.25	0.25	0.25	0.25	0.25
Default allowance	0.50	0.50	0.50	0.50	0.50
Cost of funds	10.00	8.30	6.45	4.47	2.32
Total expenses	11.75	9.05	7.20	5.22	3.07
Net income or loss	−3.75	−2.41	−2.04	−1.65	−1.21
Addendum					
Present value of subsidy[b]	−8.81				

Source: Authors' calculations as explained in the text. Figures are rounded.
a. Loan amount = $100; interest rate = 8 percent; cost of funds = 10 percent.
b. Present discounted value of future income using the cost of funds as the rate of discount.

Table 7-3. *Illustrative Asset and Liability Statement on a Subsidized Loan*[a]
Dollars

Assets		Liabilities	
Net loan receivables	91.19	Borrowings	100.00
Government receivables	8.81		
Total	100.00	Total	100.00

Source: Authors' calculations as explained in text.
a. Loan amount = $100; interest rate = 8 percent; cost of funds = 10 percent.

Under cash-flow accounting the government would simply report an initial outlay of $100, followed by five years of negative outlays equal to $25.05, with the interest and principal repayments being allocated to separate accounts. In fact, it appears that government gets back more than it paid out.

Within an income and expense statement, however, only the interest payments are reported as income. Expenses consist of administrative and default costs and a cost of funds, which is the amount that the agency pays to borrow funds to finance the outstanding balance of the loan. The default allowance is the estimated probability of default times the expected loss in the event of default. The result is a negative net income report for each year of the loan—the annual amount of the required subsidy.

The government could report the subsidy on an annual basis, but a more relevant cost accounting for decisionmaking is provided by requiring a one-time payment to the loan agency at the time the loan is made. With a cost of funds of 10 percent, the present discounted value of the subsidy is $8.81. That is the amount of a cash payment to the lending agency that, if reinvested at 10 percent, would generate sufficient additional income to meet the subsidy costs. The $8.81 is also the cost to taxpayers that should be recorded in the budget. Furthermore, the present discounted value of the subsidy is the relevant measure of the loan's economic impact. It is equivalent to a grant of $8.81.

Table 7-3 shows the corresponding entries in the asset and liability statement. The agency would report borrowings of $100 in the first year to finance the loan. The future income receipts, minus expected administrative and default costs, would have a value of $91.19 as an asset. Together with a subsidy payment of $8.81 from the government, total assets would be $100.[15]

Implementation

Critics of this approach say that government agencies cannot make these types of prospective cost calculations, particularly for defaults; yet private firms do it under comparable circumstances. As pointed out above and demonstrated in the case of Small Business Administration and student loans, many loan programs have been around for a long time, and they have histories that can be used to assess default risks. New loan programs would require more detailed analyses. The important issue for default projections is that they be unbiased, not that they prove to be exact. And there must be an opportunity to average the actual default experience across a portfolio of diverse loans, so that the vagaries of individual loans cancel out.

For these reasons it would be desirable to collect all government loans into a common set of accounts, operated by an independent agency. Thus we would suggest the establishment of a separate agency (such as

---

15. In actual practice the asset could be recorded in a variety of ways. For example, it might be carried at its face value of $100, with a negative offsetting contingency fund of $8.81. The details of accounting practice are not the issue here.

the Federal Financing Bank) that is charged with assessing the default risk on government guarantees and collecting a fee either from the sponsoring agency or the borrower (for unsubsidized loans). An independent agency would have an unbiased perspective with an incentive, unlike those of the program agencies, to estimate defaults and other costs as accurately as possible.

A more substantive issue is raised by the question of the discount rate that agencies should use. The Treasury borrowing rate is essentially a riskless rate of interest. If government lending agencies were allowed to use that rate, they would obtain a competitive advantage relative to private lenders, and the subsidy costs would be understated. In part the risk is handled in the income and expense account by establishing a reserve against bad debts. In that sense the appropriate discount rate is not the market rate of interest on private securities, because the market rate includes no such adjustment. On the other hand, the allowance for a default reserve does not reflect the variance of possible outcomes: the uncertainty of the actual income stream. The appropriate rate is closer to that paid by private lending agencies, and it should be for a maturity that nearly matches the average maturity of the loans being financed.

Information on the appropriate magnitude of the risk premium can be obtained by comparing the cost of funds for commercial banks with the cost of Treasury borrowings of comparable maturity. For example, from 1970 to 1984 the secondary market yield on certificates of deposit averaged about 0.5 percentage point more than the Treasury bill rate, except in periods of severe monetary restraint.[16] If risk premiums are constant across the maturity structure, the cost of funds for federal credit programs would equal the Treasury rate on a bond of comparable maturity plus 0.5 percentage point. The government might wish to set the rate slightly higher to prevent excessive competition with private lenders who must earn a profit.

Finally, the effectiveness of this whole system as a means of budgeting for the credit programs depends on their loan activities being *excluded* from the unified budget. If lending is included, the payment of the subsidy to the credit agency would be an interfund transfer without influence on total budget outlays. In addition, the inclusion of loans in the budget as

16. Authors' calculation based on unpublished data from the Board of Governors of the Federal Reserve. The comparison was made on the basis of three-month bond-equivalent yields. Normally, Treasury bills are quoted on a discount basis that overstates the yield differential.

outlays, and their repayment as negative outlays, would continue to cause confusion in the distinction between expenditures and loans.

Under our system, lending would be accounted for in the federal budget as an outlay (appropriation) to the off-budget credit agency equal to the estimated present discounted value of the subsidy at the time the loan is made. Interest rate risk would be avoided by matching the maturity of assets and liabilities. Some errors in estimating actual default rates are bound to occur, but they would be averaged across all programs, and any resultant net profit or loss would be returned to the budget in future years as net income or loss of a wholly owned government enterprise. If all loan originating and servicing is assigned to the off-budget agency, the budget outlay would include the full subsidy costs of each year's loans at the time they are made.

In essence the budgetary and accounting system proposed here is the same as that currently used by the government-sponsored agencies. The chief reforms are to expand the system to the direct-lending and guarantee agencies, and to allow for the reporting of explicit subsidy costs on a present-discounted-value basis. Implemented with those changes, the system would clarify the costs of the loan programs for better public decisionmaking, improve their internal management, provide a basis for comparing loans and expenditures, and increase the short-run control of the public budget by fully funding the loan liability costs at the time loans are made.

CHAPTER EIGHT

New Directions in Government Credit

THE ANALYSIS OF previous chapters has focused on the existing credit programs of the federal government. Expanding activities in two new areas also deserve attention: state and local government programs that use tax-exempt bond issues to finance heavily subsidized credit for industry, housing, and student loans, and proposals to use the federal credit programs as part of an industrial policy of restructuring the U.S. economy, along the lines of the Reconstruction Finance Corporation of the 1930s.

State and Local Government Credit Programs

During the last decade, the annual volume of tax-exempt bond issues used by state and local governments to finance private activities has expanded tenfold, to $88 billion in 1985. Indeed, direct lending programs of state and local governments now exceed those of the federal government.

The interest on state and local bond issues has long been exempt from federal income taxation. Initially, this exemption was used only to finance public construction. In the 1960s, however, state and local governments began to use tax-exempt bonds to raise funds for private entities—particularly in the areas of home mortgages, industrial development, and student loans. Interest rates on bonds that are exempt from federal taxation are substantially lower than those on taxable bonds, so that groups with access to such funding receive a substantial government subsidy.

The programs are popular with state and local governments because they pay none of the direct subsidy costs. The costs are borne, instead,

Table 8-1. *Tax-Exempt Bond Financing, Selected Fiscal Years,*
1975–85
Billions of dollars

Category	1975	1980	1984	1985
Private-purpose bonds				
Housing bonds	1.4	14.0	20.5	26.7
Private entity bonds	1.8	3.3	11.7	19.4
Student loan bonds	*	0.5	1.2	1.1
Pollution control bonds	2.1	2.5	8.1	7.1
Small industrial bonds	1.3	9.7	18.3	19.3
Other industrial bonds	2.3	2.5	14.1	14.8
Total	8.9	32.5	74.0	88.4
Public-purpose bonds	21.6	22.0	41.7	89.8
Total new issues	30.5	54.5	115.7	178.2

Source: *Special Analyses, Budget of the United States Government, Fiscal Year 1987*, p. F-52; and *Special Analyses, Fiscal Year 1985*, p. F-38.
* $50 million or less.

by the federal government in the form of lost tax revenue. In 1985 alone the revenue loss is estimated to have been $7.7 billion.

During the last decade private-purpose bond issues have come to dominate the tax-exempt market. In 1975 these bond issues amounted to $8.9 billion, or about 30 percent of the total (see table 8-1). By 1984, $74 billion was devoted to private purposes, 64 percent of the total. Although the private-purpose share of the market declined in 1985 because of a surge in the public-purpose segment, the volume of private-purpose issues continued to rise to $88 billion.

Tax-exempt bonds support a wide range of projects. In the 1980–85 period, 30 percent of the $333 billion in new issues was used for mortgage financing, for both single-family mortgages and multifamily rental units. These programs are not primarily aimed at assisting low-income families. Ceiling price limitations on the homes that are eligible for such financing is 120 percent of the median sale price in low-income neighborhoods and 110 percent elsewhere, and only 10 percent of the funds need to be used in low-income areas. The income limits for qualifying borrowers are usually well above state averages.[2] Local governments often grant developers access to the tax-exempt market when they require the

1. *Special Analyses, Budget of the United States Government, Fiscal Year 1986*, pp. G-38–G-42.
2. Congressional Budget Office, "Mortgage Revenue Bonds in 1982," special study prepared at the request of the Senate Finance Committee (1983).

developer to pay the capital costs of new public services—roads, water, and sewers.

Tax-exempt financing has also become a principal tool in the competition among state and local governments to attract new industry. From 1980 to 1984, tax-exempt issues represented about 25 percent of corporate bond financing. In another area, higher education, states attempted to use such bonds to finance the purchase of federally guaranteed student loans. The spread between the interest rate paid by the federal government on student loans and the tax-exempt bond rate made such activities highly profitable. Congress acted in 1980, however, to restrict this use.

Although the major cost of the subsidy to private-purpose bonds is paid by the federal government in lost tax revenues, there are costs to state and local governments also. Their bonds carry a lower rate of interest because of the tax exemption, but as the volume of bonds outstanding rises, they begin to saturate the market among high-tax-bracket investors. The tax exemption is worth progressively less to taxpayers in lower brackets. Thus as the volume increases, the interest rate on all tax-exempt bonds must rise to provide the marginal investor with a yield equal to the after-tax return on taxable bonds. In effect, all public-purpose bonds must pay a higher interest rate because of private-purpose bonds.[3] There is, however, no incentive for an individual state to limit its use of private-purpose bonds because its own issues have a minuscule effect on rates.

Throughout the 1980s repeated efforts have been made to restrict the use of tax-exempt bonds for private purposes. Once the programs are in place, however, pressure from their constituencies makes it hard to abolish them. The U.S. government now prohibits the linking of these tax-exempt instruments to federal guarantees, except for FHA and VA mortgages, and the 1984 Deficit Reduction Act placed limits on the volume of industrial development bonds.[4] The volume limits on private-purpose bonds were tightened considerably under the Tax Reform Act of 1986.

Federal Credit in Industrial Policy

The debate over the need for a U.S. industrial policy raises the question of new business credit initiatives as one of the government's

3. See the discussion in the appendix for an empirical estimate of the magnitude of the effect on the tax-exempt bond rate.
4. *Special Analyses, Fiscal Year 1986*, pp. F-46–F-49.

potential tools. Proponents of industrial policy argue that American capital and labor should move more quickly into areas where the United States has or can develop an international comparative advantage. The government's role is to foster the transition by easing the painful rationalization of industries with overcapacity and by encouraging the movement of resources toward promising new uses.

Of course, government credit is only one tool in a workbox that also includes trade policy, tax incentives, and federal grants for job training and research and development.[5] Credit programs do, however, have several features that make them attractive for certain tasks. They can be selective. Loans and loan guarantees are among the few forms of assistance that the government can bestow on individual firms, rather than all firms in a given class or industry. Also, credit programs appear to give a large return on a relatively small investment of federal funds. Loan guarantees, in particular, are highly leveraged.

Although mention is often made of using loans and loan guarantees, proposals have generally not been specific. One of the few that has been described at length was put forward by Felix Rohatyn, who advocates creating a central lending agency reminiscent of the Reconstruction Finance Corporation to help revive moribund basic industries.[6] The Chrysler Corporation loan guarantee illustrates this point.

Credit for New or Growing Industries

Most proposals for using federal lending or guaranteeing powers as a tool of industrial policy envision moving capital toward small but fast-growing firms that produce technologically advanced goods or services. Computer and biotechnology firms are mentioned most often. A biotechnology firm, for example, may need financing to move from its product development stage to a higher production stage. There are assumed to be many such firms ready to move, but too little capital ready to supply financing.

In evaluating the potential of a loan program to address the needs of these prototypical high-technology firms, the first question is why are

5. An overview of the industrial policy debate, with citations, can be found in the Congressional Budget Office, *The Industrial Policy Debate* (CBO, 1983).

6. Felix Rohatyn, "Reconstructing America," *New York Review of Books* (March 5, 1981), p. 16. An expanded version is proposed in the Center for National Policy, *Restoring American Competitiveness: Proposals for an Industrial Policy,* Alternatives for the 1980s no. 11 (Washington, D.C., 1984).

funds scarce: are credit markets malfunctioning? The usual answer is that banks (or bond markets) are unwilling to take on enough risk, not that they overestimate the amount of risk. If the target firms are indeed too risky for private lenders, there is an argument that it is in the public interest to fund these credit programs. That is, the future value of the successful firms will outweigh the losses of those that fail, and only by funding many new firms will the most worthy be identified. The public has a long-term interest in the future value of a whole industry, while debt holders have only an interest in the ability of their particular borrower to repay.

Once it is agreed that the real reason for government assistance to new high-technology firms is an externality associated with investment in high-growth industries, the choice of credit as the indicated treatment should be questioned. The use of government assistance depends on whose behavior—financier or firm—is to be altered.

Debt arrangements in private credit markets have a built-in mechanism to keep out frivolous applicants; namely, bankruptcy is usually a greater calamity for the owners of a small firm than for the lenders. Hence there are only a few reasons why a biotechnology firm that has decided to seek credit will find credit markets unwilling to lend. First, lenders may rate the chances of success lower than do the owners. Second, lenders may be more risk-averse. Third, the payoff to lenders if a firm is successful is less than the payoff to owners, lowering the expected value of the outcome for lenders. Finally, lenders may view the owners' equity stake as too low to motivate them to avoid default. For the biotechnology firm whose owners cannot find financing for one or more of these reasons, a government program aimed strictly at making credit available would clearly induce investment that would not otherwise be made.

By contrast, owners whose analysis of their future prospects agrees with that of private market lenders will not assume more risk simply because the government makes credit available, other things being equal. In order to encourage investment by new firms that see eye-to-eye with lenders, or whose own basic creditworthiness is not at stake, a new credit program will have to rely on subsidies, just as the Export-Import Bank does when it moves from a focus on encouraging the participation of banks in export financing to encouraging foreigners to buy American products. But subsidies are unavoidably expensive. The short history of the energy development credit programs illustrates the process. The programs provided loan guarantees to firms to commercialize previously experimental techniques for producing nonpetroleum fuels. In many cases, the firms that had developed these techniques were affiliated with major oil corporations. The barrier to movement to a higher stage of production was not creditworthiness per se, but rather the risk that the price of oil would someday plummet, making nonpetroleum fuels uncompetitive and unprofitable. Access to guaranteed credit would not alter such a decision. For these reasons, the Synthetic Fuels Corporation has switched its plans from loan guarantees to price guarantees (and higher subsidies) as its preferred form of aid.[7]

If a credit program for growing business avoided direct subsidies, offering only guaranteed loans, it would be in a position similar to that of the Small Business Administration, aiming mostly at new and independent firms whose owners and bankers assess their creditworthiness higher than financial markets do. Moreover, if it relied on banks to select borrowers, it would receive only information leading it to a bank's conclusions. A program to foster high-technology firms would have one advantage over the Small Business Administration: it would have a more precise profile of its target firm. In order to choose well, however, it would need expertise not only in credit, but also in the industries being financed.

Whether subsidized or not, a new-business credit agency would, like the Small Business Administration, have to enter a credit market that is already operating and attempt to select among the marginal applicants. If it gave banks or its own officers incentives to act conservatively, it would simply substitute government-backed debt for private debt and become a competitor to private lenders rather than a support or extension. Given that government administrators receive little credit for successes but substantial blame for failures, it is hard to visualize a government program being more innovative than private suppliers of venture capital.

Credit for Declining Industries

Many basic U.S. industries such as steel and automobiles are undergoing a steady decline that, it appears, will reduce the capital and labor devoted to them, resulting ultimately in a smaller industry. Government

---

7. See chapter 2 for further discussion of issues in the use of government credit for energy development.

aid is sometimes contemplated to speed the changes, especially by coping with the potential losers.

The Chrysler Corporation loan guarantee was aimed at allowing the corporation to shed its unprofitable old assets while protecting jobs and avoiding the shock to financial markets that would have occurred if Chrysler had entered bankruptcy. What the government did in the Chrysler case is more accurately described as a bankruptcy or reorganization action than as a credit program.

A financial event created the initial crisis, because the first constraints on Chrysler's ability to operate took the form of a refusal by commercial banks to offer it short-term credit. The credit refusal was only a manifestation of underlying problems, including inefficient plants and lack of demand for its large, gas-thirsty automobiles. Yet Chrysler did have several potentially valuable assets—the modern plants that made its successful small car, the Omni-Horizon; its already advanced plans to produce a line of fuel-efficient sedans, the K-cars; and the human and intangible assets stemming from the organization itself. These assets would be lost if they remained tied to the unproductive plants, outmoded products, and the company's past debt burden. The challenge was to free these assets with a minimum of disruption.

The loan guarantee allowed Chrysler to continue to borrow and invest, but the crucial aspects of the plan were the conditions attached to the guarantee. In a crisis that is primarily financial, such as that of banks in 1934 or, to a lesser extent, of thrift institutions in 1982, the government's guarantee of solvency is the main ingredient in producing solvency. Government intervention in these cases prevents losses. In Chrysler's case, however, one purpose of the intervention was to allocate already incurred losses among Chrysler's claimants: banks, bondholders, suppliers, dealers, and employees. Further conditions included an investment plan, particularly for the K-cars, that would produce profits and raise a large amount of private, unguaranteed funds. The government took the lead in organizing creditors and extracting concessions from them, and then in evaluating Chrysler's future operating plans.

All the government's actions could have been taken by the lead creditors and judges in a reorganization proceeding. Even the guarantee is the functional equivalent of a buyout of portions of the company by a highly creditworthy firm. Such a private reorganization is illustrated by the case of International Harvester (now Navistar), another large vehicle-manufacturing firm facing default. Private creditors were able to organize and agree on a plan of action without government assistance. The government may have special advantages as the head of a reorganization proceeding, such as speed in organizing the massive number of creditors, or greater leverage in persuading them to accept their share of loss, but the Chrysler and International Harvester cases appear to differ mainly in the success of their lobbying efforts in Washington.

The greatest potential drawbacks to government bailouts include shielding those who have made faulty decisions and being too lax about future plans for regaining profitability. The precedent-setting effect of overgenerosity establishes a new tenet in the marketplace: creditors of major corporations will not be allowed to lose money. Investors become less wary, management less efficient. Nevertheless, provided that the tendency to be too soft could be overcome, the strategy the government followed for Chrysler, of allocating loss and requiring change, could be a suitable paradigm for future federal credit assistance to declining industries.

In general, however, the problems that industrial policies seek to address, easing the decline of the older industries and promoting the expansion of the new, are not the result of financial-market failures. Throughout this study we have found little evidence that private lenders are unable or unwilling to accept risk. More commonly, their perception that the probabilities of default are high has proved to be correct.

Industrial policies usually deal with situations requiring a subsidy, and the question arises whether credit assistance is the most efficient delivery mechanism. We are inclined to believe that it is not. To be effective a credit program would have to remain focused on firms or industries that could successfully emerge as competitive enterprises in the future. Yet as the analysis of previous chapters has shown, credit programs originally intended for a specific situation have, in general, outlived their cause and spread out into other areas.[8] Credit programs face a serious problem of simple substitution with private credit, and they create several forms of adverse incentives for borrowers and private lenders who participate in the program. Much of their popularity seems to result from peculiarities of their treatment in the government budget, which obscures their costs to taxpayers.

8. See also Charles L. Schultze, "Industrial Policy: A Dissent," *Brookings Review*, vol. 2 (Fall 1983), pp. 3–12.

Concluding Comments

The U.S. government originally entered the credit business when private financial markets collapsed in the 1930s. Since then its credit activities have grown enormously both in magnitude and scope. Such growth has occurred despite the recovery and ever-increasing sophistication of private markets, developments that would seem to reduce the need for a government role. However, significant market imperfections in some areas prevent us from concluding that all credit programs are redundant public replicas of private markets. Similarly, wide variations among the programs in the degree of subsidy they provide make it hard to reach any universal conclusion about their desirability. Instead, we have emphasized the need to evaluate the programs on an individual basis.

One key aspect of such an evaluation is to accentuate the subsidy component as the critical yardstick of the cost to the public and the chief indicator of the potential for distorting resource use. Another key is to insist that the benefits of the programs can be evaluated only if there is clear agreement on their objectives, distinguishing among the correction of credit market failures, resource reallocation, and income redistribution.

At present, none of these factors are stressed in the federal budget or in the congressional evaluation of individual programs. The budget mistakenly focuses on the dollar volume of loans, while failing to identify the subsidy costs. The individual agencies do not maintain an accounting system that can provide the information needed to measure costs or to compare program performance against objectives.

Most of all, we have been struck by the wide diversity of standards that are applied to the credit programs and the costs they impose. Some programs, particularly those in the housing market, are largely unsubsidized and aim at improving the performance of credit markets. The main issue they raise is whether they are still needed, or are they simply competing with private lenders who could perform their tasks equally well? This issue can be resolved by a close scrutiny of the programs to ensure that they do not incorporate a subsidy—a net cost to the government. As shown in previous chapters, that objective has been followed with the government-sponsored agencies by a progressive withdrawal of special treatment, converting them into private institutions.

In other cases, however, programs set up to improve access to credit have evolved into mechanisms for transferring large subsidies to specific groups and activities. Student loans, agricultural credit, and business lending have become extremely costly to taxpayers through the government's failure to raise loan rates in step with market rates and to include administrative and default costs in the price of the service.

This state of affairs is not beyond remedy. Nevertheless, today's confused and ineffective oversight of existing loan programs does not bode well for suggestions that they be extended into new areas where their objectives are defined at best as vague notions.

The Segmentation of Capital Markets

THIS APPENDIX PROVIDES a survey of previous empirical research on the extent of capital market segmentation together with a report on our own efforts to reconcile the divergent findings of those studies.

Previous Research

The empirical research aimed at distinguishing between the two interpretations of how capital markets operate—as a homogeneous whole, or as a collection of segmented individual markets—has proceeded along two different lines. Analysts who view the markets as undifferentiated have tended to emphasize direct measurement of the interest rate structure. They have estimated statistical regressions relating the interest rate in one market to rates of return on competing assets, and then tested to determine if the addition of measures of the composition of the outstanding debt adds explanatory power. Many of their studies embody reduced-form models of the determinants of the interest rate structure because no attempt is made to distinguish between demand and supply factors.

Alternatively, analysts who view the markets as more segmented have preferred to estimate separate structural equations for the quantities supplied and demanded of various assets, with some disaggregation by categories of borrowers and lenders. The resulting system of equations can then be solved to obtain predictions of interest rates. Unfortunately, the two approaches have yielded contradictory conclusions.

The comparison of the two approaches is facilitated by considering

177

the following simple portfolio model of the market demand for financial assets:[1]

(A-1) $\qquad \ln(Q_1^d/W) = \alpha_1 + \beta_1 R_1 - \gamma_1 R_2 + \delta_1 Z$

(A-2) $\qquad \ln(Q_2^d/W) = \alpha_2 - \beta_2 R_1 + \gamma_2 R_2 + \delta_2 Z,$

where

Q_1 = the quantity of the first asset

Q_2 = the quantity of the second asset

W = total financial wealth including a third asset, money

R_1 = the interest rate on the first asset

R_2 = the interest rate on the second asset

Z = a vector of other factors affecting the demand for Q_1 and Q_2.

The sign of the own interest elasticities of demand, β_1 and γ_2, is positive, and because the assets are assumed to be gross substitutes for one another, the cross elasticities, β_2 and γ_1, have negative signs. By subtracting the second equation from the first and solving for the first interest rate the result is

(A-3) $\qquad R_1 = \dfrac{\alpha_2 - \alpha_1}{\beta_1 + \beta_2} + \dfrac{\gamma_1 + \gamma_2}{\beta_1 + \beta_2} R_2$

$$+ \dfrac{1}{\beta_1 + \beta_2} \ln(Q_1/Q_2) + \dfrac{\delta_2 - \delta_1}{\beta_1 + \beta_2} Z.$$

If the two assets are of roughly equal substitutability with other assets, such as money, the coefficient on the second interest rate will be approximately unity and the two rates will move together.

The important point to note, however, is that if the sum of the interest rate elasticities, β_1 and β_2 in the portfolio equations, is large, the relative quantities, Q_1/Q_2, will have little or no effect on the interest rate differential in equation A-3. Similarly, large interest rate elasticities imply that other factors, Z, will also have little effect on the interest rate structure. In this illustration the quantity and interest rate equations represent alternative versions of the same demand relationship. Large coefficients on interest rates in the quantity version (equations A-1 and A-2) imply a high degree of substitution or arbitrage between markets.

1. This illustration is a variant of a presentation by Richard W. Lang and Robert H. Rasche, "Debt-Management Policy and the Own Price Elasticity of Demand for U.S. Government Notes and Bonds," *Federal Reserve Bank of St. Louis Review*, vol. 59 (September 1977), pp. 8–22.

They correspond with small coefficients on quantities in the interest rate equation (equation A-3).

Supply equations also can be introduced into the model. The major difference is that the own-rate coefficients are negative and the cross-rate coefficients are expected to be positive. Although a change in relative quantities has a positive correlation with interest rate differentials in the demand function, a change in relative quantities has a negative effect on interest rate differentials if the equation is interpreted as a supply function. Thus in empirical applications of the quantity version it is critical to know whether the underlying relationship being estimated is that of demand or supply.

The distinction between demand and supply is less critical for the empirical studies of interest rate differentials. Let the demand and supply for a specific asset be specified as

$$(A\text{-}4) \qquad \ln(Q^d/W) = \alpha + \beta R_1 - \gamma R_2 + \delta Z$$

$$(A\text{-}5) \qquad \ln(Q^s_1/D) = a - bR_1 + cR_2 + dX,$$

where D is the total financial debt of borrowers, W is total financial wealth of lenders, and Z and X are other factors affecting demand and supply, respectively. Demand and supply are then set equal to each other, and the model is solved for the *reduced-form* interest rate equation that embodies both demand and supply factors:

$$(A\text{-}6) \qquad R_1 = \frac{a - \gamma}{b + \beta} + \frac{c + \gamma}{b + \beta} R_2 + \frac{1}{b + \beta}\left(dX - \delta Z + \ln\frac{D}{W} \right).$$

In this case the relative quantities of financial assets do not appear in the equation, and the test for market segmentation involves finding significant roles for the predetermined variables of the supply or demand relationships, D, W, Z, and X. However, the absolute magnitudes of the interest rate coefficients in the demand and supply equations reinforce one another.

Consistency of conclusions in the empirical results requires either (1) large interest rate coefficients (absolute value) in the quantity equations *and* small quantity coefficients (absolute value) in the interest rate equations, or (2) the reverse combination. As will be shown, however, a survey of the existing empirical studies finds significant but small coefficients on interest rates in quantity equations and a small or zero coefficient on quantities in interest rate equations. Thus opinions about the effect on the interest rate structure of shifts in the composition of debt instruments vary widely depending on the specific type of empirical research that individual economists find most credible. The inconsistent nature of the results is evident in (1) the research on the term structure of interest rates (the relation between long- and short-term interest rates for assets of comparable risk), (2) studies of specific asset markets, and (3) large-scale models of the whole financial system.

Term Structure Studies

The "expectations hypothesis" of the relation between short- and long-term interest rates is one of the purest versions of the undifferentiated-markets viewpoint. An individual investor with a one-year planning horizon will, in evaluating assets of different maturities, compare the interest rate on a one-year asset with the interest rate plus the expected capital gain at the end of one year on a long-term asset of comparable risk. The equalization of expected returns leads to a formulation of the long-term interest rate as representing a geometric average of the current and expected future short-term interest rate.

Culbertson provided an early version of a segmented-markets interpretation of the term structure. He argued that institutional investors would attempt to match the maturity composition of their assets and liabilities, which implies that the demand for assets of a particular maturity would be unrelated to yields for other assets with different maturities.[2] Modigliani and Sutch articulated a modified version in which investors had preferences for specific maturities but were willing to shift if yield differentials became sufficiently large.[3] These models imply that changes in the relative supplies of assets in the different maturity ranges will affect the term structure of interest rates.

Studies that estimate direct interest rate equations usually support the undifferentiated-market view in finding a small or zero effect on the term structure of changes in the maturity structure of the debt. The most influential of those studies were done by Modigliani and Sutch.[4] They

2. J. M. Culbertson, "The Term Structure of Interest Rates," *Quarterly Journal of Economics*, vol. 71 (November 1957), pp. 489–504.

3. Franco Modigliani and Richard Sutch, "Innovations in Interest Rate Policy," *American Economic Review*, vol. 56 (May 1966, *Papers and Proceedings, 1965*), pp. 178–97.

4. Ibid.; and Franco Modigliani and Richard Sutch, "Debt Management and the Term Structure of Interest Rates: An Empirical Analysis of Recent Experience," *Journal*

used current and lagged values of the short-term interest rate as proxy measures of expected future short-term rates in an equation that successfully explained a large proportion of the variation in the long-term interest rate on government securities over the period of 1952–65. They allowed for a potential effect of debt management policies by adding a measure of the average maturity of public debt to the equation.[5] Although the coefficient was generally positive, it was small and statistically insignificant—implying that variations in relative quantities of the debt had little effect on the interest rate structure. A similar formulation, with minor modifications, continues to explain accurately the much wider variation of long-term interest rates during the 1970s and early 1980s.[6]

If arbitrage is so successful in equalizing holding-period rates of return among assets of similar risk but different maturity, it might be plausible to argue that similar activities dominate in the areas of our primary concern: the determination of interest rate differentials between assets of similar maturity but different risk.

A study by Roley illustrates the alternate view that significant market differentiation exists.[7] He estimated a model of the government securities market by using separate demand equations for ten investor categories (such as households, commercial banks, and life insurance companies) and two maturity classes of government debt (leaving a third class as a residual). Assuming that supplies in each maturity class were determined exogenously, the simulation of the overall system implied that changes in the composition of government debt would sharply alter the interest rate structure.[8]

---

of Political Economy, vol. 75 (August 1967, *Supplement*), pp. 569–89. Similar conclusions are reported in Arthur M. Okun, "Monetary Policy, Debt Management and Interest Rates: A Quantitative Appraisal," in Commission on Money and Credit, *Stabilization Policies* (Prentice-Hall, 1963), pp. 331–80. Somewhat larger effects for debt-management policies were reported in Gail Pierson, "Effect of Economic Policy on the Term Structure of Interest Rates," *Review of Economics and Statistics*, vol. 52 (February 1970), pp. 1–11.

5. In effect, they assumed that the supply of securities in the individual markets was predetermined. Thus, the Modigliani-Sutch equation can be interpreted as a demand relationship expressed in terms of interest rates, as in equation A-3 above.

6. The version of the "Quarterly Econometric Model of the Federal Reserve" (November 1982) incorporates revised estimates of the interest rate equations. Their predictive accuracy is discussed in Albert Ando, "A Reappraisal of Phillips Curve and the Term Structure of Interest Rates" (University of Pennsylvania, July 1982).

7. V. Vance Roley, "A Structural Model of the U.S. Government Securities Market," (Ph.D. dissertation, Harvard University, 1977).

8. A shift of $2.5 billion of debt between the two- to four-year maturity class and

Models of Specific Capital Markets

In studies of the corporate bond markets, Friedman and Roley evaluated the relative merits of reduced-form interest rate equations and the structural approach of estimating separate demand and supply equations in quantity terms.[9] They concluded that structural demand-supply models provided more accurate forecasts than alternative reduced-form interest rate equations. Unfortunately, the comparison of the two forecasts was not based on equivalent information. The structural quantity models they developed included other long- and short-term interest rates as predetermined variables, whereas the reduced-form equations excluded other interest rates. In effect, the structural models were limited to determining the relative structure of interest rates, while the reduced-form equation had to determine the structure plus the level of interest rates.[10]

Although Friedman found significant interest rate coefficients in the quantity equations of his structural model of the corporate bond market, the coefficients were sufficiently small to imply that a change in the outstanding quantities would substantially alter the structure of interest rates. Thus his research indicates that, at least in the short run, asset swaps can have a significant effect on relative interest rates, even in two such closely related markets as government and corporate bonds.

Cook and Hendershott provided a contrasting study to Friedman's.[11]

the over-twelve-year maturity class changed the interest rate differential between the two categories by an average of 87 basis points during a simulation running from 1960 to 1975. See V. Vance Roley, "Federal Debt Management Policy: A Re-examination of the Issues," *Economic Review of the Federal Reserve Bank of Kansas City*, vol. 1 (February 1978), p. 20.

9. Benjamin M. Friedman, "How Important Is Disaggregation in Structural Models of Interest Rate Determination?" *Review of Economics and Statistics*, vol. 62 (May 1980), pp. 271–76; and Benjamin M. Friedman and V. Vance Roley, "Models of Long-Term Interest Rate Determination," *Journal of Portfolio Management*, vol. 6 (Spring 1980), pp. 35–45.

10. Their conclusion that disaggregation by category of investor did not improve the prediction of interest rates may be the more significant finding because it would seem to provide evidence against the argument of the "preferred-habitat" hypothesis that different classes of investors have strong preferences for specific types of assets. It suggested that knowledge about the allocation of credit among investors with different portfolio preferences did not have a major effect on the prediction of interest rate differentials.

11. Timothy Q. Cook and Patric H. Hendershott, "The Impact of Taxes, Risk and Relative Security Supplies on Interest Rate Differentials," *Journal of Finance*, vol. 33 (September 1978), pp. 1173–86.

They emphasized the importance of such technical factors as risk, callability, and taxes in accounting for different movements in interest rates. They were able to explain the yield on AA utility bonds over the period 1961–75 with a standard error of about 20 basis points, using as explanatory variables a tax-adjusted yield on government bonds, several indicators of default risk, and a measure of the probability that a bond will be called before maturity. They concluded that variations in the relative supplies of corporate and U.S. bonds had no significant effect on interest rates.

The mortgage market has been the focus of much of the research on market segmentation. The cost of gathering information about the financial conditions of individual borrowers is believed to limit the attractiveness of the assets to all but a few specialized mortgage-lending institutions. Legal deposit rate ceilings often prevent the mortgage-lending institutions from expanding their lending to the point where the expected return on mortgages is equal to that for other assets, and the institutions are constrained by regulation from varying the mix of their portfolios in response to relative interest rates.

A paper by Jaffee and Rosen presented a small-scale model of the mortgage market.[12] Their study is of interest because it incorporated a reduced-form, interest rate equation in which quantity-type variables were found to have statistically significant effects on the mortgage interest rate. The authors included interest rates on several alternative financial assets (Treasury bills, three- to five-year government bonds, and corporate bonds) as measures of opportunity costs on both the supply and demand side of the market. They found significant negative coefficients on the rate of deposit inflow into thrift institutions and on the quantity of government agency lending in the market. The magnitude of the estimated quantity effects was quite small, however, since a rise of $10 billion in agency financial support in 1978 would lower the mortgage rate by approximately 0.10 percentage point.

A major factor limits the usefulness of studies of individual capital markets for the issue raised here about arbitrage between markets: the studies are not capable of tracing out the different routes by which adjustments might take place in response to a shift in the composition of assets. Lending institutions can shift their portfolios, borrowers can

12. Dwight M. Jaffee and Kenneth T. Rosen, "Mortgage Credit Availability and Residential Construction," *Brookings Papers on Economic Activity, 2:1979*, pp. 333–76. (Hereafter *BPEA*.)

seek out alternative sources of funds, and depositors can change their portfolios as the financial intermediaries vary the deposit rate they can afford to pay. These issues are more easily addressed within the context of larger-scale models of the overall financial markets. Those models, however, can become so complex that it is difficult to understand fully the adjustments that occur or to be confident that the results of various simulations are not the product of some seemingly minor assumption of the model builders.

Financial Market Models

Several large-scale empirical models of the financial markets were developed during the 1970s. Despite that research effort, the models continued to embody widely different views about the extent of substitution between financial assets, and thus about the effectiveness of policies based on an exchange of government claims for private financial claims.

At one extreme, the current version of the model used by the Federal Reserve assumes full arbitrage between markets and the absence of any significant effect of relative quantities of financial claims on the structure of interest rates.[13] The model includes two short-term interest rates, Treasury bills and commercial paper, but both rates are explained as linear combinations of current and past values of the federal funds rate, with no significant effect from either flows or stocks of financial assets. The federal funds rate, in turn, is explained as a function of the demand and supply of money balances. The term structure of interest rates, both private and government, is based on a pure expectations model: long-term rates arc related to an average of past short-term rates and inflation. Even the mortgage and commercial loan rates are explained as linear combinations of other interest rates, with only minor roles for quantity-type variables. By definition, this model assumes that exchanges of financial assets, such as those engaged in by the federal credit agencies, have no effect on interest rates or economic activity.

A financial market model under development at Yale University takes the segmented-markets perspective.[14] The model includes ten separate

13. Board of Governors of the Federal Reserve System, "The Quarterly Econometric Model" (November 1982).

14. An illustration of the model is provided in David Backus and others, "A Model of U.S. Financial and Nonfinancial Economic Behavior," *Journal of Money, Credit and Banking*, vol. 12 (May 1980, *Special Issue*), pp. 259–93.

asset markets and nine categories of financial agents. In each case the demand and supply of specific assets are formulated within the framework of a portfolio allocation model in quantity terms. The model is limited to explaining behavior in financial markets and does not include equations for actual decisions on expenditure. Thus it can be used to evaluate the effect of credit policies on interest rates but not their effect on expenditure. A preliminary version of the model was used to simulate the results of a swap of $1 billion of mortgages for long-term government debt.[15] The analysts reported a reduction in the interest rate differential between mortgages and government bonds of 16 basis points in the first year and 13 basis points in the second year after the policy action. This is almost thirty times greater than the effect reported earlier for the mortgage market model estimated by Jaffee and Rosen.[16]

The Yale model finds a more modest interest rate effect from changes in the maturity distribution of government debt than Roley does. However, the effect is sufficient to imply that the change in the maturity structure of the federal debt had an important influence on the term structure of interest rates over the post–World War II period.

Two older financial market models—Bosworth–Duesenberry and Hendershott—also reported the results for a similar exchange between mortgages and government securities.[17] Both the models include equations to measure the response of expenditures to any induced change in interest rates. Because their assumptions about the underlying monetary policy differ from each other, they do not provide comparable measures of the effect of changes in credit policies on the overall level of interest rates. However, they can be compared in terms of the shift in the interest rate structure.

The simulation reported for the Bosworth-Duesenberry model of a $1 billion exchange of mortgages for government securities shows an initial large decline of 13 basis points in the mortgage-government interest rate differential, but the differential narrows sharply in the second and

15. Ibid., pp. 288–92.
16. The reported simulation of the Yale model is based on a version of the model that incorporates their own views of the parameter values (priors), which are intended as inputs into a later Baysian estimation of the model's parameters.
17. Barry P. Bosworth and James S. Duesenberry, "A Flow of Funds Model and Its Implications," *Issues in Federal Debt Management*, Conference Series 10 (Federal Reserve Bank of Boston, 1973), pp. 39–149; and Patric H. Hendershott, *Understanding Capital Markets*, vol. 1: *A Flow-of-Funds Financial Model* (Lexington Books, 1977).

subsequent years.[18] Although the model displays damped oscillations of behavior, the long-run effect of a shift in the composition of assets approaches zero. Thus the short-run effect is about half that implied by the Yale model, and the models differ substantially in the long-term implications. The Bosworth-Duesenberry model supports a segmented-markets interpretation of capital markets in the short run. But because the limitations on arbitrage are primarily the results of lags in portfolio adjustments, in the long run the model comes closer to supporting the undifferentiated markets view.

The Hendershott model produces results similar to those of the Yale model. The magnitude of the change in the interest rate differential declines over time but not as rapidly as in the Bosworth-Duesenberry model. Even after lags in the adjustment of portfolios are taken into account, there are significant effects of credit programs on the interest rate structure.

Summary

It is disappointing to find such widely different conclusions among these studies. But, as noted earlier, the studies that adopt a structural framework to explain quantities within the confines of a portfolio allocation model have some consistency. They tend to reach a common conclusion that there are significant barriers to arbitrage among markets, at least in the short run. By contrast, the studies that begin with the objective of explaining interest rate changes find little or no empirical role for relative quantities.

The differing assessments seem to result from the statistical method of analysis used—reduced-form, interest rate equations versus structural specifications of demand and supply in quantity terms. The interest rate studies are criticized because they ignore differences in the demand for assets among different categories of investors. They are, therefore, unable to incorporate directly the regulatory and institutional influences that advocates of the segmented-markets hypothesis wish to empha-size.[19] Moreover, the interest rate equations are often reduced-form relationships that comingle supply and demand influences. Thus it is not

18. Bosworth and Duesenberry, "Flow of Funds Model," pp. 94–99.
19. Friedman, "How Important Is Disaggregation?" The study by Friedman, however, suggests that variations in preferences among investor categories are not a significant source of the difference. He found that aggregate versions of the demand for and supply of corporate bonds performed as well as his more disaggregate model.

possible to take account of the constraints on investor decisions that can be derived from a portfolio allocation model, where the decision to purchase one asset necessarily implies the sale of another.[20]

Studies of portfolio allocation also encounter significant statistical problems. Estimating separate demand and supply relationships is a much more ambitious task than identifying the relative role of interest rates. The potential problems of misspecification are compounded by the simultaneous determination of both demand and supply. Furthermore, the modeling of quantity responses in the portfolio decision between assets of varying maturity is particularly difficult because of the need to adopt fairly simple measures of the expected future short-term interest rate that may inadequately reflect the expectational elements. In this respect the determination of the term structure of interest rates is a particularly difficult application of a portfolio allocation model.

Furthermore, arbitragers, who are critical to the undifferentiated-markets view, cannot be identified as a specific investor category. It is plausible to argue that, though most investors may behave as the preferred-habitat hypothesis suggests, scattered among the categories are a few who are active arbitragers, or who become arbitragers when interest rate differentials reach certain levels. Estimating a stable demand or supply relationship for a group with such heterogeneous behavior can be difficult, and average relationships may underestimate the magnitude of interest rate response in the market as a whole.

Finally, the quantities of assets held by specific sectors are measured with much greater error than interest rates are. Such error in measurement results in significant bias when relative quantities are used as explanatory variables in interest rate equations—an argument favoring the structural specification in quantities. However, because portfolio equations require other quantities as explanatory variables—including the lagged value of the dependent variable—they also encounter problems with measurement error. Thus it is difficult to favor one method over another on a priori statistical considerations.

Determinants of the Interest Rate Structure

In this section we report some additional empirical results. Our analysis differs from the previous studies in that we attribute the

---

20. William C. Brainard and James Tobin, "Pitfalls in Financial Model Building," *American Economic Review*, vol. 58 (May 1968, *Papers and Proceedings, 1967*), pp. 99–122.

Figure A-1. *Interest Rate Differentials, 1960–83*

Percentage yield

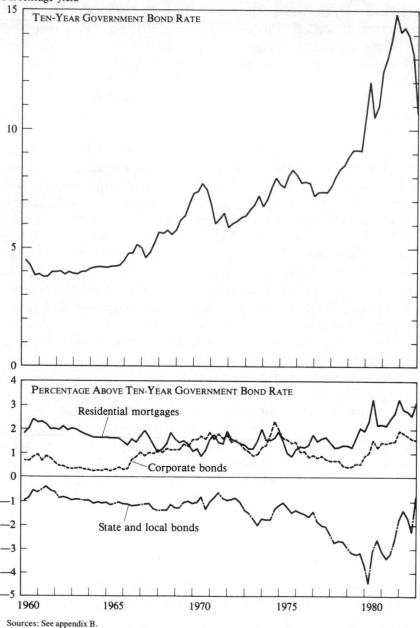

Sources: See appendix B.

dichotomy between the interest rate and quantity versions to statistical problems. We have made an effort to estimate both versions in a form that allows direct comparison of the results. The differences are then ascribed to biases introduced by measurement errors in the variables and intercorrelation between mutually determined endogenous variables. As such, the two estimated versions are indicative of the upper and lower bounds of the probable effect, and an instrumental variables estimation is used to reduce the range of possible values. As a result, the two versions can be brought into closer agreement. Our statistical analysis also benefits from the much wider range of observed variation in interest rates over the last decade.

The level of U.S. interest rates increased more than threefold over the period 1960–82 and underwent several severe cyclical fluctuations. Yet, as illustrated in figure A-1, the relative structure of interest rates among assets of comparative maturity remained surprisingly stable. The yield on residential mortgages stayed within a band of 1 to 3 percentage points above the rate on U.S. government securities, and the equivalent premium on corporate bonds fluctuated between 0.5 and 2.5 percentage points.[21] State and local securities showed a greater range of fluctuation, but that is believed to be related to their tax-exempt status: an increase in the relative quantity of such assets must be accompanied by an increased yield in order to maintain the after-tax return for marginal investors with progressively lower tax rates.

Although interest rates in individual markets have tended to move together, the range of observed variation in yield spreads, if due exclusively to variations in relative security supplies, would imply significant economic effects for credit policies that seek to control relative quantities. But many technical factors such as risk, maturity differences, and taxation also contribute to yield variations. Thus changes in interest rate spreads alone do not imply that securities are imperfect substitutes for one another.

Our initial model draws heavily on previous work by Cook and Hendershott and uses an interest rate representation of the portfolio choice as illustrated in equation A-3.[22] We restrict the analysis to the

21. In figure A-1 the yield differential is measured as the arithmetic difference between two rates. It is equally reasonable to express the differential in percentage terms. In percentage terms there is some evidence of a secular decline in the differential. In the later empirical estimates, both arithmetic and ratio formulations of the differential are allowed.

22. Cook and Hendershott, "Impact of Taxes." See also Ray C. Fair and Burton

demand side of the market. We assume that differences in real-sector variables, such as government deficits, corporate cash flow, and investment, have generated significant changes in the relative supplies of different securities for which it is possible to observe the response of the demand side. If no evidence of market segmentation can be found under these circumstances, we do not consider the possibility of arbitrage between markets by suppliers.[23]

Our general procedure is to begin with a yield on low-risk, highly marketable U.S. government securities and to relate variations in the yield premium of specific private securities over that yield to technical factors and changes in the relative supply of those securities. To reduce the influence of changes in the term structure, we restrict the comparison of yields to securities of comparable maturity. Furthermore, wherever possible, the measure of the yield refers to new issues so as to eliminate the effects of favorable capital gains tax rates on the yields of seasoned bonds when their coupon rates are below the current market rate.

For several reasons, as Cook and Hendershott pointed out, the reported market yield on U.S. government bonds must be adjusted for the effect of taxes. First, since no long-term bonds were issued during the 1963–73 period, all U.S. bonds sold at a discount, and the resulting differential between the purchase price and the redemption value was taxed at a low capital-gains rate. Thus the market rate was abnormally low during much of that period. Second, nearly all U.S. bonds issued before 1971 are redeemable at par for payment of estate taxes, and before 1976 the capital gains on these bonds were exempt from taxation. Cook and Hendershott provided a measure of the U.S. bond rate that was corrected for these factors.[24]

G. Malkiel, "The Determination of Yield Differentials Between Debt Instruments of the Same Maturity," *Journal of Money, Credit and Banking*, vol. 3 (November 1971), pp. 733–49.

23. Our examination of several large flow-of-funds models implied that there should not be a serious statistical problem of identification in estimating either demand or supply relationships. Variations in general business-cycle conditions create wide variations in the supply of new securities. And though the major autonomous demand factor, wealth, changes only slowly over time, variations in the quantity of other securities can be used as identifying factors in any individual securities market.

24. Details of the rate adjustment are provided in Cook and Hendershott, "Impact of Taxes," pp. 1174–79, 1186. The tax factors are less important after 1973 because the United States began to issue new long-term bonds. For the empirical work discussed later in this appendix, Cook and Hendershott's series was linked to the twenty-year bond rate to extend it beyond 1975, the last year of their series.

Technical Factors

The principal technical factors responsible for variations in the yield spread for private securities are default risk, call risk, and differences in the timing of the cash payments. We used several proxies, suggested by the earlier studies, to adjust for changes in investors' perceptions of default risk. They include simple cyclical variables, such as the unemployment rate and a survey measure of consumer sentiment. In addition, as a more direct measure of the risk premium on private debt, we used the observed yield differential in the short-term market between commercial paper and Treasury bills in some of the long-maturity bond rate regressions.

In the case of many private securities—mortgages and corporate bonds, in particular—the borrower can exercise the option of calling the bond before its maturity if future market interest rates should decline. To compensate investors for this risk, the yield spread for newly issued securities should rise when current interest rates are high relative to expected future rates. Several previous studies used the yield spread between long- and short-term government securities (the term structure) as a proxy measure of the probability that rates will fall in the future and that the borrower will exercise the call provision. Yawitz and Marshall developed a more precise measure of this probability for corporate bonds based on expected future interest rates at the time the bonds are issued.[25] We use both measures in the following statistical estimation.

Finally, a comparison of security yields is complicated by differences in the timing of interest and principal payments. Interest on corporate and government bonds is paid semiannually, and the principal is paid on the day of maturity. In contrast, mortgage contracts call for monthly interest payments, and the repayment of principal is amortized over the life of the loan. Thus mortgages generate a larger cash flow over the life of the asset that must be reinvested at uncertain future market interest rates. Furthermore, differences in the frequency of payment can substantially affect the yield spread when interest rates vary over a wide range.[26] In the following analysis we measure all interest rates on an

25. Jess B. Yawitz and William J. Marshall, "Measuring the Effect of Callability on Bond Yields," *Journal of Money, Credit and Banking*, vol. 13 (February 1981), pp. 60–71.
26. See Patric H. Hendershott, James D. Shilling, and Kevin E. Villani, "Measurement of the Spreads between Yields on Various Mortgage Contracts and Treasury

annual bond-equivalent rate basis that adjusts for differences in the timing of the payments.

Relative Security Supplies

The quantities of financial assets that must be held by the private sector is defined by the total issue of each type of security minus holdings of the federal government, the government-sponsored credit agencies, the Federal Reserve, and state and local governments. The total portfolio essentially includes all debt instruments issued by domestic, nonfinancial sectors as reported in the flow-of-fund accounts.[27] That portfolio is divided into seven asset categories: (1) state and local government securities, (2) residential mortgages, (3) commercial mortgages, (4) corporate bonds, (5) consumer credit, (6) short-term business loans, and (7) U.S. government and agency securities.

If the segmented-markets hypothesis is correct, the relative structure of interest rates should reflect shifts in the composition of the private sector's portfolio of financial assets. A rise in the proportion of a particular asset in the portfolio will require an increase in its relative yield. It is not possible, of course, to include all these quantities in a single statistical equation. Thus we restricted the tests to different combinations of variables. For example, the corporate bond rate equation uses the proportion of corporate bonds in the total portfolio, and corporate bonds as a proportion of all long-term instruments. In most cases we found a significant role only for the proportion of the specific asset in the total portfolio.

Basic Empirical Model

We assume that investors seek to allocate a portion of their total portfolio to a specific asset on the basis of its yield relative to a riskless

---

Securities," *American Real Estate and Urban Economics Association Journal*, vol. 11 (Winter 1983), pp. 476–90. The authors found that the failure to adjust for cash-flow differences lead to an understatement of the rise of the mortgage-yield differential of 30 basis points between 1978 and 1981.

27. Corporate equities and a category of other nonmarketable loans that corresponds to no reported interest rate are excluded. All the data are from the historical data file of the flow-of-funds accounts of the Board of Governors of the Federal Reserve.

government yield of comparable maturity as well as on their perceptions of the risk of default or early redemption:

(A-6) $V_i^* = a + br_i - cr_g + dX,$

where

V_i^* = the desired proportion of financial portfolio devoted to the ith asset

r_i = the effective yield on the ith asset

r_g = the yield on government securities of comparable maturity

X = a set of variables used as measures of the risks of default and early redemption.

The adjustment of the actual to the desired proportion is incomplete within a single time period, so that

(A-7) $V_i - V_{i-1} = \gamma(V_i^* - V_{i-1}). \quad 0 \leq \gamma \leq 1$

Thus the quantity version of the relationship is given by

(A-8) $V_i = \gamma a_o + \gamma br_i - \gamma cr_g + \gamma dX + (1-\gamma)V_{i-1}.$

The relationship renormalized with the interest rate as the dependent variable is given by

(A-9) $r_i = -\dfrac{a}{b} + \dfrac{c}{b}r_g - \dfrac{d}{b}X + \dfrac{1}{\gamma b}V_i - \dfrac{1-\gamma}{\gamma b}V_{-1}.$

A high degree of asset substitution among markets would be represented by a large value for the coefficient b, though the initial effect might be reduced by a pattern of slow portfolio adjustment indicated by a small value for γ. Thus the interest rate effect of a change in the quantity of assets outstanding in a specific market is measured by the term $1/\gamma b$ in the short run; and by $1/b$ in the long run.

Equations A-8 and A-9 represent equivalent methods of estimating the same behavior. Both equations encounter several estimation problems. First, the error term of equation A-8 is likely to exhibit autocorrelation, which will lead to biased coefficient estimates in the presence of a lagged dependent variable. Second, interest rates and, particularly, quantities are likely to be measured with error, so that if either is used as an independent variable, the estimated coefficient will be biased downward. Moreover, if equation A-8 is thought to be the correct specification with an independently distributed error term, the estimated coefficients of equation A-9 will be biased. If equation A-9 is the correct specification, the coefficient estimates of equation A-8 will be biased. Thus the estimates of equations A-8 and A-9 will differ, but there is no basis for choosing between the two. Finally, both quantities and rates are endogenous variables within an overall demand-supply system. As a result, the inclusion of either on the right-hand side of the equation can be expected to result in simultaneous equation bias in the estimated coefficients.

In the subsequent analysis we first illustrate these statistical problems by presenting ordinary least-squares estimates (OLS) of the two versions, which highlight the dichotomy in the conclusions about asset substitution. We then deal with the major statistical problems by using an instrumental variables method of estimation—two-stage least squares. That is, the financial variables on the right-hand side of equations A-8 and A-9 are replaced by their predicted values as obtained from a set of instrumental variables that are uncorrelated with the error term.

The choice of those instrumental variables is made difficult by the twin concerns that they be correlated with the endogenous financial variables but uncorrelated with the error term. If the correlation with the financial variables is weak, the variance of the estimated coefficients will be very large. But if they too are endogenous, they will be correlated with the error term. We resolve this trade-off by assuming that the current-quarter correlation of the error term with real-sector variables that determine the supply of securities would be low. Thus besides exogenous variables within each equation the list of instruments included unborrowed reserves as a measure of monetary policy, gross national product (GNP), the four-quarter change in the price deflator for GNP, the unemployment rate, and a time trend.[28]

Corporate Bond Rate

A basic estimate of the corporate bond rate equation is reported in table A-1, together with the major parameters of interest for that and several variants. For the period 1960–82 it is possible to explain the

28. For a simple, one-variable regression or for very large samples the instrumental variable estimation would produce a single coefficient estimate regardless of which variable is on the left-hand side. That is not true for multivariate regressions with small samples, however. An alternative estimation technique—limited information, maximum likelihood—would produce a single estimate, but the evidence is that the estimated coefficients have very wide variance. See J. Johnston, *Econometric Methods*, 2d ed. (McGraw-Hill, 1972), pp. 278–91, 380–93, 412.

Table A-1. *Corporate Bond Rate Equations, 1960–82*[a]

	Interest rate equations			Quantity equations	
	Ordinary least squares	*Ordinary least squares*	*Two-stage least squares*	*Ordinary least squares*	*Two-stage least squares*
Coefficient	*(1)*	*(2)*	*(3)*	*(4)*	*(5)*
b	0.379	0.137	0.108	0.019	0.093
γ	0.293	0.244	0.178	0.060	0.038
$1/\gamma b$ (short run)	9.0	29.8	52.1	882.7	281.9
$1/b$ (long run)	2.6	7.3	9.3	53.4	10.4

Note: The standard deviation of $VCB = 0.0065$, $= 0.0063$ (deviation from trend).
Sources: See appendix B.
a. Basic equation (t-statistics in parentheses):

$$RIND = -0.40 + 1.05\,RUS20 + 1.61\,CALL + 0.10\,\Delta RU$$
$$\quad\;\;(-0.6)\;\;(71.6)\qquad\quad 3.9\qquad\quad (3.3)$$

$$\quad + 0.41\,(RCP - RUS3M) + 9.0\,VCB - 6.36\,VCB_{-1}$$
$$\qquad\;\;(2.9)\qquad\qquad\quad (0.4)\qquad (0.3)$$

Standard error $= 0.15$; $\bar{R}^2 = 0.99$; Durbin-Watson $= 2.05$; $\rho = 0.58$;

where $RIND$ is the effective yield on new-issue corporate bonds; $RUS20$, the effective yield on twenty-year government bonds; $CALL$, the index of the probability of early redemption; ΔRU, the four-quarter change in the unemployment rate of married men; $RCP - RUS3M$, the two-year average of the interest rate differential between commercial paper and Treasury bills; and VCB, the share of corporate bonds in financial portfolio of private economy.

corporate bond rate with a residual standard error of only 15 basis points. Besides the long-term government bond rate, the unemployment rate and a two-year average of the difference between the commercial paper rate and the short-term Treasury bill rate are both significant as measures of default risk. The measure suggested by Yawitz and Marshall of the probability that the call provision will be exercised is also important. The relationship explains about 75 percent of the variation in the yield differential between corporate and government bonds. There is evidence of autocorrelation in the residuals, but an adjustment for autocorrelation has no significant effect on any of the estimated coefficients.[29]

The inclusion of the relevant quantity variables does not prove the statistical fit of the equation, and, as shown in column 1 of the table, the coefficients are so small as to suggest a trivial influence of quantities on the relative interest rate structure. It can be argued, however, that the interest rate differential in the short-run securities market reflects changes in the relative quantities, and the deletion of the difference between the commercial paper and Treasury bill rate, shown in column 2, does improve the significance of the quantity variables. The short-run effect of interest rates is more substantial, but the long-run effect is still very small.

29. Throughout the analysis we used an iterative search procedure to find the value of ρ, the autocorrelation parameter, that minimized the sum of squares for error.

The initial ordinary least squares estimate of the quantity equation, shown in column 4, tells a different story.[30] Because the coefficients on the interest rate variables are small, the equation implies that the changes in the relative quantity of the bonds outstanding have a dramatic effect on the interest rate structure, approximately thirty times larger than the results from the interest rate equation. Much of this difference can be attributed to a low estimate of the adjustment coefficient, but even in the long run the effect on the interest rate is about eight times larger.

Both versions of the relationship, however, are sensitive to changes in the estimation procedure. The use of instrumental variables to adjust for simultaneous equation bias increases the role of the relative quantities in the interest rate version, column 3, and sharply reduces the role in the quantity version, column 5. The result is to bring the two estimates of the interest elasticity of corporate bond demand, b, into much closer agreement with each other. In the long run at least, both versions now imply that a one standard deviation of the relative quantity variable from its mean will increase the interest differential by only 6 basis points (10 × 0.006).

There is still a substantial difference in the estimated short-run effect because the quantity version has a much lower estimate of the speed of adjustment (0.038 versus 0.178). That might be expected because of the estimation bias inherent in equations having lagged dependent variables. If the quantity version is estimated with a polynomial distributed lag on interest rates, rather than an assumed proportionate adjustment (a method of eliminating the lagged dependent variable), the value of b is close to that obtained from the interest rate equation and the instrumental variables version of the quantity equation. The interest rate version is also much more stable than the quantity rate version when they are fit to different subperiods.

Mortgage Rate

The residential mortgage market has historically been viewed as the principal example of a segmented market that has limited interaction with other financial markets. That conclusion is supported by the empirical results, but variations in relative quantities are still of limited

---

30. Both the unemployment rate and the interest rate differential and the short-term security markets were eliminated from the quantity versions because of a lack of statistical significance.

Table A-2. *Mortgage Rate Equations, 1960–82*[a]

| | Interest rate equations | | | Quantity equations | |
Coefficient	Ordinary least squares (1)	Ordinary least squares (2)	Two-stage least squares (3)	Ordinary least squares (4)	Two-stage least squares (5)
b	0.106	0.090	0.076	0.039	0.076
γ	0.150	0.087	0.091	0.058	0.091
$1/\gamma b$ (short run)	62.6	128.1	144.3	445.2	144.3
$1/b$ (long run)	9.4	11.1	13.2	25.6	13.2

Note: The standard deviation of $VMTG = 0.011$, $= 0.009$ (deviation from trend).
Sources: See appendix B.
a. Basic equation (t-statistics in parentheses):

$$RMTG = -1.97 + 0.82\,RUS20 + 0.85\,RCOST + 0.23\,\Delta RU$$
$$(-2.7) \quad (16.6) \qquad (17.4) \qquad\quad (3.0)$$

$$-0.12\,(RUS20 - RUS1) + 62.6\,(VMTG - 0.85\,VMTG_{-1}) - 0.3\,TIME$$
$$(-3.9) \qquad\qquad\qquad (3.3) \qquad\qquad\qquad\qquad (9.8)$$

$$\text{Standard error} = 0.24;\ \overline{R}^2 = 0.99;\ \text{Durbin-Watson} = 0.90;$$

where $RMTG$ is the effective interest rate on conventional mortgages; $RUS20$, the effective yield on twenty-year government bonds; $RCOST$, the effective cost of funds to savings and loan associations; ΔRU, the one-quarter change in the unemployment rate of married men; $RUS20 - RUS1$, the effective yield differential between twenty-year and one-year government securities; and $VMTG$, the share of residential mortgages in financial portfolio of private economy.

importance in determining interest rates. The basic statistical results are shown in table A-2. The best-fitting OLS equation resembles the corporate bond equation in that the change in the unemployment rate (used as a proxy for default risk) and the difference between the long- and short-term interest rates on government securities (a proxy for the probability of early repayment) are both statistically significant.[31] However, the cost of funds to deposit institutions plays an important role as would be expected in a segmented market in which lenders base their lending rate on borrowing costs rather than on the yield on equivalent assets. The relative quantity of mortgages is also statistically significant, even though it was necessary to constrain the value of the adjustment coefficient, γ, because the unconstrained version was negative.[32] The value of γ is strongly affected by the inclusion of the interest rate differential between long- and short-term government securities, and the differential was not significant in the quantity equations. Thus it was dropped from the

31. A high long-term rate relative to the short-term rate implies that rates are expected to rise in the future. Thus a rise in the differential should reduce the probability of early prepayment. Both the foreclosure rate and the ratio of new loan value to per capita disposable income were insignificant as alternative measures of default risk.

32. The value of 0.15 for γ was obtained from an equation in which the estimation period was shortened to 1970–82, a period with a more homogeneous regulatory structure.

equation shown in column 2. The result is to increase the significance of the quantity variables, produce a positive estimate of γ, and eliminate any evidence of autocorrelation in the residuals.[33]

A quantity version of the mortgage-demand equation is shown in column 4. Although it has the same specification as the interest rate equation of column 2, the effect on the interest rate of a change in quantities is three to four times larger—the result of a decline in the estimated values of both b and γ. There is a smaller discrepancy between the two equations with regard to the long-term effect of changes of quantities—11.1 versus 25.6.

As with the corporate bond equation, an instrumental variables estimation substantially reduces the disparity between the two versions of the mortgage-demand equation—primarily by altering the estimated coefficients in the quantity version. In this case the two equations yield identical estimates of both the long- and short-term effects. The statistical analysis implies that a significant degree of market segmentation exists, but that it is largely the result of lags in the adjustment of investor portfolios. If the share of mortgages was increased by one standard deviation, it would raise the interest differential by about 1.5 percentage points initially, but by less than 15 basis points in the long run.

We made an effort to include other quantity variables in the regressions. In contrast to Jaffee and Rosen, we found that the rate of deposit inflow of the mortgage-lending institutions was not statistically significant.[34] We also found that the proportion of mortgages incorporated into mortgage pools was not significant, which implies that market innovation has not significantly reduced the costs to borrowers.

Surprisingly, there is little evidence that the amount of market segmentation is declining over time. If the estimation period is restricted to 1970–82 or 1975–82, the coefficient on the cost of funds declines only slightly, and the quantity variables remain statistically significant, whereas the negative coefficient on the trend variable becomes small and insignificant.[35]

33. It should be noted that excluding the cost of borrowed funds variable does not increase either the magnitude or the significance of the quantity variables. On the other hand, the cost of funds variable was of major significance for all subperiods and alternative formulations of the equation.

34. Jaffee and Rosen, "Mortgage Credit Availability."

35. We could find no evidence in the empirical data that the rapid growth of mortgage pools after 1975 had reduced the relative cost of new mortgage loans. Such a conclusion

State and Local Government Bond Rate

The chief distinguishing feature of state and local government securities is the exclusion of the interest receipts from income taxation. Equalization of after-tax returns implies that the yield on tax-exempt bonds should be equal to the yield on equivalent taxable bonds, multiplied by one minus the marginal tax rate:

$$R_{exempt} = (1 - \tau)R_{taxable}.$$

In an economy in which marginal tax rates vary across investors, this factor alone can be expected to create a positive correlation between interest rates and variations in the quantity of securities outstanding. New issues will have to be made attractive to new investors with progressively lower marginal tax rates. Thus the relative interest rate should rise as the quantity is increased. In general, these securities are most attractive to commercial banks and other corporate investors that face high tax rates. Once that demand is satisfied, the securities must be absorbed by the household sector, where the range of effective marginal tax rates is greater.

In principle, these factors could be measured by including an estimate of the tax rate applicable to the marginal investor. But when the definition of the marginal investor changes with variations in the amount of securities that the market must absorb, such a rate is difficult to measure. Furthermore, effective marginal tax rates are altered by the creation of other new, low-tax investments, as well as by legislative changes in tax rate schedules. Thus there may be little or no correlation over time with a measure of the marginal tax rate for investors in a specific income bracket. Finally, previous efforts to construct an index of the trend in marginal tax rates as a weighted average of the statutory rates indicate that those rates have varied very little over the last several decades.[36] In the estimated equations none of the available measures of effective tax

---

seems to be contradicted by the evidence that the formation of mortgage pools is profitable and has obvious attractions to investors. But given the scale on which these operations are undertaken, profit can be earned on a very narrow interest rate spread without translating into major gains to the borrower. However, it is also possible, given the low quality of the data, that such other factors as risk perception have changed during the period to offset the gains from the creation of mortgage pools.

36. Barry P. Bosworth, *Tax Incentives and Economic Growth* (Brookings, 1984), pp. 75–79.

Table A-3. *State and Local Government Bond Rate Equations, 1960–82*[a]

Coefficient	Interest rate equations			Quantity equations	
	Ordinary least squares (1)	Ordinary least squares (2)	Two-stage least squares (3)	Ordinary least squares (4)	Two-stage least squares (5)
b	0.011	0.018	0.012	0.016	0.013
γ	0.810	0.514	0.560	0.068	0.233
$1/\gamma b$ (short run)	109.8	109.2	153.6	916.0	321.1
$1/b$ (long run)	88.9	56.2	86.0	62.0	74.8

Note: The standard deviation of $VGSL1 = 0.006$, $= 0.002$ (deviation from trend).
Sources: See appendix B.
a. Basic equation (t-statistics in parentheses):

$$RGSL = -14.12 + 0.72\,RUS20 + 0.35\,RUS20_{-1} + 0.09\,RU$$
$$(-13.0)\quad(10.8)\qquad\quad(5.1)\qquad\qquad(2.4)$$

$$+\ 0.02\,MOOD + 63.6\,VGSL_{-1} + 109.8\,VGSL1 - 20.9\,VGSL1_{-1}$$
$$(5.2)\qquad\quad(8.3)\qquad\qquad(3.5)\qquad\qquad(-0.6)$$

$$\text{Standard error} = 0.28;\ \bar{R}^2 = 0.99;\ \text{Durbin-Watson} = 1.32;$$

where $RGSL$ is the effective yield on new-issue municipal bonds; $RUS20$, the effective yield on twenty-year government bonds; RU, the unemployment rate of married men; $MOOD$, the index of consumer sentiment; $VGSL$, the share of state and local government bonds in the financial portfolio of the private economy; and $VGSL1$, the share of state and local government bonds held by households and mutual funds as a proportion of the financial portfolio of the private economy.

rates was statistically significant. Therefore we did not include explicit measures of the tax rate.[37]

An equation that emphasizes the household sector's demand for state and local securities is shown in table A-3. It includes the share of total financial assets accounted for by the household sector's holdings of state and local securities in both the current and earlier periods. The total stock of state and local bonds held by all investors is included as a separate variable. Both the unemployment rate and the index of consumer sentiment are significant measures of default risk, but the measure of consumer sentiment has an unexpected positive coefficient. Its deletion from the equation affects only the coefficient on the unemployment rate.[38] Furthermore, preliminary estimates indicated that industrial revenue bonds are viewed by investors as identical to other state and local government issues; for this reason they are included in the measure of the total stock. The state and local bond equation differs from those of other markets in that a very rapid speed of adjustment (column 1) is

37. This exclusion limits the usefulness of the statistical results in any situation in which a major tax rate change is anticipated.

38. An alternative measure of default risk, the general fund deficit of state and local governments from the national income accounts, was not statistically significant.

implied, so that the effect of quantities on the interest rate spread declines much less over time.

An alternative specification (column 2) models the total demand for state and local bonds. It includes total state and local securities as a share of all assets in both the current and earlier periods, and the earlier-period value of household holdings is used as a measure of the composition of total demand. In the short run this version implies almost the same effect on interest rates as the household demand version, but if additional bonds are absorbed entirely by institutions other than households, the long-term effect is smaller.

As with the previously examined markets, a quantity version of the household demand for state and local bonds (column 4) implies a much larger short-run effect on interest rates and a much slower portfolio adjustment than the interest rate versions. Again, however, the use of instrumental variables (columns 3 and 5) sharply reduces the divergence between the interest rate and quantity versions. There is little disagreement about the long-term effects, which are substantially larger than those found for mortgages and corporate bonds. A change of one standard deviation in the amount of these securities to be absorbed by households would raise the interest rate by 1.0 to 1.8 percentage points in the short run and by about 0.5 percentage point in the long run.

Commercial Bank Loan Rate

Two measures of the interest rate charged on commercial loans are available. The first is simply the average of the prime rate publicly reported by banks, and the second is based on a survey of lending rates actually charged by banks. It is widely believed that a substantial difference exists between the two rates because of discounts to preferred customers and variations in other loan terms, such as requirements for compensating balances. However, the use of time-series data from the survey is hampered by several alterations in the survey design in past years and by the fact that data are available only for a single week within a quarter. In the preliminary empirical estimates the prime rate appeared to have a more systematic relationship to other financial market rates, and that is the version used in the reported equation. The qualitative results, however, are not seriously affected by the measure of lending rates chosen.

The basic OLS estimate of the interest rate version is shown in table

Table A-4. *Commercial Bank Loan Rate Equations, 1964–82*[a]

Coefficient	Interest rate equations			Quantity equations	
	Ordinary least squares (1)	Ordinary least squares (2)	Two-stage least squares (3)	Ordinary least squares (4)	Two-stage least squares (5)
b	0.156	0.456	0.111	0.013	0.013
γ	0.150	0.054	0.120	0.236	0.203
$1/\gamma b$ (short run)	42.8	40.3	74.8	325.2	372.5
$1/b$ (long run)	6.4	2.2	9.0	76.9	75.4

Note: The standard deviation of $VLOAN$ = 0.023, = 0.018 (deviation from trend).
Sources: See appendix B.
a. Basic equation (*t*-statistics in parentheses):

$$RCL = -2.52 + 0.54\,RCOST + 0.44\,RCDTB + 0.32\,RCDTB_{-1}$$
$$ (-5.0) \quad (4.8) \qquad\qquad (5.0) \qquad\quad (10.3)$$

$$+\ 0.19\,RU + 3.03\,D8002 + 42.8\,(VLOAN - 0.85\,VLOAN_{-1})$$
$$ (2.7) \qquad (9.9) \qquad\quad (3.4)$$

$$\text{Standard error} = 0.32;\ \overline{R}^2 = 0.99;\ \text{Durbin-Watson} = 1.84;\ \rho = 0.54;$$

where RCL is the prime loan rate charged by commercial banks; $RCOST$, the effective cost of funds to commercial banks; $RCDTB$, the average of effective yields on three-month government bills and three-month certificates of deposit; RU, the unemployment rate of married men; $D8002$, the dummy variable for effect of credit controls in second quarter of 1980; and $VLOAN$, commercial and industrial loans as a share of total commercial bank deposits.

A-4. A simple average of the secondary market rate on commercial paper and the Treasury bill rate provides the most effective measure of alternative market rates. In addition, a weighted average of the yields offered by banks on different types of time deposits (passbook accounts, large negotiable certificates of deposit, and small time deposits) is highly significant. The regression also includes the unemployment rate and a dummy variable to adjust for credit controls in the second quarter of 1980. The quantity variable is the ratio of commercial loans to total demand plus time deposits.

The effect of quantities on interest rates is comparable to that reported previously for other markets. Although the coefficient seems large, the quantity variable has a much larger variance than in the other equations. A change of one standard deviation would raise the interest rate by about 1 percentage point in the initial period and 12 basis points in the long run. In the first equation the adjustment coefficient, γ, is constrained to a value of 0.15 because it is highly unstable with respect to minor variations in the equation specification. An unconstrained version is shown in column 2. Note that when the value of γ declines, there is an offsetting rise in the estimate of b; so that the short-run interest rate effect is unchanged but the long-term effect is substantially reduced.

Again, the quantity version (column 4) yields a much lower estimate of the interest elasticity of demand and thus implies a much larger role for quantities in the determination of interest rates. In this case the ambiguity is not resolved by the use of instrumental variables (columns 3 and 5).[39]

Finally, survey data are available since 1972 for the interest charge on automobile loans by commercial banks. Our effort to find a role for relative quantities in an equation for that market was unsuccessful. The best empirical relationship was found by relating the auto loan rate to a twelve-quarter polynomial lag on the prime loan rate, though the same lag structure applied to the market yield on five-year government securities worked almost as well. The statistical significance of the long lag in adjusting to changes in yields on other assets suggests market segmentation, but there is no evidence that the volume of loan demand influences the interest rate.

Summary

The principal conclusion that emerges from our empirical analysis is that segmentation of capital markets is primarily a short-run phenomenon related to lags in portfolio adjustments by investors. Thus, in the short run, variations in the relative quantities of financial assets can strongly affect the interest rate structure, but such changes are of minor long-run importance. In the long run, interest rate differentials are dominated by technical factors, such as the cost of servicing the loans and investors' perceptions of the risk of default and early repayment of the loan. The state and local bond market does exhibit lasting effects from changes in relative quantities, but that appears to be the result of a progressive tax system, in which rates of return to the marginal investor must be equated on an after-tax basis. Additions to the stock must be held by new investors for whom the tax exemption is a less attractive feature. Thus a correlation between interest rates and quantities would be observed even if arbitrage completely equated after-tax rates of return.

As for the homogeneity of capital markets, we found that statistical problems of estimation seem to account for much of the conflict between the empirical studies that focus on changes in quantities and those that emphasize interest rates. It is not possible to eliminate all the contradic-

39. If the purpose is to model the behavior of the lender, it seems more sensible to view the bank as setting the interest rate and the borrowers as determining the volume of loans. On that basis the interest-rate version might seem to be a more plausible representation of bank behavior.

tion between the two approaches, but certainly the range of disagreement is narrowed substantially by the use of instrumental variables in the estimation.

Also, all of the empirical results apply only to the demand side of the market: the determination of the quantity of securities to supply to the market is not part of the model. As such, the results represent an upper limit on the potential effect of changes in quantities on the relative interest rate structure. A comparable sensitivity to relative interest rates by borrowers that have access to alternative markets would substantially reduce the overall effect.

Such results have important conclusions for government credit programs. They suggest that efforts to purchase private assets financed by the sale of government securities will have a largely transitory influence on the cost of credit to borrowers in that market. Although the programs have the potential for a substantial role as tools of short-run stabilization policy over the business cycle, they have seldom been designed or used with that purpose in mind.

Definitions of Variables
and Data Sources

MOST OF THE data used in the regressions summarized in tables A-1 through A-4 came from the following: Board of Governors of the Federal Reserve System, *Flow of Funds Accounts, Second Quarter 1983: Annual Revisions,* and unpublished historical data (hereafter FOF); unpublished data from the Federal Reserve Board model (hereafter FRB model); Board of Governors, Statistical Release G.13, "Selected Interest Rates" (hereafter FRB G.13); Salomon Brothers, *An Analytical Record of Yields and Yield Spreads,* 5th ed. (New York: Salomon Brothers, 1979) (hereafter Salomon Brothers).

CALL: Index of the probability of early bond redemption. Computed using the yield on ten- and thirty-year-maturity U.S. government securities (Salomon Brothers) according to the procedure outlined in Jess B. Yawitz and William J. Marshall, "Measuring the Effect of Callability on Bond Yields," *Journal of Money, Credit and Banking,* vol. 13 (February 1981), pp. 60–71.

D8002: Dummy variable to adjust for the effects of credit controls in the second quarter of 1980.

MOOD: Index of consumer sentiment, 1966 = 100. U.S. Department of Commerce, Bureau of Economic Analysis, *Business Conditions Digest,* vol. 24 (January 1984), p. 97.

RCDTB: Average of the effective market yield for U.S. government three-month bills and the effective secondary market rate on three-month certificates of deposit (FRB G.13).

RCL: Effective prime rate charged by banks (FRB G.13).

RCOST (mortgage equation): Effective cost of funds to FSLIC-insured savings and loan associations. Federal Home Loan Bank Board, *Savings and Home Financing Source Book* (Washington, D.C.: FHLBB, various issues). Quarterly series was derived through interpolation.

RCOST (state and local government equation): Effective cost of funds to commercial banks. Computed as the weighted average of the interest rates paid on certificates of deposit, passbook deposits, and small time deposits as a share of total deposits at commercial banks. The weights are the respective shares of each type of deposit in the total (FRB model).

RCP − RUS3M: Two-year average of the interest rate differential between the money rate on prime three-month commercial paper and the market yield on three-month Treasury bills (FRB G.13).

RGSL: Effective yield on new-issue AA municipal bonds. U.S. Department of the Treasury, *Treasury Bulletin* (Fourth Quarter, Fiscal Year 1983), p. 32, and earlier issues.

RIND: Effective yield on new-issue, deferred-call AA industrial bonds. Effective yield is calculated from the average of beginning-of-month and end-of-month bond yields. Salomon Brothers, pt. 2, table 2, pp. 3–5; table 2B, p. 1; table 3, p. 1. For the period before 1969, the rate is the new-issue AA utility bond yield minus 0.22 percentage point.

RMTG: Effective interest rate on conventional mortgage contracts (FRB model).

RU: Unemployment rate of married men. U.S. Department of Labor, Bureau of Labor Statistics, seasonally adjusted household data published in *Employment and Earnings,* various issues.

RUS20: Effective yield on new-issue equivalent U.S. government bonds, mid-month average yield. For 1961–75, Timothy Q. Cook and Patric H. Hendershott, "The Impact of Taxes, Risk and Relative Security Supplies on Interest Rate Differentials," *Journal of Finance,* vol. 33 (September 1978), p. 1186; for 1960 and 1976–83 the average yield is computed from a regression that excludes the 1967–72 period: $0.04789 + 1.00582 \cdot RMGFCM\text{-}2ONS$. ($RMGFCM\text{-}2ONS$ is the annual yield on twenty-year constant maturity Treasury securities from FRB G.13.)

RUS20 − RUS1: Effective yield differential between new-issue twenty-year government bonds and one-year constant maturity Treasury securities (FRB G.13).

TIME: Trend variable, first quarter 1954 = 1.0.

VCB: Share of corporate and industrial revenue bonds in the financial portfolio of the private economy (FOF).

VGSL: State and local government obligations and industrial revenue bonds as a share of total private holdings of financial assets (FOF).

VGSL1: State and local government obligations held by households and mutual funds as a share of total private financial asset holdings (FOF).

VLOAN: Commercial and industrial loans as a share of total deposits at commercial banks (FRB model).

VMTG: Residential mortgages as a share of total private holdings of financial assets, seasonally adjusted stock (FOF).

Index

Aaron, Henry J., 48n, 63n
Accounting practices. *See* Budget; Cash-
flow accounting; Income-expense
accounting
Adjustable rate mortgages (ARMs), 54,
64, 68, 69, 78
Agricultural credit program, 1; development, 108–09; direct loans, 12, 13;
projected debt write-offs, 112–13;
subsidies, 108, 109. *See also* Farm
Credit System; Farmers Home Administration; Rural Electrification Administration
Agriculture: crisis of *1980*s, 108, 112,
113–14; dependency on credit financing, 111; tax policy effect on investment in, 119–20
Agriculture, Department of, 4, 114
American Bankers Association, 82
Ando, Albert, 181n
Angly, Edward, 82n
Arbitrage: across financial markets, 19,
26, 27, 30, 183, 184; and interest rates,
181, 187
Armington, Catherine, 89n
ARMs. *See* Adjustable rate mortgages
Asset exchanges, 6, 24; in homogeneous
versus segmented markets, 26–27,
177–78; interest rates and, 27–28; and
resource allocation, 27, 29–30

Backus, David, 184n
Baron, David P., 99n, 106n, 107n
Barth, James R., 41n, 60n, 63n
Bonds: interest rates of, 181, 182,
194–96; as source of business credit,
79–80, 86; tax effect on yield of government, 190; tax-exempt state and local,
4–5, 166–68

Bosworth, Barry P., 185, 186, 199n
Brainard, William C., 187n
Breneman, David W., 137n
Brooks, Stephen H., 74n
Buckley, Robert M., 61n
Budget, federal: deficit, 5, 154, 160;
treatment of credit programs, 19–21,
22, 23, 24, 150–65, 174
Business credit market, 2; development,
83; government role in, 80–81; justification for, 83–84; private sector role
in, 83, 86–87; sources of financing,
79–80

Capitalization ratio, 32
Capital markets, 15–16; federal credit as
percent of, 1, 5–6; government credit
programs effect on, 14–15, 29; imper-
fections in, 7–8; variations in, 7. *See
also* Federal credit programs; Private
capital market; Segmented capital market; Undifferentiated capital market
Carron, Andrew S., 54n
Cash-flow accounting, 19, 21, 151,
152–53
CCC. *See* Commodity Credit Corporation
Certificates of Beneficial Ownership, 154
Chrysler Corporation, 2, 13, 43, 44n, 83,
169, 172–73
CMO. *See* Collateralized mortgage obligation
Cohen, David L., 86n
Collateralized mortgage obligation
(CMO), 54, 55, 71–72
Commodity Credit Corporation (CCC),
11, 108, 109–10n
Congressional Budget Office, 37n, 146n,
157

209